HOT BUTTONS

HOW TO RESOLVE CONFLICT AND COOL EVERYONE DOWN

SYBIL EVANS WITH
SHERRY SUIB COHEN

First published in the UK in 2001 by
Judy Piatkus (Publishers) Limited
5 Windmill Street
London W1T 2JA
e-mail: info@piatkus.co.uk

The moral right of the author has been asserted

A catalogue record for this book is available from the British Library

ISBN 0 7499 2184 6

This book has been printed on paper manufactured with respect for the environment using wood from managed sustainable resources

Data manipulation by Phoenix Photosetting, Chatham, Kent

Printed and bound in Great Britain by
Mackays of Chatham PLC Kent

SYBIL EVANS:

For Richard W. Shevlin, who gives me unconditional support, challenges my thinking, and offers me a chance to practise each day.

SHERRY SUIB COHEN:

This one's for Ben. A tranquil, growing little boy.

Contents

Preface

The Conflict Coach™

by Sherry Suib Cohen

I was writing an article on relationships for a major women's magazine, and I was stumped. Interviewing enraged couple after couple, I was struck by how helpless they seemed—how few had a clue as to how bitter and accusing they sounded. All I could hear was anger. I needed an expert to tell me what was happening—one who could give people the power to change their own lives.

Another writer gave me an article Sybil Evans wrote dealing with conflict resolution—the art of teaching angry people to solve their differences creatively. My colleague referred to Sybil as the *Conflict Coach.*

I found Evans in front of a large group of women who'd gathered together to learn how to deal with the hot tempers of their partners and other irritating people in their lives. She was a force. Making them laugh, making them sit on the edge of their seats in excitement, making them nod their heads as they welcomed new insights, Sybil moved through that group with such energy, such passion. These women were eager to save their relationships—and Evans was giving them the tools to do it.

The next time I saw Sybil, she was giving a workshop to businesspeople. With the same common sense and verve, she offered cutting-edge techniques to managers and their subordinates on how to deal with the daily stresses of the workplace. And here's the thing: In each group, she was just so appealing. As she lectured about the furies that cripple us, we all came to feel enormously hopeful about deactivating the hot buttons in our own lives.

After the workshop, I grabbed her for a few private moments to hear her story. I was curious. How did she come to spend her whole life with angry people?

"I grew up in an angry household," she told me. "My parents argued constantly and when they divorced, I dreamed about their reconciliation. That never happened, but as the messenger and the mediator caught between these two raging people, I began to understand that I was good at helping people turn off their hot buttons."

It was awhile before she realized quite how good. She earned a master's degree in social studies from Teachers College, Columbia University, and became a popular educator in three New York City high schools. Gradually she worked her way up to assistant principal and quickly discovered her strengths at handling myriad conflicts among students, teachers, parents, and administrators—all from different cultural backgrounds.

It soon became clear that what worked in the educational arena would work in the rest of the world. She was invited to serve as a consultant to the International Center for Cooperation and Conflict Resolution at her alma mater, Teachers College, Columbia University. Shortly thereafter she established her own training and consulting firm, Sybil Evans Associates. She began to present her conflict resolution skills to such Fortune 500 companies as AT&T, Avon, Campbell's Soup, Consolidated Edison, Lucent Technologies, McGraw-Hill, and other organizations including Memphis Diversity Institute, Meridian Health System, New Jersey Transit, and the United States Tennis Association. They all asked her to train them to unruffle each other's feathers in their personal and professional relationships.

The Conflict Coach was born.

So I found out what a Conflict Coach was. Sybil Evans gives us simple but fascinating tools to gentle anger in others and to dissolve our own bitterness. She teaches us how to turn off the hot buttons of difficult people with grace, integrity, and humor and to manage our anger rather than have it manage us. She helps us rise above a world of strife, misunderstanding, and the most annoying people!

On a personal note: I feel a bit strange about writing the following because as the coauthor of this book, I clearly have a bias. Still, I hope you take me at my word.

I'm a journalist who often writes about relationships, and I've become very wary of simplistic, manipulative advice offered by experts who promise the world. This advice may look good on paper, but it rarely works because people are such complicated, individual creatures. During the many months spent writing this book with Sybil Evans, in my own life I've tried every single technique she taught me. I was enchanted to see that in almost every difficult situation, anger was defused.

I've gotten to be pretty popular. Conflict resolution works. Evans has given me true power. It's comforting.

Acknowledgments

Most of all, we acknowledge and thank a publishing legend, the incomparable Diane Reverand, publisher and editor in chief of Cliff Street Books, HarperCollinsPublishers. Our hero. She has impeccable vision, heart, wit.

Deepest thanks from Sybil to Kent Beaty, Elizabeth Capen, and Barbara Deane, who have, from the beginning of my entrepreneurial life, lovingly shared their mentoring, talents, and generosity. To the memory of Donald Kaplan and Simpson Sasserath, who taught me to reach for stars. To my dearest brother, Henry Mellman, and to the memory of Helen and Murray Mellman.

Gratitude also to those who have been great advocates of conflict resolution, and who have supported *Hot Buttons* with scenarios, materials, advice, ideas, and marvellous enthusiasm, especially Richard Alpert, Barbara Appel, Marjorie Austrian, Lisa and Mike Baviello, Dana Boettinger, Leonard L. Burgess, Lolita Chandler, Lois and Ed Cogen, Adam M. Cohen Esq. (of Kane Kessler, P.C.), Gay Norton Edelman, Wendy Edelson, Edward N. Gadsden, Jr., Richard S. Gaskins, Bryan E. Gingrich, Blake Goldstein, Josh Goldstein, Don K. Jones, Sally Koslow, Liz MacGillivray, Alison Meisel, Karon R. Moore, Rory Mullett, Deborah R. Pierce, Leslie Saunders, Michael Shevlin, Teri Seidman, Liz Smith, Ellen Stoianoff, Barbara Wiggins, Frank Wilson, and Carol

A. Young. Thanks especially to the students and teachers in New York City who questioned Sybil's assumptions and were a constant source of growth.

Blessings on the extraordinary stars at HarperCollins: inspired art director Joseph Montebello; the gifted Mary Ann Smith for a perfect cover design; the creative Richard Rhorer, director of retail marketing; the galvanizing Pam Pfeifer, director of public relations, and Leslie Cohen, senior publicist; and the greatest star of all, Larry Ashmead, vice president and executive editor of HarperCollins, who keeps his friends supplied with books, laughs, and the very best stories. We also enormously appreciate the wonders who oil the wheels on Cliff Street—Margaret Meacham; Keva Mosher, assistant to the publisher; the wonderful Janet Dery, editor; and Douglas Didyoung, editorial assistant.

Thanks to Sherry's spurs: Larry, always Larry. And Josh, Rebecca, Ben, Jennifer and Steven Goldstein, Susan Gross, and Julia and Adam Cohen—not one of them ever boring.

Finally, love for Connie Clausen who pushed so many buttons by dying too soon—and without even saying good-bye.

1

What's a Hot Button?

We live in angry times. It no longer shocks us when we hear about a teenager shooting up his own school, a motorist breaking the jaw of someone who took his parking spot, or a mother who shook her infant to death because his crying drove her crazy. Were all these people crazy? Or only crazy for a few minutes because they didn't know how to turn off their hot buttons?

A hot button is an emotional trigger. Hot buttons get pushed when people

- call you names.
- don't respond to you.
- take what you think belongs to you.
- challenge your competence.
- don't respect you.
- give you unsolicited advice.
- don't appreciate you.
- are condescending.

When someone pushes one of your hot buttons, it makes you a little crazy. That's all it takes. You explode. Not all explosions are loud, and maybe no one can see your eruption, but you still explode inside. Has it happened to you this week, this month? You know it has. And it has damaged you—and anyone who's been on the receiving end of your rage.

Fallout from a Pushed Button

If one of your hot buttons has been pushed, you feel brutalized—even if there's been no physical attack. Aside from a sense of being savaged, your ability to assess a situation and decide how to react in a way that will do you the most good are obstructed. Your emotions carry such force that they rule your actions before you cool off enough to think about doing the right thing. When you're emotion-driven, you make mistakes you can't take back. You irrevocably hurt other people—and yourself.

It's not terrific to get your buttons pushed—or to push someone else's. The scary part is that hot-button rage is happening more and more. Our buttons seem to be closer to the surface. The degree of insult we can take before we blow is diminishing.

Jennifer tells me about her "Telemarketer Rage." The fourteenth telemarketer of the week interrupts her as she's feeding her baby and he starts his pitch—what he calls a "courtesy call." When Jennifer says she's not interested, the telemarketer keeps right on pitching. When she says she really must hang up, he becomes cursingly abusive and hangs up on her. "This is a courtesy call?" she says in fury to the dead phone. Her hot button has been pushed—hard.

Marsha tells me about her "Mobile Rage." "On the train, coming to work, I want to hit the woman talking so loudly on her mobile—oblivious to the rest of us trying to read our newspapers in peace. I don't hit her, but the man sitting opposite me who puts his dirty shoes up on my seat gets the brunt of my anger. 'Would you mind?' I brusquely ask him. When he hurriedly moves and apologizes, I can't believe I've been so crummy." Marsha's hot button was pressed.

At the gym, someone stays too long on a treadmill and gets killing looks, or one lap swimmer brutally kicks another who's moved slightly over into her lane. "Gym Rage."

I could go on. It's everywhere. It's as if we're on the edge. It's as if we all have overflowing reservoirs of anger. It's as if the world's hot buttons are suddenly all exposed.

Can We Blame It on Global Warming?

What's happening around here? No one really knows why we feel angrier lately. Perhaps it's a matter of territory: In a shrinking world, we feel we must claim our space or lose it. Perhaps it's a matter of time: With crushing deadlines and little time to unwind, we lash out at anyone who threatens to make us late. Perhaps machines are threatening us: Everything is supposed to work and nothing does. A computer crashes—and all the work you've created during the last year is on that computer. We've just embraced a brand-new millennium and can't get a human voice when we telephone a company—just a menu of directions, none of them having anything to do with the reason we called.

But no matter what's behind all this accumulated rage, if you're a kid with a hunting gun and someone says you look ridiculous, your hot button gets pushed and you explode. If you're a husband and your wife tells you you don't know what you're talking about, your hot button gets pushed and you explode. If your colleague pointedly ignores your ideas, your hot button gets pushed and you explode.

What makes *you* crazy? Perhaps it's when someone says

Calm down. Maybe it's when your mother tells you what to do, or your boss messes you around, or your friend keeps you waiting for twenty-five minutes.

Now think. When was the last time you erupted with anger, lost your cool? When did you get so irritated that you lashed out at a salesperson because you felt ignored? When was the last time you hurt your partner, child, parent, pal, or colleague because you couldn't find common ground on which to meet? When was the last time you blew?

Whatever made you lose it, one thing is clear: Your hot button was pushed, and it was not a pretty sight.

When was the last time you pushed someone else's hot button—and hurt yourself in the process? You might have said exactly the wrong thing to your best friend or to your colleague at work—and now he's furious with you. You might have touched the secret nerve with your teenager when all you meant to do was help, but no matter, there she goes stomping off to her room. You feel despair, and your own hot button is dangerously close to being pushed.

Do Your Buttons Explode Differently from Mine?

Yes. There are so many different expressions of a pushed hot button: There's explosive anger and contemptuous anger, revengeful anger and embarrassed anger, repressed anger and expressed anger—and they all look different. Besides overt anger explosions, pushed buttons also can set off other kinds of behaviour we hate in ourselves. For example, when their buttons are pushed, some women revert to childlike, submissive behaviour—"*Okay, I'll do it, I'll do it!*"—submerging rather than releasing their anger. We feel flustered and defensive when that happens. Other people who submerge their anger when their buttons are pushed are avoider or peace-at-all-costs personalities. They'll pretend nothing happened to hurt them—but inside? Inside they're fuming. Submerged anger can smoulder and resurface in the most ugly ways. Hurt to the core, some of us even withdraw and shut off all communication when our buttons are pressed.

Depending on where you live, you react to pushed buttons in different ways—regional rage. In the city you might react with icy sarcasm to the same insult that makes a country dweller curse, or perhaps you are more likely to withdraw and silently brood over a pushed button.

Wherever we live, we share a common human trait: if someone misunderstands, insults, ignores or irritates us, we feel hot surges of anger in varying degrees. Whether we live in a leafy suburb or the inner city, we know that the second millennium is leading to anxious season. The increasing popularity of yoga, meditation and other relaxation techniques comes as no surprise.

Something new is in the air and we all feel it: We know that relationships seem to be more fragile, that random violence is with us more, that hot-button issues crop up more easily than ever before.

Behind the Buttons— What's Fuelling the Explosion?

A sense of conflict is behind a pushed button. When you clash with someone, when he insults you or steps on your toes, your button is pushed and that releases blinding smokescreens of rage and feelings of impotence. These smokescreens not only prevent *us* from seeing clearly, they also blind and irritate anyone in our path.

Let's be clear: Conflict is not all bad—not at all. When

harnessed, conflict can be a gift of energy. Some of the greatest friendships, love affairs, and inventions were born from certain kinds of conflict. Still, the conflicts that keep us from realizing the fullest relationships, the conflicts that put up glass ceilings at work beyond which we'll never progress, the conflicts that ripple and cripple and push our buttons till we see red—those are the conflicts we want to banish.

The Birth of a Hot Button

Hot buttons are born from our earliest experiences in dealing with conflict. It takes years to develop a pattern of behaviour—and the patterns that are cultivated from childhood are used as weapons and defences throughout our lives when we're faced with trouble.

For example: Darlene says, "When I was growing up, my dad was a dictator. When he shouted at me, I cringed and did whatever he said." Whenever anyone shouts at Darlene today, she still cringes. Her hot button is pushed by loud voices and angry manners, and what will she do? *She'll do anything to gain peace at all costs.*

Lucy says, "When I was a little girl, my parents fought constantly. They'd ignore me, so I'd run into my room and hide under the covers to get away from the sound of their voices." When Lucy sees conflict coming on, when someone insults or pushes her button by ignoring what she says, she still runs the other way because *she is an avoider.*

Nancy says, "When I was small, there were mean kids in second grade. I learned that the only way to survive was by attacking back. The minute I attacked, they folded." Nancy's hot buttons are still pushed by the first sign of conflict, and then she instantly lashes out with an eruption. *She's an exploder.* First she attacks, then she thinks, because that's the way she's learned to deal with conflict.

> It's important to know what your conflict style is: Before you can turn off your buttons, you have to be clear about what's turning them on and how you'll probably respond.

Whatever your style, most people feel hopeless when they're blinded by anger, locked into the old patterns of hot-under-the-collar behaviours that are so hard to break. Frankly, it's nothing new—there's always been rage in the world, wars, lethal enemies, and global hot buttons ready to be pushed. What is new is that it's happening more and more. Life is increasingly complex, weapons easier to obtain, children more difficult to understand, relationships more intricate, and emotions much closer to the surface.

This book is not meant to solve the cosmic problems, but it can teach you how to turn off the triggers to boiling points. And that's plenty.

Do the Same Old Things Work?

No. Anyone who feeds you the following platitudes when he sees you're upset will probably just press another one of your hot buttons:

- "Say to yourself, 'It's not the end of the world.'"
- "Tell yourself the person who got you angry didn't mean it."
- "Calm down."

We live in complicated times, and platitudes won't work anymore. Knowing how to cool down someone who's out of control will change your life—I promise.

Larry used his inborn sense of humor a couple of years ago to cool down a cab driver who was ready to take a club to him—but he's lucky. Today, that cab driver might have knocked him silly. He'd stopped for a red light, but as the light changed to green, a little old lady began painstakingly to make her way across the street in front of his car. Behind him, a taxicab driver began to honk. He leaned on his horn and never let up—"The light's green, jerk!" he yelled out his window. "Move or I'll break your nose!" Larry quietly took his keys out of the ignition, walked slowly back to the cabbie, and offered them. "Here, you run her over—I haven't the heart," he said with a sweet smile. The cabby couldn't help laughing. He didn't apologize, but his button was defused, and both he and Larry went on their ways with a good story. Larry's nose remained intact. Today? Larry would be a fool to try it. The cab driver might think he was being made fun of, and he could react with violence.

Choose to Defuse

Even if times are more sensitive, you still have a choice. It's your call. Attitude is a choice. If you choose to react to your own pushed buttons with an attitude of blinding anger, you'll get nowhere. If you understand why people incite your rage and what you need do to turn off your (and their) anger, you'll react another way and find a solution. Choose to defuse—defuse the red heat and move on.

I'm so happy you hold this book in your hands. If you have tools to turn off sudden angers, you have power. I mean to give you those tools.

The Five-Step Formula

What follows is one of the most important tools I can offer you. Throughout this book, I will give you many approaches to resolve conflict. These techniques reflect the precepts of this vital cornerstone formula. The Five-Step Formula has within its core many of the secrets to turning off hot buttons. Don't worry about memorizing it—as you read through the many hot-button scenarios to come, the five steps, or variations of them, will become almost second nature to you.

The Basic Process in Five Easy Steps

The process always differs slightly, depending on the players. A confrontation with a colleague or a child will not play out the same way as a confrontation between a husband and wife. Here's one example of the way anger can be defused and a hot button turned off within a marriage.

A HOT-BUTTON SCENARIO BETWEEN MARRIAGE PARTNERS

DON'T JUMP DOWN MY THROAT!

Your husband, John, walks through the front door at 10:00 P.M. and you expected him for dinner at 6:00. He never called. Your hot button has been pressed good and hard. You move in for the kill. He sees trouble coming.

"I know what you're going to say, don't jump down my throat, don't give me a hassle, just leave me alone," he shouts. What's the first thing you do?

You don't move in for the kill. Instead, you move into the first step of the process.

STEP 1: WATCH THE PLAY

Remove yourself from the action, stand back in your mind for just a minute, put a spotlight on the players (in this case, you and your husband), and watch the scene that's unfolding as if it's a play and you're the audience. This enables you to see the whole picture more clearly than if you were part of the play.

"Watch the play" is a metaphor for creating a mental attitude of detachment and objectivity. When one of your buttons is pushed, the trick is to try not to let your anger go, but to just put it aside for a moment. Even if you watch the play for only a moment, you can then begin to restore your balance and react coolly and not with rage.

Step back and join the audience.

What do you see on the stage? You see a man on the defensive—worried that his wife's going to kill him. Because he feels guilty, he's on the attack. "Leave me alone!" he yells to his wife, whom he knows must be furious because he's been inconsiderate. Now his hot button is just screaming out to be pushed—as his wife's was.

But you will not push a hot button because the next step is to . . .

STEP 2: CONFIRM

This is an easily learned skill for defusing other people's anger and eventually your own by confirming the validity of their points of view. Even though you feel righteous anger because your own hot button has been pushed, you defuse the fire by acknowledging that the other person must have had a valid reason to have set you off. What you want to get across is this: "Hey, even though I feel as though I'm the victim, I think you must also feel really frustrated and upset about what happened here."

Though you feel put-upon and unappreciated, confirming your husband's point of view tells him you don't think he's crazy, evil, or stupid to have done what he did or to feel the way he does. Confirming and validating others brings a measure of calm to your antagonist.

Notice that as you defuse his hot button, yours also begins to turn off.

It's starting to look as if this situation may just end up without murder or mayhem.

Here's what you might actually say to your husband, confirming him: "John, you sound so upset and angry. I'm *not* going to jump down your throat or give you a hassle—I promise. I know something must have happened to make you so late and to stop you from calling me. We've got to talk so I can understand."

The aim here is to convince your husband you're ready to hear him—really hear him—without judging. Bottom line? At this step, you want to disarm your husband. Disarming others means you take away their weapons. You disarm your husband—you take away his weapon of defensiveness by confirming his actions and telling him you don't know why he did what he did, but you're ready to listen.

STEP 3: GET MORE INFORMATION

Once the other person's anger is defused, he or she may be willing to talk more. Getting information about the situation is essential.

Steer the situation toward understanding by asking your opponent open-ended questions. An open-ended question gives a person an opportunity to answer you in different ways, rather than by just a yes or no response. This stimulates conversation—and provides information.

Do not say: "Couldn't you find one lousy moment to call? Don't you know that I worry?"

These are not open-ended questions. They will not provide satisfying information.

You should say: "John, what kind of pressures were you under today? What happened to keep you from calling?"

STEP 4: ASSERT YOUR OWN INTERESTS AND NEEDS

In the previous steps, you've begun a conversation. Your husband is less defensive because he sees you're not on the attack. He may even say something like, "Look, of course I knew you'd be worried, but I didn't have five seconds to find a telephone, my client was on the warpath, and I had to block out the new contract. . . . I looked for a phone, but the queues were long."

He gives you his side. You listen hard.

Remember, this is not a one-sided deal. When he feels he's gotten his point of view all out and you understand him, he'll be more ready to hear you. Then it'll be your turn to discuss the situation from your perspective.

When it is your turn, try to pick up on information cues from his story and link them to your own interests, goals, or opinion.

"John, I hate that your client is giving you grief—it sounds like it was World War Three in your office. I can understand your pressure, honey—I can, believe me. Now just listen to how it felt on this end."

This is your turn to gently assert your interests and needs, and talk about your own concerns to him. You might say: "Let me tell you why it upset me when you didn't call to say you'd be late. First, I imagined you under the wheels of a bus. Second, your boss called and asked me when you'd be home and I was embarrassed because I didn't know. Third, if you'd have called, I could have planned my own evening."

You give him your side. He listens hard—because you've listened hard.

STEP 5: FIND COMMON GROUND FOR A SOLUTION

At this stage in the process, both your buttons are almost turned off. Now you need to identify issues of mutual concern and areas of common interest to resolve the conflict. It's time to shift the conversation and make the transition to the problem-solving mode by finding common ground. You might say, "We're both concerned about each other's state of mind—I know we are. We both want to do the right thing by our marriage, right? Let's make a deal on how we'll handle this kind of thing in the future, okay?"

It's time to start brainstorming solutions.

He might say: "Maybe I should anticipate problems and give you an early call even if it's just a warning that I might be late."

You might say: "Maybe we could get each other mobiles for our anniversary."

Eventually you reach common ground—a solution that sounds reasonable, even if it's not perfect.

And there we are—the Five-Step Formula in action. It may not be necessary to use all five steps during every conflict. Sometimes just one step will turn off a button and start a dialogue. For example, in the following scenario, only Step 3, Get More Information, was necessary.

Rome—If We Ever Make It There

Sheila and Mac are planning a vacation to Rome. At dinner, Mac begins to tell Sheila about a package deal his friend recommended. Sheila interjects, saying she hates group travel, and begins immediately to talk about her own idea that would save them money. As she speaks, she sees Mac frowning and shaking his head. "What's the matter?" she asks. "What do you want me to do now?" Mac responds by saying, "I want you to let me finish, I want you to LISTEN."

What happened here? Sheila pushed Mac's hot button by interrupting him and prejudging his suggestions. She needed to turn off his hot button to ward off an argument.

So Sheila asks Mac, "What intrigues you about your friend's deal? Why is it good for us?" (Step 3: Get More Information), and that's all it takes. Mac is now able to tell the full story about the package deal, which answers most of Sheila's concerns. In fact, group travel was not even involved. When Mac feels satisfied that all his issues are addressed, he asks Sheila, "Can you tell me more about your ideas on how we can save money?" She tells him.

Mission accomplished: Hot buttons turned off.

Win/Win—Everyone Wins!

There's a premise in which I believe—and I must state it right up front. I think that in a conflict, everyone needs to feel like a winner for resolution to occur. Win/win—not win/lose, not compromise/compromise—is the way to go.

Much of the art of turning off people's hot buttons depends on whether they perceive themselves as being a winner or a loser in a conflict. We live in a society in which we've been taught that winning is all, but that means one person must lose if the other wins. The trouble with this is that losers never really get their buttons turned off, even though they may lose fair and square. Resentment rules when you lose.

Compromise

Conventional wisdom tells people always to compromise during a conflict—each one gives a little and neither wins. Sometimes compromise is the only way to go. Occasionally it works, but more often it doesn't. People tend to compromise too soon—and then feel dissatisfied. If they'd only dug beneath the surface of the conflict a bit more, they would have found more complete solutions. People who compromise often end up feeling they've made more concessions than the other. Finally, agreements tend to be temporary—no one really commits to the compromise because the solution is a far cry from what each really wanted.

Collaboration

There is another way—collaboration—one that leads to everyone being a winner. I'm firmly convinced that collaboration—where we go beyond each of our hard-and-fast positions to look at the underlying needs, perceptions, and concerns of everyone involved—brings us to a win/win position, which feels much better than compromising and certainly better than losing. It usually takes more time, energy, and mutual willingness, but in the end, collaboration is the finest way for each to emerge from a conflict feeling each has won.

Finding out what the other person thinks and wants, then finding common ground where your needs connect, is what we must strive for, the feeling that we're partners, not adversaries. I'll be honest: It doesn't always work, but what does? Still, win/win works more often than any other solution to turn off hot buttons permanently.

What really is win/win? Here's the classic example given to explain collaboration to achieve a win/win situation.

The Orange Story

Two kids both want the last orange. They fight over it. They reject a compromise—cutting it in half—that won't satisfy either, really. Mum walks in. She knows about collaboration and win/win.

She knows she has to find out their needs, try to be fair, and come up with options so that each child feels she has won.

"*Why* do you want the orange?" she asks one child. "I'm thirsty—I want juice," is the answer. "And why do *you* want this orange?" she asks the other. "I want the rind to make orange icing for my cake" is the answer.

Mum gives all the rind to one child and the whole orange to the other. Both win.

Sure, this is an easy one, but the principle of win/win can be expanded to more complicated situations. I'll tell you about a win/win experience for my husband and me.

Richard's passion is photography. Mine is jazz. For a long time we each tried to compromise—I'd walk the city with him carrying his lenses and his camera bag, and he'd go with me to jazz concerts. Neither of us loved the compromise. Worse, we began to feel irritated with the other. His camera bag started to weigh a ton, and he so dreaded the concerts, he found every excuse not to go. We did want to spend time together, but it seemed we'd hit a brick wall.

One day I got smart. I suggested he bring his camera to a concert and afterwards, with their permission, photograph the musicians. What a spectacular evening! Now he had a reason to be there—to watch the musicians as they played to figure out his best shots. We went to subsequent concerts, and Richard began giving some of the photographs to the musicians. I loved watching the process and became fascinated with the personal contact we now had with jazz. He, miracle of miracles, began to get a feeling for the beat and the sound of jazz.

That's win/win. We blended our interests, we each got just what we wanted—and we grew together as a result. Win/win. It will be the basis for resolving every kind of conflict you read about in these pages.

Strangers and Other Dangers Out There

Rest assured, there are many kinds of conflict. Throughout this book we'll concentrate on how to reduce feelings of anger in yourself and in others with whom you have developed relationships. For those rages, there are marvellous tools you can use to disarm anger and open up people to hearing your side. But unstable hot buttons belonging to strangers are out there everywhere, and we ought to address those right now. Whether it's a woman pushing your buttons in a movie or deranged passerby whom you've unintentionally set off, you ought to get a feel for what to do in potentially eruptive situations with imperfect strangers. Because you have no relationship with these people, it's almost impossible to use the tried and tested techniques of conflict resolution, but you can still turn off the hot buttons that are everywhere with a few well-chosen words.

2

Hot Buttons Everywhere!

The Dalai Lama Conquers the World

Where does rage hit us hardest? Everywhere.

It all started with road rage. In the early 1990s, drivers were found to be making rude hand signs much more often than in the past when someone tailgated or didn't signal a turn or drove too slowly or, God forbid, cut them off at the pass. These were always automotive sins, but before nobody seemed to get so furious when they happened. Soon we began to notice drivers who cursed uncontrollably when one snared a parking space away from the other or didn't move fast enough as a red light changed to green.

Then cursing didn't seem to be enough. My coauthor was driving with a friend who honked at a Volkswagen Jetta blocking her path. The driver from the Jetta emerged from his car, waved a six-inch knife in her face, spat at her, then broke her windscreen with a shock absorber. Rage released, the Jetta Vigilante returned to his car and drove off.

Soon came drivers who punched each other's noses for honking or jockeying the other out of position at a red light. The newspapers began to tell of people who got clubbed with a bat or killed with a handgun for not getting out of the fast lane.

The term "Road Rage" was born.

It was the times. Experts opined that car commercials and movies made aggressive driving seem cool. More cars on the same roads, gridlock, less space, and feelings of territoriality ruled the day. People just had shorter fuses, it seemed.

In the mid-1990s road rage spread to the office, where employees were asked to be creative from tiny cubicles. For privacy, the staff had to get out on the street with their mobiles. Enter "Cubicle Rage," where nerves are on edge daily and workers' hot buttons are pushed by the slightest infractions. Cubicle Rage spread to "Air Rage" and that morphed out to "Telemarketer Rage" . . . and there we are.

It keeps growing, a whole society filled with rages we don't know how to control. Last week I heard people talking about "Slope Rage," which happens when skiers sit down right in front of other skiers to adjust their gear or jump in front of another in the lift queue. There's not a person online who hasn't complained about "Internet Rage"—when your computer cuts off after you've waited for an eternity for a special site. In the newspaper, I read about a new one—"Beach Rage," which happens when someone kicks sand on your blanket or plays his boom box too loudly or steals your wave when you're both surfing.

It's no surprise that in the West the Dalai Lama attracts increasingly massive crowds wherever he goes to spread his message of Buddhist calm. We live in a very angry, very violent society—and a lot of us want relief.

Bigotry

I have to say a special word about discrimination—the bigotry that may be the most potent hot-button presser of all time. This chapter cannot even begin to address the myriad examples of discrimination that create rage. Just imagine the anger that's sparked when someone is treated contemptuously because she is disabled or dresses differently. Imagine the bitterness and rage someone feels when she's followed by a distrustful salesperson in a department store or she can't get a bank loan or even a taxicab because of the colour of her skin. These are huge issues requiring huge societal and legal changes and cannot be fairly addressed in the brief pages that follow, but I ask you to be acutely aware of such discrimination.

What follows are some of the furies of less cosmic origin that every one of us has grown to know—if not to love—and they're just the tip of the iceberg.

I'm Out of Here

There are some kinds of rages on which you can't lay a finger, no matter how adept you are at conflict resolution. A wide-eyed, ranting maniac passes you on the road, and you're not going to empathize with him, you're not going to check his perspective, you're not going to dissect your differences. You're out of there; you're going to try to make the smoothest, fastest getaway without further inciting. He may be the guy with the knife. There's no resolution of the problem. There's only transcending it. Your only concern should be your reaction—not the other's stupidity. In such threatening confrontations, the civilized response is to consider how much more you have going for you, and thus to lose, than a driver with steam coming out of his ears. You just let him win, let him have his pathetic little kicks.

Here are some basic tips:

- Strangers react better when you imply that you know they don't intend to offend you—that their annoying behaviour is somehow just "happening." You allow them to save face.
- Don't ever blame strangers or tell them they're bad or wrong because that sets them up for fury. If possible, empathize with their situation.
- Always retain your own dignity and niceness. You want to live in a civilized society, and the world, fast reeling the other way, needs some of us to dig in our heels. Rarely will niceness fail totally, except maybe in the case of telemarketers

HOT-BUTTON HINT

WHAT PUSHES STRANGERS' BUTTONS?

Someone had better be prepared for rage.

—Robert Frost

Road Rage

What is it? Road rage is the furious response that occurs when another driver seems to pick on us, irritates us, or drives in a way that puts our safety at risk.

R.R. Behaviour	**How to Deal with It**
• Another driver won't let you in his lane, gives you the finger, or in other ways exhibits truly irritating driving behaviour.	Be meek and turn the other cheek. Let the idiot pass you and get out of your life. Although we know someone who keeps a huge picture of a horse's ass in the front seat of his car to hold up when this happens, don't do it. Also, don't hold up the sign that says STUPID or JERK or MOVE OVER or BACK UP—no matter who tells you that humour or defensive tactics soften the hearts of crazy drivers. Communications with wild-eyed drivers can be misinterpreted. It could get you killed.
• You do something wrong—accidentally cut someone up, slam on your brakes without warning, or double-park and block another car.	Contriteness is the *only* way to go. Don't be defensive or explain the good reason why you double-parked. Consider this: Dr. David Givens, the Director of the Center for Non Verbal Studies in Spokane, has come up with the *Bowing Thumb Waggle*—you display the open palm and wave gently with the fingers spread slightly apart and the thumb folded across the palm. He says it's a perfect hand signal to counteract road rage because it's a world-used gesture to signal contriteness and helplessness. *Automobile associations say the best way to avoid being the target of an aggressive driver is to follow these rules:* • Don't make eye contact with aggressive drivers. • Don't make obscene gestures. • Don't tailgate other drivers. • Use your horn sparingly.

- Don't block the fast lane.
- Don't block the righthand turn lane.
- Don't take more than one parking space (no wheels over the line).
- Don't take a parking space if another driver is about to move into it.
- Don't let your car door hit the car parked next to it.
- Don't inflict loud music on others.
- If you drive slowly, stay in the left lane.
- Don't use a mobile phone when driving.
- Don't stop in the middle of the road to talk to someone—move to the side.

Movie Rage

What is it? Movie rage is the result of inappropriate behaviour people bring to public places that ruins the entertainment for others. Treating the public place as their living room, they eat loudly, talk whenever they feel like it, or cough incessantly.

M.R. Behaviour	How to Deal with It
In the movies, the couple next to you is . . .	
• Eating or talking loudly or rattling wrappers	Say firmly but with a smile as soon as the film/play starts, "I know you don't mean to disturb others, but the acoustics here aren't the greatest and your voices (the noise from your chocolate) are louder than you think. I'd love it if you could keep it down."

M.R. Behaviour	How to Deal with It
• Coughing, sniffing, or making other disgusting noises	Always come prepared, especially in flu season, with an unopened pack of tissues or cough drops—unopened because people don't like to share with a stranger. It's a small investment and can be the difference betwen a hands-clenched experience or a happy movie time for you. Say, "I see your cough (cold) is really annoying you. I'd be so happy if you'd take these—they're unopened."
• Smooching	"I'm really sorry to interrupt. I see that you two really care about each other and it's lovely to see. Still, would you mind embracing at another time because it's so distracting? Thanks a million."
• People who arrive late, asking you to change your seats of choice to accommodate them	"Oh, I wish we could, but we got here especially early just to choose the seats most comfortable for us. I don't like being uncooperative, but I'll have to refuse your request—I'm so sorry."
• Or worst of all—piled up their coats on the adjacent seats, which they're "saving" for friends	You first must say, "Is that seat taken?" If the answer is, "Yes—my husband's sitting here," you must find another seat. If the answer is, "I'm saving it for friends," you have every right to nicely assert, "Well, the movie's about to start and since I'm here and your friends are not, I think it's only fair that they find other seats—thanks." Then sit down.

Shopping Rage

What is it? Shopping rage usually derives from workers in stores who are supposed to be serving your needs and aren't. Of course, you also may feel anger when clothes are mislabeled or when sale items are fought over by fellow shoppers, but shopping rage happens most when we are ignored or dismissed by store employees.

S.R. Behaviour	How to Deal with It
• Persistent salespeople who want to score a commission and don't leave you alone	Say, "Thanks for offering to help. I prefer to look around on my own, and I'll call you when I need assistance."
• Salesperson in an expensive store who's not paying attention to you, or any salesperson who pretends she doesn't see you	Your own attitude counts here. Even if you're not dressed elegantly, stand straight, look the salesperson in the eye, and with a smile say, "I'd appreciate your help. I'm sure you don't intend to ignore me, but I've been waiting for quite a while."
• Salesperson who takes phone calls while you wait	Wait till the call is finished. Then say with a smile, "Your call may have been important, yet I was kept waiting. I hope you can give me your undivided attention now. I'd appreciate that."

Expert Rage

What is it? When doctors, lawyers, accountants, or other experts intimidate us, we forget to question their advice. Because we're nervous, we don't hear half of what they say. Because we need them, we listen silently to stuff we don't understand. Then we get angry at them for what we see as arrogance and feel rage at ourselves for being afraid to ask questions.

E.R. Behaviour	How to Deal with It
• Your doctor has rattled off a diagnosis and a suggestion for cure—and you've been so nervous about your problem, you've missed most of what she's said.	Bring a note pad or a tape recorder with you. Prepare some questions in advance—you'll have more as the expert speaks. If you don't understand something, ask for clarification. Say, "It would be helpful if you just explained what you said in layman's terms so I can better understand." When the session is winding down, ask, "Is there anything else you think I should know?" At home, listening to the tape or checking your notes, you'll see what you missed in the office.
• You get a large bill from your lawyer. For what? He tells you your EBT [examination before trial] is next week. What's that? You realize you have no idea of the status of your case.	Lawyers' jargon has done you in. If there's a term you don't understand, ask what it is. Write everything down, or tape the session. You must also ask three questions of your lawyer before you hire him/her: 1. What expenses are included in the retainer you ask for—and what are not? 2. What's the law involved in my case—and what are our chances of winning? 3. How long will it be until my case comes to trial?
• The expert makes you wait too long.	Say, "I realize that it's difficult for you to keep to appointment times when emergencies often arise, but it's terribly inconvenient for me to wait so long. What can we do in the future to avoid this? Perhaps I can call an hour or so before my appointment to see if you're running late?"

• You want to get a second opinion. Your doctor is looking mighty miffed.	Get another doctor. No kidding. No good physician will ever get insulted when a patient seeks another opinion. He must be unsure of himself.
• Your health plan or medical group has denied your claim.	You can always appeal the decision. First speak to your own doctor and ask his/her recommendations. Then contact the group's customer service department (or your "ombudsman") and ask to have the reason for the denial put in writing. Find out exactly what things you must do to create an appeal—and in what order. Generally, you'll have to write a letter describing why the health plan was wrong to turn you down and why you need the disputed procedure for your health.

Air Rage

What is it? For many years, flying passengers have been subjected to delays and cancellations of their flights, lack of information when the plane acts funny, missed connecting flights, lost baggage, wrong information, abysmally long queues, increasingly cramped seating, people who recline their seats all the way back and stay that way even after the food has arrived, overhead bin hoggers, odours . . . an endless list of air horrors. It makes our blood boil.

A.R. Behaviour	How to Deal with It
• Passenger in front of you is reclining almost into your lap.	If a polite request doesn't work, this will: Say, "I'm about to be sick—would you very much mind not reclining?"

A.R. Behaviour	How to Deal with It
• The food is terrible.	Airlines are spending less on food: In America in 1990, \$5.51 per passenger was the norm, and in 1998, \$4.49 was spent. Really outrageous. If it's a problem for you, bring your own sandwiches, or call the airlines twenty-four hours in advance and order a specialized meal—kosher, vegetarian, low-cal, low-salt, low-fat.
• You're at the airport and you've just heard there's been a serious delay or cancellation of your flight.	Do not wait in the endless line. Pull out your trusty mobile and call the airline for more in-depth information and/or to rebook for the next flight; you'll be hours ahead of the person who waited in that line.
• You need to catch a domestic flight, but the queues are endless.	Go to the international counter if the queues are shorter. Politely ask if you can check in for a national destination. Almost always the answer will be yes.
• You're really having a terrible time on the whole flight—and you don't even know that your baggage is going to be lost.	Don't get mad, get even. Soften your rage by thinking about the letter you're going to write to the CEO of the airlines. Get his/her name by phoning your carrier. You will almost surely get an apology—along with some free miles, sometimes a whole free flight for you and a companion.

Cubicle Rage

What is it? Today, 58 percent of US office workers labour in cubicles—four and sometimes three-sided tiny box work-stations with the thinnest of walls. As work cubicles grow even smaller, cubicle rage grows in proportion. In many large companies, even the cubicle is a blessed memory. Today, many are asked to inhabit even tinier spaces called pods.

C.R. Behaviour	**How to Deal with It**
• The person in the next cubicle has been sighing, schmoozing with her boyfriend on the phone, and banging her rolling chair on your adjoining wall as she slides back and forth.	You need to say, "Listen, Sue—I'm working very hard on this project, as we all are. You may not be aware of it, but your chair is banging on our mutual wall and it's driving me nuts. These walls are so thin I can hear everything from your office." That's all. You can afford to be subtle and not list every one of her annoying behaviours. She'll get the message. In a couple of hours, stick your head into her cubicle and thank her for being so understanding.
• The closeness of this place is oppressive—you feel like you're ready to scream.	Take a full lunch hour. According to a new study, only 17 percent of all workers take that full hour, which can be the key to diffusing cubicle rage. You need time to yourself. And leave the cubicle. A change of scene for only a few moments takes the focus off the work scene and helps you be more productive and even-tempered when you return.
• An officemate keeps borrowing. And borrowing. And borrowing. She's forever popping in to take a pencil, a coffee cup, an extra computer disk.	One of the reasons that cubicles so enrage us is because our privacy is perennially overrun. We have no space, no tools, no atmosphere to call our own. Therefore, we become supersensitive to invasions. Try this. Invest a few dollars and buy a coffee cup (perhaps with the annoying person's name

	How to Deal with It
	on it), a box of disks, and a package of pencils and give it all to your officemate, saying, "I bought you some presents, Sally—I hope they'll hold you for a while." Be very careful how you say this because you do not want it to be interpreted as sarcasm. Smile warmly. She'll get the idea.

Queue Rage

What is it? No matter what queue we choose, the other queue always moves faster. This causes rage to build because we feel trapped. When the bank teller is agonizingly slow, people try to cut in front of you in a movie queue, or a thirty-item woman precedes you on the ten-items-only checkout queue, you're a candidate for queue rage.

Q.R. Behaviour	How to Deal with It
• She says, "I'm in a terrible hurry—may I just go in front of you with these few things?"	You say with a smile, "I'm sure you're in an enormous hurry—but I am, too. Try to understand."
• There are too many customers and too few checkout staff.	Ask to speak with the store or bank manager and request additional help. You'll almost always get satisfaction.
• He crashes the queue (at the airport, movie, supermarket).	Confront him in a polite way, but allow him to save face. Say, "I think perhaps you didn't realize it, but the queue starts here—thanks so much for understanding."

Phone Rage

What is it? Phone rage is the result of the telephone-based aggravations that set our teeth on edge and are the bane of civilized society. I think more people complain about the indignities unleashed on us from telemarketers, mobile abusers, and automatic voice mail menus than anything else.

P.R. Behaviour	How to Deal with It
• The infuriating telemarketer calls to sell you something and won't take no for an answer.	Gently but firmly say that you never respond to telephone solicitation and you're going to hang up. "I hope you understand. I know you have a tough job." Then hang up.
• The solicitor for the charity gives you guilt along with irritation.	Say, "We've already made our decisions about our contributions this year, but thanks for your good work."
• You're trying to reach a person or department by telephone. You get an automated menu (press this number if you want, etc.). But none of the numbers deals with your problem.	This is automation gone wild, and it is the most complained-about rage. As soon as the recorded message comes on, press ZERO for operator—even before you listen to the litany of choices. That will usually get you a live person to help. Many companies don't even mention this option because they don't want to encourage the use of a live operator, which costs them more money. OR: When the recorded voice says, "If you're dialing from a rotary phone, dial—," press that number even if you don't have a rotary phone. That will also get you a live person with whom to talk.

P.R. Behaviour	How to Deal with It
	If all else fails, press any option the menu offers that sounds like it will get you a real person. Then depend on the kindness of strangers. Say, "I'm desperately trying to reach the radiation department of this hospital—can you connect me or look up the extension for me?" Little-known statistic from Prudential Insurance: Twelve percent of people say by the time they get through to a live person, they've forgotten why they've called.
• Someone puts you on hold. It lasts forever.	Be equipped with personal button-soothers before you call. Have a newspaper handy, make your to-do list, decide who to invite to the party, empty the dishwasher, meditate. Sometimes you have to play their game, but at the very least, you can be in control of what you do with the wait. It makes you less angry.
• Mobile abusers. This problem is so endemic, we're devoting a great deal of space to it!	• Item: A German businessman infuriated fellow restaurant-goers by refusing to turn off his mobile phone. A fight broke out, and he was clubbed to death. "He spoke really loud," said one witness. • Item: Broadway's *Death of a Salesman* is interrupted three times a week by chirping mobile phones. Once, enraged, the leading man stepped out of his character and said to the audience, "Turn that damned phone off!" • Item: Last week someone's mobile phone rang at a funeral,

and she proceeded to answer it and talk throughout the service!

Clubbing someone to death is a bit extreme, but some would disagree. Mobile phone rage is taking over the world. When we feel trapped—having to listen to the woman making endless calls on the train when we want to read, having our dinner disturbed by the very instrument we've run from in the office—we feel that clubbing is a reasonable response.

But it isn't. Here's what to do: Don't just stare at the mobile phone user with a look of disapproval, as too many of us do. If someone is making or receiving excessive numbers of phone calls in a public place like a restaurant, bus, movie, or library, say, "I see you're a very busy person, but I'd appreciate your turning off the mobile phone and using it elsewhere where it won't interfere with my meal (my privacy, my reading, etc.)." Always complete your request with a sincere thank-you. If the person refuses, you have a perfect right to ask a person in authority to take over. Many mobile phone users, believe it or not, don't realize you don't have to yell into a mobile phone. Say, "It would be helpful if you could please lower your voice."

- What if it's your mobile?

Bottom line: In public places such as restaurants and theaters, unless you're a doctor with an emergency, civility demands you keep that phone turned off. If you are a doctor, it's vastly more considerate to wear a phone or a

How to Deal with It

beeper with a vibrate function that won't disturb others—and you can return the call outside. If you're in a public place such as an airport lounge or bus, limit your calls to three minutes or so, and speak in a low voice so tempers don't flare around you.

This is an issue that's so inflaming others that companies are already selling devices to disable mobile phones by using radio signals to block communications between handsets and their base stations. The outrage of trapped listeners may encourage restaurants and theaters to install them.

Restaurant Rage

What is it? We become furious when the dining we've been looking forward to as a pleasure becomes a battle for courteous service and good food. We feel anger when imperious or stupidly friendly waiters take the joy out of dining.

R.R. Behaviour	How to Deal with It
• Reservations are not honoured.	Call in advance to confirm to avoid problems. If they're still not honoured, consider the restaurant as truly derelict in duty. It gives you permission to nicely suggest to the maitre d' that you plan to write a letter to the editor of a prominent newspaper telling what happened, and that you'd greatly appreciate a strong effort to find a table. Bad press is anathema to restaurants. They'll find a good table for you.

• You're dissatisfied with the food that appears.	You will always feel fury with yourself if you eat something you dislike because you don't want to "make a fuss." Well, don't make a fuss, but quietly and nicely tell the waiter, "I feel annoyed and frustrated because I've been looking forward to this meal and the food is cold." Give the waiter your specific complaint, and ask for your food to be replaced. The chef won't be shocked—it happens all the time.
• You're placed at a table right near the kitchen, bathroom, or other undesirable spot when more attractive tables are vacant.	Say, "We would like a better table—how about that one—or that one." If you're told they're reserved, ask how long before a satisfactory table is available. By being persistent in a gentle but assured manner, you're pressing your point, making your needs clear. You usually get what you want if you're willing to wait a few moments. If you don't, you still have a choice: Stay or leave. The only untenable choice is to stew, fume, and hate your experience.
• This is the worst service! After requesting it, your waiter doesn't bring you bread or respond to your request for water. He brings an inferior wine—not what you ordered. Perhaps he thinks that two women alone don't know any better. He is slow, sometimes arrogant, sometimes dismissive.	Act immediately to correct the problem. With great courtesy you need to say, "It seems as if you either are very busy or have had a long day. If that's so, it explains the way you've overlooked us." Then specifically state your complaints. If the rest of the meal is not smoother, don't leave any tip. That will get his attention.

Starbucks Rage

What is it? Coffee shops like Starbucks have sprung up nationwide, and although they're supposed to be lovely places to hang out for a leisurely fifteen minutes or so, they can be a source of burgeoning anger. Perhaps because there are no rules, perhaps because they're low-maintenance operations (custom has it that you clear your own table), too many people walk away with coffee nerves instead of a smile.

S.R. Behaviour	How to Deal with It
• Someone's dozed off in the only comfortable armchair or is nursing an empty cup of coffee while doing her homework—and you're waiting for a table.	Don't wake up a dozing person because you don't know if he's dozing because he's ill, homeless, or even somewhat mentally unbalanced. In a city, you have to use street smarts. If this is important to you, inform the manager of the problem and say, "I'd appreciate it very much if you could speak to that person because I've been waiting for a while to use that wonderful chair." If someone's writing a letter or doing homework at a table in a crowded coffee shop, she either is not aware of your presence or just doesn't get it: Coffeeshops are not extensions of school or office. Speak to her directly and say, "I've been looking forward to my cup of coffee and there are no other tables available—will you be using yours much longer?" You've put her on notice in a pleasant way, and she'll probably leave shortly. Everyone doesn't have to love you.

Gym Rage

What is it? The whole world is working out. The gym is a particularly intimate place. We're all dressed in almost nothing, we sweat and strain together, and the atmosphere is rife for simmering anger and smouldering resentments.

G.R. Behaviour	How to Deal with It
• The swimmer brutally kicks you as she passes you in your lane.	She doesn't know the lane rules—or doesn't care. She should have gently tapped you on your foot at the end of the lane to show she wanted to pass. Tell the lifeguard. He should keep a "book" on her. Too many transgressions and she should be asked to resign from the gym.
• The woman next to you leaves the residue from her sweaty palms all over the bicycle handles. • The guy next to you leaves heavy weights on the weight bars—and you can't even lift them to remove them. • Your locker room neighbour is monopolizing the treadmill. • Someone on a treadmill is watching TV or listening to a radio, and the sound is so distracting you want to die.	The following applies to *all* the behaviour on the left: Every good gym is run by rules. If the management of your gym has not posted signs like the following, you must politely ask them to do so. If they refuse, get militant. Organize a petition drive signed by the members threatening not to renew membership if the following rules are not enforced fairly and consistently: • Please be courteous and clean your sweat off the machines when you're finished. • Please remove weights from weight bars when finished. • Thirty-minute limit on treadmill if someone is waiting. • Earphones required for TV and radio. What if someone pays no attention to the sign? Most people are reasonable. Say, "This is apparently a very popular machine, and I know there are limits on its use (point to the

How to Deal with It

sign). Have you any idea when you'll be finished so I may have a turn? Thanks."

Danger Lurking

Why is all this important? Why should we bother about resolving conflicts when others are making us furious? Why not just walk away?

We've said that you definitely should walk away from a few isolated situations where hostile strangers can pose a real danger to our well-being. When you're dealing with relationships, however, unresolved conflict can push your buttons and make you very, very angry. It can also do something even worse.

It can make you very, very sick.

3

Hot Buttons: Hazardous to Your Health!

When my hot buttons are pushed, I get angry. So . . . big deal . . . I get angry. It's not going to kill me. Well, maybe not right away. If you're experiencing rage and frustration regularly—two to four times a week or more—chances are good that it's going to make you sick. I'm not exaggerating.

Fight or Flight

The natural reaction that helped primitive people survive stress—the *fight-or-flight syndrome*—can actually damage us greatly in more modern times. When our ancestors' hot buttons were pushed and they needed to defend themselves or flee to safety, hormones such as adrenaline and cortisol, which prepare the body to respond to stress, were sent rushing into the ancestral bloodstream to give the needed burst of energy. Bodies geared up to face the challenge (fight) or muster the strength to move out of trouble's path (flight). All this was terrific if you were a caveman and the wild boar was right behind you, but today, wild boars are not our biggest problem. Anger more than fear gets those hormones racing, and that same anger can really destroy your health.

Because modern stress levels tend to stay at a near-constant high and the fight-or-flight reaction occurs every time your hot buttons are pushed, we have a problem if they get pushed a lot. "You're giving me a headache," your mum used to mutter every time you exasperated her. Well, people really can get sick from pushed buttons.

What does getting sick from anger feel like? Try to remember the last time your hot button was pushed by your husband, your teenager, the rude salesperson:

Did you feel heart palpitations?
Did your stomach turn over?
Did you get that sour taste in your mouth?
Did your muscles tighten up?
Did your face feel flushed and hot?
Did your hands get cold and clammy?
Did you develop a headache or a backache soon afterwards—even pimples or a rash?

If you said yes to any of these reactions, your body was responding to stress caused by rage. And this is exactly the kind of stress that attacks health.

Body and Spirit

"The body and spirit are twins," wrote the poet Algernon Swinburne. What happens in your mind and your spirit gets to your stomach and your heart—believe it. Exactly what does happen in your body when a perfect stranger gives you the proverbial finger as he accelerates past you on the highway?

Your heart rate and your blood pressure jump, sometimes sky-high. A new study at the Ochsner Clinic in New Orleans reports that high levels of hostility existed in many heart attack victims, and that these hostile patients also had higher levels of weight, cholesterol, anxiety, and depression. Enough guys with raised middle fingers and it may well lead to your own heart disease—and heart disease kills one of us every twenty seconds. As we know well enough, though, it's not just crude strangers who wind us up.

Arguing with a respected partner or a beloved relative who knows exactly where your jugular lies is the most common and surefire way of raising blood pressure. We love our kids, but no one can infuriate us more: Those particular pushed buttons can always be counted on to jog the heart to beat abnormally fast.

Large-scale studies have also shown that the workplace can damage our health. Stress from conflict at work often leads to colds and coughs and even musculoskeletal disorders.

When a button is pushed, your body instantly feels tense, tight, overworked. Your mind reads **R A G E** in red letters. As you feel this rage, your blood, carrying oxygen and nutrients, is redirected to organs such as the brain and muscles, which now need more energy to function with the anger-induced stress. Because less blood goes to the stomach and skin, your stomach may be tied up in knots and your skin may break out. Stress brought on by feelings of impotent rage can also affect memory, creativity, and even sleep. Stress increases our respiration rate—you know that because the angrier you get, the more heavily you feel yourself breathing.

The immune system—and your susceptibility to infectious diseases—can also be compromised. Someone made you feel furious yesterday, and you've started to sneeze today? Not surprising. Experts tell us that during episodes of stressful anger, bacterial infections increase, and we're more prone to upper respiratory viral infections like flu.

Marital conflicts do more than bruise feelings and break hearts metaphorically. They also narrow blood vessels and encourage hypertension, atherosclerosis, and acute coronary heart disease say recent studies. And here's the killer: As couples exhibit negative fighting behaviour—including sarcasm, disapproval, nastiness, and dismissal—their levels of immunologic agents that ward off viruses and tumours dip lower.

Could it be that it's not the rage that kills so much as the ways we display our rage during conflicts?

In women, brittle bones are a common fallout of stressful anger because anger and depression may actually decrease bone minerals. And speaking of depression, the vast majority of depressions today are caused by anger turned inward against the self, anger daily stirred up by pushed buttons.

Not only can a hot button push you toward poor health, but it can even affect your sex life—try feeling amorous when you're in a fury.

Finally, pushed hot buttons can harm our bodies directly, but they can also lead to health-impairing behaviours such as alcohol and drug abuse. If the anger or tension you're expressing or suppressing cannot be made to melt away, how about a drink, a pill, a cigarette? How about two—or three?

So we should contain our anger, right? We should not respond when people push our buttons, right? Wrong. Research shows that both "extreme expressors and extreme suppressors of anger" are more likely to develop health problems than those who learn to release their feelings moderately. The way we don't display our rage can harm us: Unexpressed anger greatly increases the odds of contracting heart disease because anger drives up blood pressure.

In the next chapter, you'll begin seeing how deactivating your hot buttons and releasing your feelings in acceptable but satisfying ways can preserve your sanity—and your health. Here's the question you should ask yourself at this point: Am I close to getting sick with anger? Is my health hot-button prone? Try the following self-assessment exercise to see how near to the surface your hot buttons actually lie.

Rate each experience listed below on a scale of 1–5 as directed. Then check the analysis that follows.

ARE YOU HOT-BUTTON PRONE? AN EXERCISE

I EXPERIENCE THE FOLLOWING:

ALMOST NEVER	RARELY	SOMETIMES	QUITE OFTEN	ALWAYS
0–1	2	3	4	5

The Way I Move Through My Day

When I hang up the telephone, I feel frustrated __

I have interactions with strangers on the street, in stores, or at parties that aggravate me __

My family doesn't understand me __

I find myself close to tears __

My work colleagues are jealous of me __

I can't seem to express myself without someone getting angry at me __

I feel powerless or frustrated __

I'm scared __

Nothing seems to work anymore __

People tell me I'm oversensitive __

I feel attacked __

People blame me when things are not my fault __

The people around me are neglectful __

People try to take advantage of me __

I Feel These Physical Symptoms

I live with anxiety __

My heart beats too fast __

When I'm not exercising, I start to hyperventilate or breathe very heavily __

My stomach is tied up in knots __

I regularly take antacid tablets __

My back hurts __

I'm exhausted __

I get muscle twitches __

I have embarrassing wind __

I'm constipated or I have hemorrhoids __

My doctor has told me I have some form of heart problem __

I'm accident-prone __

I've got headaches __

My skin breaks out __

I have a "lump" in my throat __

I Notice That

I bite my nails __

I want to hurt people who get me furious (but I don't, of course) __

I *do* hurt people who enrage me __

I can't sleep __

I'm not in the mood for sex __

I find myself reacting loudly, angrily, or aggressively when someone winds me up __

I've been drinking, smoking, or taking pills __

My memory is troubling me __

I lose my temper __

I indulge in repetitive behaviour when I feel frustrated (tap my foot on the floor or my fingers on any surface) __

I'm close to tears __

I sigh __
I grind my teeth __
People are so damned stupid __
I find myself clenching my fists __
People are so damned inconsiderate __
I've been fighting with someone close to me __
People want to change me __
I fantasize about killing someone __
Everyone gets mad at me __
I feel angry — very angry __

NOW: Add up your number responses.

Did You Score Between 170 and 249?

You are very hot-button prone. Those buttons are right there on the surface, pulsating and waiting for someone to set them off. You're enormously vulnerable to being insulted or "dissed," and way too often you find yourself trembling with rage. This poses a real threat to your physical health—but your emotional health is also subject to the anger you feel at people who don't understand you or respect you.

You need to take charge of the conflict that's threatening to make you ill. Your score tells you to learn to defuse your own buttons and rechannel the negative energy you feel when someone does or says something that enrages you. Instead of becoming hostile, aggressive, or defensive, you can redirect all that angry passion into resolving the conflict.

This score is in the danger zone and should be a warning signal. Your health is threatened by your hot buttons.

Did You Score Between 90 and 169?

You're somewhat hot-button prone, but this score is right on the edge. You can easily learn how to turn off hot buttons, but

- right now, you still find it hard to take criticism.
- you often have difficulty having a discussion without it becoming a fight.
- too much of your day is spent thinking of what you could have said, should have done. RIGHT?

So there are still too many abrasive confrontations in your life—and this takes up much of your precious time. It also makes your stomach hurt and gives you headaches. Don't cage yourself in and threaten your health by having volatile hot buttons. Learn how to navigate difficult conversations and confrontations. Read on.

Did You Score Between 40 and 89?

Not bad at all. Your health is not under direct threat from pushed hot buttons because you're pretty good at resolving misunderstandings. If you ever felt helpless, ill, or depressed by having your hot buttons pushed, that's probably no longer the case. Still, you have more work to do—and you sense it. Unfortunately, some people still know how to "get your goat," you still blow more easily than you'd like, and you seem to irritate other people more than you like. The good news? Your health is not really at risk. But read on to become even more expert at soothing your own and others' hot buttons.

Did You Score Less Than 40?

You're *not* hot-button prone. In fact, you could probably write this book. The daily conflicts in your life are usually defused before they have a chance to touch your health. You know how to express your own feelings and needs in a way that does not threaten others or your own sense of well-being. In fact, your calm often helps chronic button-pushers find some calm in their own lives.

But have you told the truth? Are you sure your number responses are an accurate reflection of your deepest feelings? This score is almost too good to be true.

Hear What's Unspoken

Let's begin to see the way hot buttons and health are connected. Though people who don't like us or aren't even aware we exist can disturb our equilibrium, we can push the buttons of people we really love and cause them ill health, even when that's the last thing in the world we would wish for them. It doesn't have to be an enemy or a stranger who sets off violent anger inside you—it can be your daughter, your husband, your best friend. In fact, the typical hot-button scenario occurs when no one is bad and no one means harm. It's a fact of life.

I want you to read about Anne Coren, divorced and a senior marketing director of a telecommunications firm, and her fifteen-year-old daughter, Karen, and think about how you would defuse their pushed buttons.

Listen to Me—Even Though I'm Not Talking!

When you love another, you have to hear what's unsaid.

Anne: I saw your English teacher at the community board meeting last night, and we talked about you. She says you complain about asthma, and you're always going to the nurse with headaches. She also said your grades and your last practice SAT score are way down. I told her not to worry—you were fine. Listen—aren't things fine? I thought everything was going so well for you. Why haven't you told me about these school problems, or even that you've been feeling crummy?

Karen (angry and yelling): I really don't appreciate your talking to my teacher about me behind my back, and I don't have time to deal with all this trivial stuff like how many headaches I get a week. And anyway—I shouldn't have to tell you—someone else might have noticed her child gasping from asthma. What kind of mother are you? Listen—don't interfere in my life.

Anne: Just calm down—why are you crying? I don't think it's trivial at all. And it's not just your life—I'm your Mum, I have a right to know that you're feeling sick. But Karen, I never saw you gasping. Do you notice anything about me, like the fact that I'm shaking here? Do you care enough about your mother to think about my ulcer and how the doctor said I shouldn't get aggravated? And about your grades—I assumed you were doing well because I didn't hear differently. Listen, darling, calm down, let's stop arguing, I'll help you—we'll both feel better in the morning after breakfast, I know it.

Karen: Don't darling me, don't tell me to calm down! I won't feel better in the morning. And you won't find the time to help me with my problems—you're always complaining about how stressed you are.

Anne: That's a low blow, Karen. Don't we schedule time for talking together? Don't you think a child's health is a mother's concern?

Karen: I'm not a child—I know when to worry about my health. Yes, we do schedule twenty minutes after dinner together, but even then, you know you're always distracted, always looking at your watch, always pushing for our talk to end. You know what? I hate our talks.

Anne: That's so not fair to say that! It's you who are always looking for things to say to get at me—you resent me even though I go out of my way to please you.. Why do you have to be so unpleasant?

Karen (slamming shut her bedroom door): Forget it—leave me alone, get out of my life.

A HOT-BUTTON ANALYSIS

WHAT HAPPENED HERE?

Karen's mum always seems remote and distracted, and Karen feels she is at the bottom of Anne's priority list. Karen, hiding the fact that she's not the student Anne thinks she is, has had her button pressed because she feels betrayed by her mum, who spoke to the teacher behind her back. She also feels abandoned because her mum didn't even notice her wheezing. Her buttons are seriously pressed by the way Anne seems to avoid problems. In fact, Karen's stress level is so high, her health is in real danger. She expresses her angst by exploding. And an exploder like Karen is trouble for an avoider.

Karen's pressing Anne's button because she's making her mum face up to uncomfortable issues—that's why Anne makes light of Karen's headaches (just eat a good breakfast). Illness terrifies Anne, and she just wants it to go away. Anne's button also has been pressed because Karen never notices when she feels poorly. Anne's been pretending that her daughter's problems don't exist. The first time she acknowledged trouble was when the teacher brought her up short with the information that Karen was feeling ill and doing poorly in school. So much has been unsaid between this mother and daughter.

What to Do?

To hear each other, actually hear the unspoken words, both must recognize and defuse the different ways each expresses hurt. For starters, Karen has to level her explosions because they make her avoider mum feel frantic. Anne has to confront issues because avoiding them will make her exploder daughter feel even more ill from the stress.

Although mother and daughter have pushed each other's buttons, Anne needs to do the big work—she needs to make the first move because she's the grownup. Naturally, Anne feels hurt because she really loves her child deeply, but she also feels angry because she's been misunderstood. Still, it's Anne who needs to use the five-step model to resolve the conflict with her child. And she does.

The Five-Step Formula at Work

STEP 1: WATCH THE PLAY

Anne says to herself: "I'm not going to react to Karen's explosions; I won't even muddy the air by being defensive. First, I need to watch the play, see us on a stage as if I'm an audience to this happening. I need to take a breath and watch the play for a moment.

"What do I see? I see a slammed door. Behind it is an angry kid who looks as if she's been angry for a long time. She's mad at me. She thinks I go behind her back. She thinks I'm not there for her. She says she wants me out of her life—but I don't believe it."

STEP 2: CONFIRM

Anne knocks on Karen's door, and when it's reluctantly opened she says: "Karen, I hear how furious you are. I'm ready to listen to you—maybe you think I'm being phony about this, but I know it's time for me really to hear what's bothering you. I am going to throw out all thoughts of my work and anything else in my life so that I can listen to you as you deserve to be listened to. I know you have lots of reasons to be angry at me, and I want to hear them. I want to find out what's behind your anger. I know I need to trust your judgment more. I keep thinking of you as my baby and I'm wrong—you're almost an adult."

STEP 3: GET MORE INFORMATON (ASK OPEN-ENDED QUESTIONS)

Anne: When we're having a talk, what do I do that bothers you?

Karen: For starters, you do things that show me you're not listening. You look at your watch like you want to get away; you ask me to repeat stories I've just told you.

Anne: How does that make you feel?

Karen: It makes me feel like slamming doors! I really hate you when you don't pay attention or patronize me. You make me feel as if I'm an inconvenience to you.

Anne: That must be a terrible, terrible feeling. How do you think this affects you?

Karen: How the hell do you think it affects me? I get up in the morning with a headache and I can't breathe. And you never even notice because you're always off to a meeting—you always pretend everything's all right. Well, it's not. And guess what? I think I'm failing in school, too.

Note to reader: Anne and Karen continue in this vein, with Anne continuing to ask open-ended questions to get Karen's side. She's showing that she accepts and values Karen's point of view. Whatever Karen says, Anne always responds with understanding and never defends her own point of view—yet.

STEP 4: ASSERT YOUR OWN INTERESTS AND NEEDS

Anne: It's meant a lot to me to hear you speak from your heart. I want to mend our fences and be close—so can I just tell you what's in my heart now? (Karen nods.)

What I most need is for you not to shut me out with such loud anger—it makes me feel so helpless—and mad, too.

I'm sorry that pressures in my work life have interfered with our relationship, but I have to work to make money to support us, and I need for you to understand that. I also need to know when you're not feeling well so we can figure out ways I can help you. I felt embarrassed when your teacher had to tell me stuff I didn't know about my own child. So keep me in your loop.

What can change is that now I will consider you as an adult. And I will change the way I am when we're together—I'll be more focused, I promise you.

Karen: That's right—you need to do all that. How long have I been trying to tell you I'm not a baby? And, of course, I understand you have work responsibilities—don't you think I know that? But if when you're with me, you're really with me, it'll feel better.

Note to reader: Now Anne's building on Karen's point of view with an expression of her own needs so that both their needs can become a mutual goal. And it's starting to work. Karen's opened her door just a bit. It's enough for now—it'll open wider.

It will save their mutual health.

STEP 5: FIND COMMON GROUND FOR A SOLUTION

Anne: It looks like we both need to respect each other's judgment more and share what bothers us.

Karen: This is the first time in ages that you've really listened to me—and let me finish my sentence. Last week, when I told you I felt crappy, you told me if I ate a good breakfast, I'd feel better.

Anne: That was arrogant of me. But how about we talk specifics now. What exactly do you want me to do?

Karen: Well . . . our stupid "scheduled" after-dinner time doesn't work for me. I'd rather spend an occasional afternoon shopping and just hanging out with you. Let's do something together instead of phony scheduled time—and I think we'd share more that way. And I'd like the time with you.

Anne: Perfect—you're on. How about Saturday? And this is what I'd like: A promise that if you feel ill or have a school problem, I'll be the first to know. Well, maybe not the first—maybe the third. If you don't feel like talking, you can write a note and slip it under my door. Whatever—I just need you not to leave me out.

Karen: I'll try.

The Five-Step Formula works. It may not be perfect, and you may have to modify it to fit your situation, but it is a universally effective approach to resolve conflict.

Wrong Assumptions

Another way to turn off hot buttons is to be aware that most of us assume too much about the other's motives—and those assumptions are often dead wrong. The kind of stress that makes us ill easily comes when people attribute false feelings to us. Assumptions are beliefs we take for granted. People's beliefs are not always what you assume they are. When people make wrong assumptions, it's guaranteed to push hot buttons.

Listen to the story of Alan and Kristina. Alan and Kristina have been married three years. Kristina has started her own catering business with her office in her home. Alan's been helpful about giving her advice on what computers and telecommunications systems will cut her costs, but lately he seems to be reluctant to involve himself in her office problems.

Alan is on his way home from the office.

He's Thinking	**She's Thinking**
I wish she didn't keep bugging me all the time with those computer problems. I just bet when I walk in the door, she'll pounce on me with something new, and I'm so tired.	Every time I ask him questions about the computer, he jumps at me. I get headaches whenever I use the scanner because he makes me so nervous.
He Says	**She Says**
What a relief—I got a seat on the train. I'm really beat. What's for dinner, honey?	I had problems with the scanner, today. Dinner? It's leftover chicken.
Not chicken again! I'm not eating. And I'm losing patience with your perpetual problems.	Stop shouting at me! When you get that way, my head explodes. You're so grouchy—you jump at me before I even tell you the whole story.
I already know your whole story. I hate it.	And I hate yours.

What Happened Here?

When people get it wrong and make negative assumptions about each other, it creates havoc with relationships. Conflict is bound to spring up when we act and talk on the basis of these wrong assumptions. Alan assumed Kristina would burden him with her computer problems, so he didn't even hear her out. She was going to say that she got help—and it was all fixed! Further, his first words to Kristina were to ask what she was going to do for him—he expressed not a word of interest in her day. On her part, Kristina assumed her husband would be fatigued when he came home—and she was right, although she paid no attention to this correct assumption. Because he was tired, she assumed he'd be impatient with her. That was not necessarily so, but guess what?

Assumptions about what the other person is going to say or do often come true—even when the original assumption is wrong. Kristina assumed Alan would cut her off and not help her at all. By not listening to his tiredness or his hope for a good dinner, she's acted in a way that was guaranteed to push his buttons. Kristina unconsciously willed a self-fulfilling prophecy—she didn't expect him to be considerate or hear her out about her day—and what she expected, happened.

It was inevitable that they would push each other's buttons. If something doesn't change, their health will be compromised by their frustration. Turn off those hot buttons. But how? Step back in time. Try to rewrite the script so no one's buttons get pushed:

Alan Should

- Listen to Kristina and refrain from making assumptions. He doesn't know her whole story—maybe she's already gotten help with the scanner.
- Show some interest in her day—without prejudging what she will expect from him.
- Not assume that she's always available to make him

dinner—even though she's in the catering business. Marriage is a fifty/fifty proposition. If her workday has been terrible, he might suggest they go out for dinner, a common-ground solution since neither really wants the leftover chicken.

- Find a quiet time to discuss the way he really feels about helping her with her computer problems—and brainstorm a solution. Should she find a smart high school student to help?
- Not push her buttons with disrespect—"I already know your whole story. I hate it." That's anger talking, not accuracy.
- Understand that pushed hot buttons really do make people sick. His wife is having very real headaches.

Kristina Should

- Assume responsibility for her own business, and look for other resources to help her deal with computer problems and thus take the burden off her husband.
- Not push Alan's buttons by ignoring his words. He's tired and hungry.
- Not assume Alan would be inconsiderate.
- Not assume Alan would be interested in hearing about her problems the moment he walks in the door.
- Not assume she's invulnerable to stress—she should avoid the stress that gives her headaches. For example, she instinctively knows what her husband does not want (her computer problems)—why bait him and bring on another headache?

Change False Assumptions into Better Approaches

Here's a false assumption. Mum says to her teenage daughter Amy: "Which one of your friends gave you that awful idea? You're too young to go trekking through Ireland with just one other person."

The assumption is false because it just so happens the idea is all Amy's. She got it from no one. When her mum makes the assumption, it pushes Amy's buttons for a number of reasons. First, because the false assumption tells Amy that her mum thinks she's hanging out with friends who are a bad influence, Amy gets angry because she now has to defend her choice of friends. Second, the false assumption tells Amy that her mum thinks she's unoriginal, that she's not capable of her own ideas. Amy gets furious that her mum thinks so little of her intelligence. This one short false assumption does a lot of damage.

A better approach might have been for Amy's mum to say: "Tell me about why you want to backpack through Killarney and why you think it would be a safe and good thing to do." After she's confirmed Amy's point of view and acknowledged that it's really Amy's idea—not a friend's—and that it has some validity (Step 2 of the Five-Step Formula) and after she's gotten more information about Amy's view (Step 3 of the Five-Step Formula), she can go on to assert her own interests (Step 4)—why she thinks this particular idea is not good. Then both might more easily reach common ground (Step 5).

Let's think about assumptions—or rather, *wrong* assumptions—for a minute. Look at the following exercise, and see how to transpose a wrong assumption into a more productive communication.

False Assumption: *You Say*	What's Wrong with It	A Better Approach
I know what you're thinking.	You can't possibly know what's in her mind.	Tell me what you're thinking.
This is your fault.	It's more likely that you've both contributed to the problem.	Let's take a look at what happened, and see how we both can fix it.
You don't know what you're doing.	Maybe he knows exactly what he's doing, but you don't have the patience to listen.	Can you give me your reason for doing that—and I'm going to listen hard to understand.
You wish you were alone.	How do you really know what he wishes?	If you want to be alone, I understand perfectly.
You love to catch me making mistakes.	You should accept honest feedback.	When you're sure I did something wrong, I appreciate your comments.

Rage Surfaces—No Matter How Long It Takes

Rage festers like a nasty infection. Sometimes the infection takes hours, weeks, or months to surface. Sometimes it gets red and hot almost immediately. If you don't do something about it, you'll get sick. Listen to Marge's story.

The Tale of the Terrible Orange Juice

While out for the newspaper, Marge picked up a tiny container of what was labelled "fresh squeezed, delicious orange juice" in a corner deli and was astounded to see that it cost three pounds "I'll treat myself," she thought. Eleven blocks later, at home, she sat down for her breakfast, broke open the orange juice, and—you guessed it—the worst taste ever! The juice should have been sold a month ago.

Orange Juice rage! It may sound funny, but Marge was really furious at the tradesman who so disrespected his customers that he'd cheat them with old juice. She was angry at herself for being "taken." And she felt disappointed that her breakfast was ruined. Reluctant to face the hassle of returning the juice—not to mention the eleven-block walk back—she just poured it down the drain.

For the next two days, she felt tense. Her head ached. On the third day, she had forgotten about the juice, she thought. When she passed the deli on the way home, heartburn—from nowhere—overwhelmed her. It wasn't from nowhere.

"That's it," she thought to herself. She walked in and asked to speak to the owner. She spoke calmly but firmly. When the owner heard what had happened, to Marge's delighted surprise, he apologized and immediately offered a money return. Plus a lily.

Good-bye headache and heartburn.

Here's some food for thought:

HOT-BUTTON HINT

When anger rises, think of the consequences.

—Confucius

4

What Pushes Your Buttons?

Do You Know Your Conflict Style? A Quiz

You actually own a conflict style—the way you most often approach confrontations. It is a learned style: You started learning it in your earliest childhood. As you grew, your emerging temperament dictated the way you'd deal with personal and work conflicts.

Now, as a grownup, if your conflict style jars the people in your life, watch out. And if their conflict styles clash with yours, hot buttons will be exploding everywhere!

For example, extroverts and introverts may infuriate each other when in a confrontational situation. People who are detail-oriented push the hot buttons of those who want to hear only the bottom line or see the big picture. People who pull rank with their age, superior knowledge, or clout can boil the blood of those who hold back their accomplishments and talents. If you crave direct answers to your questions and your partner responds with *maybe, perhaps,* trouble is on the horizon. It comes down to this: People with different communication styles and different responses to conflict can get on each other's nerves.

Just as we learned a conflict style in our early years, we

can modify it if it's not working. Then we can begin to turn conflict into collaboration.

The first step is to learn a little bit more about yourself. You need to pinpoint the strategies you instinctively use in dealing with conflicts to figure out why your hot buttons are always being pushed, leaving you feeling angry and helpless. Then it's a short step to figuring out how to avoid pushing others' buttons.

Take the following quiz and check out the analysis that follows to determine your personal conflict style. What pushes your buttons?

Choose the Response That Comes Closest to How You'd Act

Be Scrupulously Honest!

1. **You tell your teenager that he can't use the car because he's been late three times in a row. Your husband overrides your veto and is about to hand over the keys. What would you do?**

   a. You smile and pretend your husband did not contradict you.

   b. You grit your teeth and stand your ground. "You are going nowhere in this car," you say to your son through gritted teeth while giving your husband the look that kills.

   c. You agree but calmly ask your son to promise he'll come home early this time.

   d. You tell your teenager you'll abide by your husband's

decision today if he agrees to a family meeting the next day at which boundaries will be firmly set. Later, you have a discussion with your husband about the importance of a united front.

e. You can't help it—tears come to your eyes at the injustice of it all. Husbands are supposed to stick by their wives. You leave the room with a heartache.

2. You're a copywriter at an advertising firm, hired for your enthusiasm. At a conference meeting, you get positively lyrical about an idea—and your boss says, "Calm down—you're acting inappropriately." You do which of the following?

a. Get very quiet and don't say another word for the rest of the meeting.

b. Respond enthusiastically: "The reason nothing gets done around here is because we're all so damn passive. More of us should show a little energy!"

c. Calmly apologize to the group with a big smile, and concede that maybe you have been a bit overexuberant.

d. After the meeting, discreetly ask the boss to be more specific about what he means by "inappropriate"—and also what he recommends to make meetings more productive.

e. Slam down your pen on the table, exhale loudly, and look heavenward.

3. A co-worker is extremely manipulative and spreads false information about your performance. You do which of the following?

a. Ignore the situation and put the episode out of your mind—maybe you're oversensitive and imagining the whole thing.

b. Confront her, saying, "You better stop talking about me. I've got some pretty damaging information to spread about you and make no mistake—I will!" You feel like socking her.

c. Try to make up with her by being more friendly ("A soft answer turneth away wrath").

d. Say to her, "I would like to discuss some things you've said about me to others because it may be keeping us from working well together."

e. Approach her but get very nervous and emotional as you tell her how much she's upsetting you.

4. Fill in the blank from the phrases below. Your best friend says: "I can't stand your always being late. I can't believe you're so inconsiderate and selfish." You probably would say something like:

a. "Sorry, babe—listen, I love the brooch you're wearing."

b. "You're arrogant and shrill and now that you bring up selfishness, let me tell you what a master of selfishness *you* are!"

c. "Whatever."

d. "We need to talk about this right now. Let's see how we can change our meeting plans to make us both comfortable in the future."

e. "How could you say such terrible things—look—I'm shaking."

5. Lucy, your officemate, is a serious bubble gum chewer/popper. You love your division, but the noise is doing you in. A likely way you'd deal with it might be:

a. Ask your boss if you can change divisions. It'll be fine—you're flexible.

b. Chew gum loudly to show what an annoying habit she has. Cut out articles on chewing gum and tooth decay and put them on her desk. Finally, complain to management.

c. Get used to gum.

d. Go out to lunch with her to discuss the problem. Tell Lucy that the gum chewing bothers you, but you also know it's not fair to ask her to stop. Say, "Could we figure out a way to work it out like—chewing just ten minutes out of every hour?"

e. Tell Lucy that your nerves are frazzled—you're going to have a nervous breakdown.

6. Your colleague says, "I keep giving you new ways to get the job done and you insist on doing it your way. Why are you so inflexible?" You answer:

a. "I don't mean to be inflexible—by the way, *your* report last week—it was great!"

b. "Do you want it done your way—or done right? Your way stinks—and this is why."

c. "Sorry—I'll do it your way from now on."

d. "Is there any part of my approach you find effective? What do you think we can do to meld my way with your way?"

e. "Damn it! You ride slipshod over everyone's feelings and I feel brutalized!!"

7. Check the response best describing your reaction to conflict. *Don't lie.*

a. I withdraw from situations where people are getting furious with each other.

b. I can usually overpower or intimidate the person who starts up with me. Frankly, I kind of enjoy that.

c. I believe that harmony in a relationship is more important than getting what you want.

d. I find that conflicts give me an opportunity to learn more about the other person.

e. When I'm having a fight with someone, my whole body reacts emotionally. It seems important that the other person know how I feel deep inside.

8. When I see hostility at work, this is what I usually think or do:

a. I try to control my feelings so hardly anyone knows what's going on in my heart. Anyway, there's rarely any hostility in my workplace.

b. I do what I have to do to win. It's more important to be respected than loved.

c. I'm tempted to give in in order to smooth things over. Losing one's temper is a sign of poor breeding.

d. I love to create an open forum and hear my opponent's point of view and try to find a solution that satisfies everyone.

e. I say what I have to say even if I lose my cool. That's me—take it or leave it.

9. Check the *two* statements that seem most true for you:

1. I reach agreements as quickly as possible so I don't have to deal with anger.
2. The meek will not inherit the earth.
3. I hardly ever express my views in a volatile situation.

4. I often plan ahead, trying to anticipate various options to deal with problems.

5. Getting really excited is not a bad argument ploy: After the storm comes the calm.

6. I can always find reasons to delay dealing with conflict; often the problem just goes away.

7. Compromises dilute everyone's side. I'd rather make an enemy than lose points.

8. I'd rather lose the argument than lose my temper.

9. I'm good at putting myself in someone else's shoes—if only for a moment.

10. If you don't express yourself with spirit, no one takes you seriously.

10. Check the following character you best identify with:

a. Pollyanna

b. Alexis (Joan Collins's character in *Dynasty*)

c. Mrs Brady of The Brady Bunch

d. Madeleine Albright

e. Bette Midler

11. Your husband avoids affectionate physical contact

with you in public. Last night, at dinner with friends, you tried to take his hand and he pulled it away. Mortified! This is your reaction:

a. Try to forget about it.

b. Get pretty testy. You probably won't sleep with him for a week—or you'll punish him in some other way.

c. Live with it. That's his style, you can't do anything about it, and anyway, he's a good provider.

d. Ask him at a quiet time, "How do you feel when I take your hand in a restaurant? Does it embarrass you? How do you think I feel when you pull it away?"

e. Tremble. He hates it when you tremble.

Scoring and Analysis

SCORING

Note: In question 9, if you checked 1 or 6—take an a
if you checked 2 or 7—take a b
if you checked 3 or 8—take a c
if you checked 4 or 9—take a d
if you checked 5 or 10—take an e

Now count the number of a's you've chosen and write it here: __

b's? __
c's? __
d's? __

e's? __
f's? __

ANALYSIS

As you read about the various types, remember: In the real world, no one exactly fits any one category. You may be a combination of types, or you may even show different styles in different situations.

However, we all have a predominant style of addressing conflict. Your answers indicate a style that is yours—at least much of the time.

IF YOU'VE CHOSEN MOSTLY A'S, YOUR CONFLICT STYLE IS AVOIDER

If you are an Avoider, *make it go away* is your most fervent wish when conflict intrudes in your life. One of the ways you've learned to make it go away is by denying that there's any conflict at all. And when you can't pretend it doesn't exist? Because you feel you'll lose in any battle, you'll run away from conflict. What if you run but can't hide? Then you'll just delay—put the whole problem on a back burner.

Avoiders equate conflict with something bad rather than seeing conflict as a normal, natural part of life. An Avoider's first assumption is that if a touchy situation is brought up, something bad will automatically happen. She avoids face-offs because she must avoid failure. She's afraid of getting the short end of the stick. When confronted with conflict, Avoiders feel they will end up being devalued in some way.

Here's your secret: You would really love to make your own points, be more assertive, and face the truth, but something's stopping you. You know you're not your own best friend—and that makes you feel guilty.

What do you sound like?

An Avoider mum: "I'm having this conflict with my son, but I don't want to ruin the holidays so I'll wait till later to deal with it."

An avoider boss: "We're a happy family; we have no conflicts, no differences." (But go ask the employees—you'll get a different story.)

An Avoider adult (about her controlling mother): "I know it's wrong to ignore my ailing, aging mum, but my brother's better at this than I am."

An Avoider girlfriend: "He flirts at parties, but I know that nothing more will happen."

An Avoider sister: "I have to talk to my sister about her drinking problem, but I'll have more time next month."

What pushes your hot buttons? When someone says, "We've got a problem and we've got to deal with it right now." (Avoiders hate being pushed into conflict.)

IF YOU'VE CHOSEN MOSTLY B'S, YOUR CONFLICT STYLE IS SLASH-AND-BURN

If you're a Slash-and-Burner, you're a tough guy, an *in-your-face* person. A Slash-and-Burner wants to cut down her opponents. You've learned to see conflict as *I win, you lose.* You take no prisoners, provide no options. Why? Because you've come to believe that if you attack fast when there's trouble, you'll have the upper hand. You genuinely feel that you're right—and that you should be able to convince your antagonist of your position. You try to barrel through a conflict so you win and the other loses by yelling, slamming doors, fighting, or being insulting.

You find yourself trying harder to come up with reasons why the other person's wrong rather than why you're right.

You do admit there are some problems. People seem to get offended because you're very impatient. If you're a woman in the workforce, you want always to look tough so others don't think you're wimpy. That seems to make you a lot of enemies—but so be it. You will not compromise your standards.

Here's a secret: You often displace your anger. You'll tell someone off at work because your husband criticized you.

Here's another secret: You have always felt cheated by life. That's why you slash and burn your way through life—it's the only way to get authority.

What do you sound like?

A Slash-and-Burn mother (to her daughter): "Wear the pearls I gave you—anything else looks disgustingly cheap."

A Slash-and-Burn friend: "You are truly stupid if you go out with that guy."

A Slash-and-Burn boss: "If you don't hand in the report tomorrow, you're history."

A Slash-and-Burn girlfriend: "I don't care if she's a business colleague, and I don't want to hear your puny excuses. If you have lunch with her again, don't bother calling me."

A Slash-and-Burn colleague: "Can't you tell when no one is even listening to you? Your work is sloppy—do it my way."

What pushes your hot buttons? When someone says, "I can't seem to make up my mind, can we let it go for a while?" (A Slash-and-Burner can't stand indecisiveness.)

IF YOU'VE CHOSEN MOSTLY C'S, YOUR CONFLICT STYLE IS PEACE AT ALL COSTS

If you're a Peace at All Costs person, you want harmony. You'll do almost anything to make sure conflict is soothed over. You tell yourself you're being unfair if you're tempted to say something critical about someone else. You hate confrontations and arguing—that's not the way you were brought up. Decent people don't fight.

You rarely express your own needs because you see the way people get crazy when they disagree. You could get hurt in a conflict—and that scares you. You could even look undignified. The fact is, you're not a yeller. Not even a loud arguer.

The truth? You often feel frustrated. Perhaps if you dare to say what you really want, people will really get angry. Sometimes you could kick yourself for not being more self-confident, but it's more important to be liked than victorious.

Here's your secret: It appears that hardly anyone loves a martyr. You seem to drive people nuts with your soft and self-effacing style—even though that hardly seems fair, right?

What do you sound like?

A Peace at All Costs pal: "Okay, okay—you win."

A Peace at All Costs employee: "I can see why you can't give me a raise—I understand perfectly."

A Peace at All Costs mother: "Sure, you can have your ears pierced even though you're only ten and I hate it. Anything not to have a scene at home."

A Peace at All Costs wife: "Okay, we'll have Thanksgiving again with your family even though my own mum is alone and she misses me—it's not worth fighting about."

What pushes your hot buttons? When someone says to you, "Stand up for your rights and fight for what you want." (A Peace at All Costs person finds it very painful to assert herself. It feels much safer to just give in.)

IF YOU'VE CHOSEN MOSTLY D'S, YOUR CONFLICT STYLE IS PROBLEM-SOLVER

If you're a Problem-Solver, arguments don't make you quake. Angry faces won't kill you. You've learned that if you look hard enough, you can usually find something in common with others who see things differently. You know that problems that seem insurmountable can usually be solved if you work at them.

A good conflict, fairly played out, jogs your creativity and imagination. It usually clears the air. When people put their cards on the table, the solution becomes visible.

You genuinely like to know what's on other people's minds—what's underneath the surface, that is, not just what they *say* they're worried about.

You know things aren't always black and white—in fact, they're usually a nice gray. If you can't find a perfect solution, you're willing to give a little.

Here's your secret: You're a great and creative listener. You know what few people know—if you show interest in what others need, they are more interested in knowing what you need.

What do you sound like?

> A Problem-Solving lover: "I think I understand why you don't want to wear a condom. It's clear that this is important to you. But I must protect myself—and I know you can understand that. It seems now that we have to talk about different methods of birth control. Do you have any ideas?"
>
> A Problem-Solving pal: "When you come late to lunch, we lose our table, it gives us less time together, and worst of all, I feel frustrated because it's inconsiderate. You know what? I hate feeling mad at you. What can we do to work this out?"
>
> A Problem-Solving employee: "I know this project is a high priority to you, yet I have to go to my son's class play this afternoon. I'll arrange to work late tomorrow night to meet the deadline."
>
> A Problem-Solving wife: "You don't feel like pasta and I do. Let's go out to dinner and you can have your chicken—and I'll get my pasta."

What pushes your hot buttons? When someone says, "There's no point in talking about this—friends don't have to be forever." (You're frustrated because you feel differences *can* be discussed rationally.)

IF YOU'VE CHOSEN MOSTLY E'S, YOUR CONFLICT STYLE IS THE EXPLODER

If you're an Exploder, you're high drama. You're emotional and demonstrative. You know that a display of emotion gets people's attention. Anyway, conflict actually does create a physical reaction in you—your heart beats faster, your palms sweat—and it somehow shows. When confronted with a problem, you cry easily, you storm out of rooms, once you stamped your feet—and you were a lot older than eleven.

Sometimes you plan out an explosive scene, but more often it just happens—you can't help it. Listen—you have to be emotional in order to have your point of view heard. You've known that ever since you were two. Maybe your mum was an Exploder.

Some people think you're out of control, but here's your secret weapon: You're not. You can control your emotions—turn them off when you wish.

Here's the bottom line: It's your opinion that if the other person feels your pain or passion, sees what it does to you, he'll understand you better. Frankly, you can't bear ice people—so cool and detached in a conflict, they have no feelings. That is *not* you.

What's your secret? Sometimes, inside, you feel so damn fake.

What do you sound like?

> An Exploder mother: Your teenager doesn't want to apply to the prestigious college of your choice. She says she's not smart enough. You get tears in your eyes and yell, "What's the matter with you—you're as smart as anyone—you're killing me."
>
> An Exploder wife: "What do you mean we have to relocate? I'll go crazy without my friends! I don't care about your promotion. Over my dead body we'll relocate!" (And you slam down the phone.)

An Exploder colleague: You have to make a presentation with someone. She proposes a cut-and-dried, boring approach. You've already written a witty, terrific pitch. "It's ridiculous to do it that way—it'll never sell! I can't bear it, Jane—you're doing this to spite me."

What pushes your hot buttons? When someone says, "Lower your voice" or "Calm down." (You need to express your emotions.)

Quick Fixes

So what do I do with all this information?

Just understanding your conflict style should make you more aware of the way you react when faced with an emotional clash. Being able to predict your own behaviour will help you cool down because you are stepping back—looking at yourself as though you were watching a play. That's the first step toward opening constructive dialogue with the person who's fuelling your fire.

What happens if you run into a confrontation with one of the above types—and need a quick fix? For more lasting changes, you need to use the techniques described later in this book, but to turn off hot buttons temporarily, try the following.

What Do You Do If You Run Into . . .

AN AVOIDER?

A person who avoids conflict has removed herself from the action for one of two reasons: Either she smugly feels she knows best—*or* she's so terrified of losing any battle, she pretends there's no battle. You deal with an Avoider by approaching the person calmly and suggesting that there is a situation that needs attention. That encourages her to face conflict without experiencing too much anxiety. When an Avoider is helped to express her feelings, they often come pouring out, and a dialogue is started—just what is needed.

A SLASH-AND-BURNER?

Don't back off; don't yell—but act forceful. Here's a trick: Subtly mirror his choppy, vigorous body language, but don't act as if you're mimicking or making fun of him. As you move into his more vehement form of expression, gradually cool down, move less forcefully, speak less intensely. Then watch to see the Slash-and-Burner follow you into your own cooler zone—it almost always happens. Tell the S-and-B quietly but firmly that there will be negative consequences to both of you if the problem can't be worked out. It puts him on notice that his techniques will hurt him as well as you.

A PEACE AT ALL COSTS PERSON?

Speak calmly and find a gentle way to discover what she really wants. The trick here is to avoid feeding into her "martyr" personality so she won't feel hidden rages at you later. Instead, ask her what she thinks ought to happen as a result of your disagreement. In order to avoid confrontation, she'll agree too easily to what you want, then probably not keep her commitment, so make sure you question the Peace at All Costs person to find out her hidden agendas. You'll avoid sulking, seething, and submerged anger if you're clear about what you need and what she needs.

A PROBLEM-SOLVER?

You've hit pay dirt. Thank your lucky stars.

AN EXPLODER?

Quietly allow her to blow off steam—she'll probably run out of rage sooner than later if you don't explode back. Acknowledge by body and facial language that you're hearing her dramatic outpourings—and you don't think they're phony. Listen to her complaints—they'll be lengthy—but focus on your own targets and objectives instead of her behaviour. Don't use "blaming" or "shaming" phrases that might escalate the explosion.

Finally, when there's a pause, ask quietly if she has anything more to tell you. If she's finished, ask if you might tell your side. She'll listen—cooled off considerably. Then, you can start a dialogue toward resolution.

5

Hot Buttons and Intimacy

Given only one wish, most of us would wish to be loved. To be able to reveal ourselves totally in front of a beloved, with all our imperfections, and still be embraced and accepted—what could be more gorgeous? Whether we're married, single, or same-sex partners, we crave connection, we need to be close, we yearn for that heart-revealing intimacy.

But, "you love me so much, you want to put me in your pocket . . . and I should die there, smothered," said D. H. Lawrence. D. H. was right. You can't put the other in your pocket, even in the name of intimacy. It doesn't work because intimacy is not the same as melting into each other. One lover doesn't own the other, nor should she blend into the other. Intimacy is not two people who turn into one, even though they connect sexually, spiritually, and intellectually.

In fact, the very dearest intimacy of all happens when each partner stays a unique individual and shares differences with the other.

Face it—there's a downside. If you're an intimate couple, expect fights. Has to happen. Two different people, loving each other, sharing time and secrets and their very lives, are also going to hit hot buttons. Every intimate couple sometimes has conflicts—and they have the potential of being more terrible than the conflicts of the worst enemies.

You Always Hurt the One You Love

Why does it hurt so much to fight with the one you love? It hurts more than fighting with anyone else because we have so much more invested in each other. When your hot button has been pressed by a lover, it's pressed. Feel rage at the persistent telemarketer? It'll last for ten minutes. Feel rage at your dearly beloved? Plan for ten hours, maybe ten months. A beloved partner goes unerringly to our most vulnerable part—and when that happens, we go on autopilot and follow the old patterns of angry reaction. Between lovers, hot buttons are raw, emotions more heightened. Here's why:

1. *Lovers have road maps to each other's hot buttons.* When we feel rage and want to get even with someone, who knows better than a lover where her partner's hot button lies? We're capable of bringing up still-raw issues that may have occurred a year or ten years ago. We're capable of being meanly judgmental. Capable of unfair criticism. Capable of saying and doing things that are guaranteed to produce a hot reaction. And we know it.

2. *Neither is the boss.* You may be the quintessential problem-solver at work, but at home with your partner, you're part of the problem. If you're the boss in your office, you can direct workers to do what you want. If you're an employee, you follow

directions. Simple. But you can't direct your intimate partner to always do what you want, nor do you want him to be the boss, nor can you tell him off, nor can you tell yourself—as you can with a colleague or an employee—that what he's saying is trivial, and you won't pay attention.

3. *You both have unreasonable expectations.* Having a fight with a loved one hurts so much because expectations are much higher—expectations you don't have about the outside world. Lovers or spouses are supposed to be perfectly loyal, supposed to listen to you, understand the most subtle nuances of your feelings, nurture you, and agree with you—right? When your love doesn't do what he's supposed to do, it's hard not to press his hot button in retaliation.

4. *You wear masks.* With those we love, ordinary conflicts have a way of turning into murderous rages because closeness often gets in the way of getting to the truth of the matter. Ironically, the closer we are, the more we tend to mask a problem, and the real issues may lie far below the obvious. Sometimes it's hard to tell what we're really arguing about—values, shared visions of the future, or a current problem.

HOT-BUTTON HINT

Think, when you are enraged at anyone, what would probably become of your sentiments should he die during the dispute.

—William Shenstone

She criticizes him for never putting the toilet seat down. He responds with a zinger about the way she put *him* down in front of their friends. But what they're really both upset about is that they haven't made love for a month. And if that never even gets brought up, how can they possibly resolve this conflict?

The exercises in this book may seem simple, but they will do just that—help you dig deeper. And then, just watch.

The Crucial Ingredient of Intimacy

Is it great sex? Well, great sex is swell—but think again. Great symmetry of ideas? Nope.

If there's anyone who knows about the chemistry of an intimate relationship, it's John Gottman, Ph.D., of the University of Washington in Seattle, who for the past three decades has been a pioneer in the field, with astonishing results from large-scale studies of couples. And do you know what Dr. Gottman considers one of his prime findings? It's this: A lasting intimacy, says Gottman, results not from a couple's ability to avoid conflict, but from a couple's skill in resolving the conflicts.

I couldn't agree more. We tend to think that the fewer the conflicts, the happier the couple. Well, we're wrong. What makes for the deepest intimacy is when each knows how to turn off the other's hot buttons. And, say the experts, it's even possible to predict whether a couple will stay happy together simply by looking at the way they deal with problems. Those who constantly push each other's hot buttons, who unfailingly go for the jugular in their disagreements, are doomed to failure.

On the very first day of a new workshop, I usually can tell which couples are going to learn the tools of conflict resolution and stay happily committed and which ones seem headed for a split. You can be the most erotically inventive lovers, but if you blame each other, criticize, or become defensive at the first sign of conflict, you're in trouble. Those partners who don't sling mud when they're furious, those who don't have to win every point, those who seem to be friends, who can make each other laugh, and who soothe each other even when they're arguing—those are the ones who can count on the deepest intimacy for all their lives.

Let's stop for a moment and consider the worst offenses of the mudslinging partners—the jibes that consistently push buttons. Well, what gets you right in the jugular? In what areas do you feel most vulnerable? The first step in turning off your own hot buttons is to recognize the sensitive spots that for many of us originated in childhood. If your father was really sarcastic to your mum, you may have unresolved childhood issues that make you blow up when someone is sarcastic to you. If you were the butt of a whispering campaign in sixth grade, the sight of your partner whispering to someone else can set you off. If your best friend constantly judged your actions and choices, when your partner comments that you were stupid to do something, it will make you see red.

The following nine triggers make us most angry.

The Nine Top Button-Pushers in the World of Intimacy

Button-Pusher	What It Does	What It Sounds Like	What You Can Say (to defuse anger, avoid a defensive answer, and start dialogue)
1. Blaming	This avoids responsibility for actions and points an accusing finger at someone else.	You gave me the wrong directions and made us late.	I need to be more careful. When I'm getting directions, tell me the questions I should ask next time.
2. Being a Know-It-All	This partner gets you furious because he has the correct (and ONLY correct) answer to everything. He must have the last word, must one-up you.	Believe me—you're wrong. I've done this a million times.	Your way works for you—I see other options I'd like to share with you.
3. Dissing (undermining)	When you diss someone, you disrespect and devalue her. You can diss someone by calling her names, but the act of ignoring a person is the worst diss of all. I take that back: Hanging up the phone on someone is the ultimate diss.	Loudmouth—you talk too much and say nothing.	Aren't you exaggerating? But I'll listen more, and let's see what happens.
4. Being Sarcastic	This is a subtle and insidious put-down—often reflected in the tone as well as the words.	Well, here comes Ms. Perfection.	I feel put down when you are snappy with me. Maybe I'm not perfect—but admit it, I can be awfully cute.

Button-Pusher	What It Does	What It Sounds Like	What You Can Say (to defuse anger, avoid a defensive answer, and start dialogue)
5. Denying	I never said that, I didn't think that, I wasn't there, I didn't hear, you didn't tell me. Denying implies your partner is stupid, doesn't listen, or is insensitive to your needs.	I never told you it was okay to call me in the office.	Perhaps I misunderstood. Why don't we go over when and where I might call you during the day?
6. Judging	This denigrates someone's choices or opinions.	That's the stupidest idea I ever heard.	What's not good about it? Be specific and constructive.
7. Condescending	A partner who is condescending puts you down by acting patronizing and superior to you.	Yes, darling, you're trying so hard to understand this complex idea, but you're not going to do it because you have trouble seeing the big picture.	Yes, I'm trying—it may be complex, but not that complex. Perhaps my view is different, and I see something you're missing.
8. Psychoanalyzing	When a partner acts as though he knows your deepest, most hidden motivation—it gets you insane with rage! He's implying he knows everything about what makes you tick.	You and your mum both love to be seen as martyrs.	I don't agree. Tell me why you feel that's so.
9. Name-Calling	A name-caller puts someone down by comparing her to something insulting or terrible.	You look like a blimp in that dress.	That statement was really hurtful—I'm sure you didn't mean to hurt me so deeply.

The Awful Zinger

When people are very close, they know just what will hurt the other the most. Going for the jugular is the specialty of intimates who thrive on pushing buttons. They give awful zingers. The awful zinger can also be the response of a partner whose jugular has been tapped. If you've pushed a partner's hot buttons (and sometimes we don't even know we've done it), expect an awful zinger back. Complete the following exercise to see how many times you've given a zinger or set yourself up to get one back.

How Many Zingers Have You Given Today? (Tell the Truth!)

By ordering: You must . . . You have to . . . You will do as I say . . .

By threatening: If you don't, then . . . You had better, or else . . .

By preaching: It's your duty to . . . You should . . . As a father, you ought to . . .

By lecturing: Here's why you're wrong . . . Do you realize . . .

By providing answers: What I'd do is . . . It's best if you . . . Nobody asked me, but . . .

By being judgmental: You're thoughtless . . . Your hair is too long . . . How could you . . .

By excusing: It's not so terrible . . . She didn't mean it . . .

By diagnosing: You need a psychiatrist . . . You try to get attention by . . .

By name-calling: You wimp, jerk, dumbhead, nobody . . .

By fortune-telling: You'll feel better by tonight . . . I know what you're thinking . . .

By expecting him to change: Why aren't you . . . Why can't you . . . Why don't you . . .

If you pressed two, that's two too many. Expect zingers back.

Zingers abound in conflict between intimates. Howard Markman, Ph.D., of the Center for Marital and Family Studies at the University of Denver has discovered in a groundbreaking study of intimate couples that it takes only "one zinger to undo twenty acts of kindness you show your partner." One harsh phrase, one hot button pushed, can wipe out months of niceness.

Want a Perfect Example of a Zinger?

"You're a damn liar, Charlie."

If you're Charlie, your button's pressed.

Charlie's been insulted by his girlfriend—called a liar. Of course, he's probably set himself up for the zinger by pushing one of her buttons, but instead of reacting to the zinger with another zinger, he can defuse her anger and save the situation. How?

BY EMPATHIZING

"I can feel how furious you are—it's terrible for you to think I'd lie to you—it must shatter all trust you have in me!" When you empathize, you're not agreeing with the zinger-giver, just acknowledging her feelings, and that shows you care. Empathy's the number one button-defuser because it usually starts a dialogue. Empathizing takes your mind off your own feelings for a moment and allows you to creep into someone else's shoes to see how she feels. What could be more calming?

BY ASKING QUESTIONS

"What have I said that makes you think I lied? Can you say a little more about why you think I've lied to you?" Asking a question does two things: It probes for more information about your partner's feelings, but just as important, it gives you time—time to cool down.

BY PARAPHRASING

"You're upset because you feel I've not been truthful." When you paraphrase, two things happen: First, by restating what your partner said, you're making sure you heard exactly what he meant you to hear. Second, you're mirroring what she had to say and that tells her you're paying attention—a button turnoff right there. It's simple to do—start with the word *you,* describe what you think she's said, but don't defend yourself or apologize.

Silent Zingers

You sense your partner's anger, but he's not talking. Silent zingers can corrode a relationship even faster than verbal ones. Do you live with a master of the silent zinger? Dr. John Gottman has extensively analyzed videos of couples, and he's discovered two especially insidious silent-zinger button-pushers that are as lethal as they are soundless—showing contempt and disgust.

CONTEMPT

The facial display of contempt is a contraction of "the dimpler"—the muscle that pulls the corners of the mouth to one side (usually the left) while the eyes roll heavenward. The body language of contempt is illustrated when your partner studies his nails or picks lint off his jacket as he says, "Go on—I'm listening." But he's not. He's showing contempt.

DISGUST

The facial display of disgust is signaled by a sneer or a curled lip, as if your partner smelled or tasted something pretty bad.

Gottman found that when a partner habitually flashes contempt or disgust zingers, not only do health problems in the other partner ensue, but chances are good that the couple will eventually separate.

No zinging (silent or otherwise) allowed.

Conflict Resolution and Why Lovers Need to Know It

Can we live without zinging each other when we're furious? We can. It's possible to unload and sound off constructively, and share gripes, criticisms, and annoyances with our intimate partners—only not with zingers. We've got to dig to find the real issues, then find dialogue that works to heal. We've got to learn how to resolve conflict.

A conflict is a disagreement. When you and your partner clash, or say or do something that gets the other truly furious, it hurts. Conflict is also the spice of life, the sexy energizer, the seductive come-on that can breathe a happy commotion into a humdrum relationship. You better believe that Masters and Johnson, Dharma and Greg, Cruise and Kidman all came up with their best work through conflicts of their own. You really wouldn't want a partner with whom you didn't have some conflict—imagine the boredom! If you're sentient creatures, if you breathe, you will have conflict. It's natural. There's no avoiding it.

Though there's no avoiding conflict, you can learn how to avoid zinging each other. If lovers figure out how to shape conflict to make it work for them, it can be turned into a gift, a motivation for change—and every intimate relationship thrives on change. When you clash, it can be an opportunity for increased intimacy and a new sense of aliveness, instead of a feeling of hopelessness. Hello, conflict—thanks for dropping in.

Conflict resolution is a learnable skill; it teaches us ways to turn anger into energy and greater intimacy. In order to do so, you've got to know three things:

1. *Conflict resolution always takes words.* Since the cradle, we've been taught that "actions count more than words," but here, the opposite is true. Although actions do count, words count more. Author Robert Fulghum pointed out that the old children's ditty—"Sticks and stones can break my bones, but words can never hurt me"—is dead wrong. Words can hurt horribly. They can also heal. Conflict resolution is the art of using dialogue and listening skills to work out differences.

2. *Conflict resolution is rarely about winning or losing, or who's right or wrong.* It's about acknowledgment of the other and an appreciative recognition of his differences.

3. *Conflict resolution can't happen if you try to avoid the conflict.* Walk around conflict, smooth it over,

pretend it's not bothering you: Avoiding conflict makes the angry feelings inside you build until you're ready to explode. All it takes then is for your partner to ever so lightly press the hot button that caps your feelings of frustration, and whoa—war.

So How Do You Turn Off the Hot Buttons?

Change the way you do things. Used to your own and your partner's destructive patterns of communication, you tend to react in the same self-defeating ways whenever conflict rears its stubborn face. And you fail at peace.

If your old habits have led you to tensions and pressed buttons everywhere, you must suspend your usual ways of interacting with each other to try something new. It won't be easy to change the old patterns of communication. If you're open-minded and willing to try a new approach, conflict resolution will work—it has never failed me yet. After a while, the new approach will come to be second nature. And then it will be easy to live and love in peace.

Take, for example, Marilyn and Art.

The Stomp-Off

Marilyn and Art are sitting in their living room. He's trying to tell her a business idea she's sure he told her before. She rolls her eyes in boredom because that's what she always does when Art repeats stories. It makes him nuts, and he gets testy as he always does—and with his fist, he pounds the couch in irritation. She accuses him of "acting like an animal" and stomps off. Arrrgh.

Using a new approach, this is the way the story can unfold.

Averting the Stomp-Off

Marilyn and Art are sitting in their living room. He's trying to tell her a business idea she assumes she's heard before. She rolls her eyes in boredom. As usual, he gets agitated and pounds the couch in irritation. But now Marilyn says, "I see you're upset—what do you want me to do right now?" And Art says, "I want you to stop rolling your eyes and making assumptions that you've heard this idea—because you have not, my darling." She laughs, she listens, she has indeed not heard the idea, and the stomping off is averted.

It may be as simple as that, or it may involve a more complicated resolution, but the exercises throughout this book will teach you how to avert stomp-offs. In this chapter, some exercises are designed with married lovers in mind and some for single lovers, but don't let those delineations scare you away. You may be married for one hundred years, but an exercise that works especially well for a single couple may be just the ticket for you, too. Be open—and think positively. Don't let your age or length of time together dissuade you from changing the way you do things. Once, in a workshop, a couple in their seventies came to me and said, "At our age, you can't teach an old dog new tricks—how are we supposed to change a lifetime of habits?"

"Just do it," I answered. They did. Don't ever be stuck in a box of habit.

Is It Worth the Work?

You want to know the truth? Maybe not.

I have two criteria: First, if your partner is not a nice person, if you know in your heart of hearts that he's selfish, uncaring, and untrustworthy and always will be, the work involved in learning conflict resolution approaches really isn't worth it. Pack it in.

Here's the second criterion: After you've tried several of the exercises in this book and after you've given it a few months, if there is no movement forward, not even the smallest improvement in the way you both approach conflict, forget it. There has to be a sign that a partner is willing to change the old destructive habits that make him walk around with clenched fists. If you're dealing with a stone, it's not in your power to transform your relationship.

If you and your partner don't meet the above criteria, conflict resolution is not going to work.

What If You're the Only One Who's Willing to Put in the Effort?

Trust me: It's okay for now. All it will take is just one success in turning around an angry confrontation with a partner to get you both excited, to get you both to understand that we're on to something here. Amazingly enough, all it takes is just one partner to get this ball rolling. In the beginning, you don't have to do this together. Experts tell us that just one person in a conflicted relationship can lead the way, make a sea-change that will lead to waves of other changes and ultimately reconstitute the whole relationship. Just one of you can start down the road to conflict resolution—the other almost always follows.

Traditionally, it's been the woman whose job it is to "fix" heartaches (face it—we're usually better at it), but no woman reading this book should feel that it's always her responsibility to fix what's broken. Either partner can be the one to take the lead. Because this is the real world, look at it this way: Secretly, do you think you're the more mature partner; secretly, do you think you're the more flexible one? Well, it may not be fair, but fairness is not the issue. It may not always work, but you—the one reading this book—you will have to be the one to start bringing conflict resolution into both your lives.

HOT-BUTTON HINT

There's never only one right thing to answer; the idea is to keep the conversation going until all sides are heard and understood.

Hot-Button Cooldowns

I don't know where I read it, but it's good advice: "Put brain in gear before putting mouth in motion." Your partner may have said something mean, unfair, or uncalled-for that pushed your button sharply, but stop a moment before shooting back an angry answer that will only push his button—and then you've got all-out war.

So, how do I encourage this beloved but irritating person to cool down?

Before we even touch on other strategies for gentling the anger of your partner, see how adept some people have become at turning away wrath. The more you do it, the easier it becomes.

Here are the stories of Lola and Bert, Tom and Mary, Ivana and Donald, Eric and Sandy, Jessica and Jerry, and Walt and Joyce.

Lola: You're hopeless.
Bert: What do I do that's okay?

Tom: You ask me so many questions—sometimes you're just too nosy.
Mary: I'm surprised you feel that way—I thought we shared everything about each other's lives. How do you see it?

Ivana: You're so evasive. I just don't think I can trust you.
Donald: That upsets me. I don't mean to be evasive. Tell me what you'd like me to do.

Eric: I never promised I'd get the gift for your mum.
Sandy: Perhaps I didn't make it clear that I hoped you'd do it.

Jessica: You say you like kids, but if I talk about having one, you change the subject.
Jerry: I'm still unsure about what I want. That's why you're getting mixed messages.

Walt: I thought we decided to date other people, but if I'm not home when you call at night, I never hear the end of it!
Joyce: I'm probably reacting harshly because I love you and I feel a little jealous, no matter what we decided. I'll be more sensitive next time.

The Cornerstone Strategies

You've already read about the Five-Step Formula, a fundamental conflict resolution tool. Here are some more wonderful cornerstone strategies to help turn off the rage that threatens your intimacy. A cornerstone is a foundation—something that's basic and essential. The following techniques represent the foundation of everything we know about conflict resolution, and that's this: We must dig deeply to unearth the secret differences between us, then talk about them in ways that bring us closer.

Let's begin.

Strategy 1: The Marvellous Metaphor

How do you feel about conflict? Before you apply the tools of conflict resolution, first discover how you secretly feel about conflict. Does it scare you, paralyze you, or do you think you can learn to transform it into opportunities?

I'm going to ask you to think of conflict as a metaphor. Metaphors are comparisons—a great way to discover our own hot-button issues because when you compare two things to each other in unlikely ways, it highlights secret feelings. Take a minute for me and look at the list of words below. Think about conflict as it applies to these words. Then describe conflict using each word as a starting point. Always start with the sentence "Conflict is a . . ."

For example, suppose I gave you the word *bridge.* You might write, "Conflict is a bridge because people are at opposite ends with vast gulfs to cross." Then again, you might write something like, "Conflict is a bridge because people can disagree, then meet in the middle." Or you might say, "Conflict is a bridge because angry people can learn to cross over to each other safely."

Now think about what conflict means to you in terms of the words in the list. And always put the word in a sentence: "Conflict is a symphony because . . ."

symphony
deserted island
mask
boxing match
sunrise
puzzle
dance
dream
cactus plant
storm
statue

Look over your responses to see if they're mostly negative or mostly positive. If you're terrified of conflict, if an argument paralyzes you, you might have said something like, "Conflict is a storm because it's raging, uncontrollable, and frightening, and you can lose everything in a storm." A negative response.

But if you understand that conflict can lead to change and provide challenge, you might have said, "Conflict is a storm because it energizes, it's stimulating, it washes things clean." A positive response. See the difference?

Count your negative and positive responses to give you an idea of how you view conflict. If you secretly feel that conflict will kill a relationship, you'll have more negative than positive metaphors, and you need to work particularly hard because major changes in your relationship are called for. If most of your metaphor sentences are up and positive, you'll take to conflict resolution like a duck to water. Whatever your innate feelings about conflict, the fact that you're reading this book says you're open to trying something different. That's so good.

Let's insert metaphor into your real life.

Remember the last big argument or difference of opinion you actually had with your partner? Simplify that same argument into five or six words, substitute it for the word *conflict,* and do the metaphor exercise all over again. For example:

> *Bob's stubbornness about using condoms is a symphony* because . . .
>
> *Luke's lying to me is a desert island* because . . .

You might have responded, "Bob's stubbornness about using condoms is a symphony because it takes many underlying notes to figure out his melody." That might lead to you thinking, "Maybe Bob was once unable to get an erection when he used a condom and so he's afraid to repeat that embarrassing situation." You've located an underlying note. Or maybe it would lead to you thinking, "Hey, what if Bob has some deeply held religious belief or macho superstition about birth control that we ought to discuss?" Another buried note. That should lead to, "Hey, we ought to talk about this."

You might have responded, "Luke's lying to me is a desert island because it makes me feel so desperately alone, because it makes me feel abandoned." Even though you feel negative and somewhat despairing, thinking like this tells you that you've got an issue to discuss. Telling Luke that you feel abandoned and alone when he doesn't tell the truth will be far more productive to starting a dialogue and ending the lying than if you simply said, "Luke, you're a lying bastard."

HOT-BUTTON HINT

Sometimes, when an issue is too hot to handle, translate it into a metaphor and tell yourself what the conflict is "like" and how it makes you feel. It's a way to open the door to better communication with your partner.

Strategy 2: The Anatomy of a Conflict

I hope that translating your frustration into metaphors has helped you start a conversation with your partner. Now you're ready for the real dialogue. Here's a conflict resolution tool that digs down deep to find real motives and differences. My workshop clients have told me it's invaluable.

On the next page, you will see a chart called "Anatomy of a Conflict." Its purpose is to dissect a conflict, much as a pathologist would dissect a body to see what went wrong. This exercise helps you creep into the other's head—and that gives you the power to heal and transform. Like the Five-Step Formula you read about in Chapter 1, it will turn off anger in order to find common ground for resolution.

Every human being has an anatomy, a structure. We're made up of blood, sweat, tears, bones, eyes, feet, and a lot of other parts. Conflict also has an anatomy. After you define the issue that's giving you grief, it consists of five basic parts. Here's how you dissect your personal conflict and start the process of resolution with the Anatomy of a Conflict exercise. I'll give you the steps, and then we'll see how two other people dissected their conflict. Then it will be your turn to do your own Anatomy of a Conflict exercise.

ANATOMY OF A CONFLICT		
ISSUE		
	POSITION	
	NEEDS	
	VALUES	
	ASSUMPTIONS	
	EXPECTATIONS	

First, define the problem by deciding on the issue or the problem.

The issue is what's making you both angry/hurt/nuts. Define the issue well—do not cast blame on either partner or give more weight to one side than another. Condense the issue to one sentence (or question).

Here are some well-defined issues that spell out problems while being fair to each side:

A well-defined issue: How much time should we spend with each other's families?

A well-defined issue: Does a commitment mean we have to live together?

Now check out these poorly defined issues:

A poorly defined issue: Bob is a spendthrift. (casts blame on Bob)

The same issue, well defined: How should our money be spent?

A poorly defined issue: The house is a pigsty. (gives only one partner's side)

The same issue, well defined: Whose responsibility is it to clean the house?

Second, check out the five parts of your particular conflict: each person's position, needs, values, assumptions, and expectations. Read the following explanation of the five parts.

1. Position: What does each person think is the right thing to happen?

Each person holds a position on an issue consisting of his or her views and demands. When you insist that your position is the only right one, you get locked into it—and that worsens the conflict.

2. Needs: What does each think he or she must have?
Needs may include privacy, a feeling of being important, a desire for recognition, a sense of security, demonstrations of love . . .

3. Values: What deep principles are important, morally true, and correct to each?
What have you come to believe is a good way to live, based on your culture and experience? One person may value beauty most, another intellect; one may most value career success and another, family.

4. Assumptions: What does each think is true about the issue and about each other?
If one thinks the house is a pigsty because the other is lazy and it's her job to clean it, he's making two assumptions that may or may not be true. We tend to make judgments about people based on our own mind-set—for example, "He doesn't call when he's late because he's callous and uncaring." Acting on assumptions in a conflict situation can be very dangerous because our assumptions can be very wrong. Many hot buttons are pressed because of wrong assumptions.

5. Expectations: What does each predict will happen?
What do you expect the other person to do? What do you expect will happen with the conflict?

Third, when you've each finished your side of the Anatomy of a Conflict, look over each other's responses. Take turns asking questions of the other to get more details and explanations from the other's perspective. Listen hard to each other. Don't interrupt or defend yourself when the other is talking. Just listen. Then explain your side.

We're ready to start. Read the following scenario carefully. Afterwards, we'll see how Paul and Alice's conflict can be dissected within the Anatomy of a Conflict.

Paul and Alice: Who Comes First—Me or Your Sister?

Paul and Alice are lovers. They've been dating each other exclusively for more than a year. Paul's brother-in-law recently died, and Paul's sister, Diana, has asked him to spend more time with his nephews. Paul does the best he can. To find time for the boys, he's had to cut down on his time with Alice. He feels guilty, for example, when he has to leave Alice's apartment early Sunday morning to take his sister's boys to church and play with them afterwards, but he knows it has to be done. He'd do anything for his baby sister, Diana—and she's in trouble right now.

Alice tries to be sympathetic—and she is—but frankly, she thinks Paul is overdoing his obligations to his sister. She feels neglected and near the bottom of his priority list. Besides the shortened Sundays, he comes late to dates, when he doesn't cancel them altogether. Even when they're together, he now seems distant. She feels there may be something more that he's concealing.

Here's a recent conversation:

Paul (on the phone): Listen, Alice, I'm really sorry. I took the kids home and got stuck on a local train. By the time I get back to your house, it'll be time to leave because I have an early meeting in the morning. So, I guess I won't come.

ANATOMY OF A CONFLICT

ISSUE: There's a downward change in our relationship

PAUL		ALICE
Most of my free time has to be spent with my nephews, and you don't understand.	POSITION	Your obsession with your sister and her problems is hurting our relationship.
I need to be a father figure to my nephews, and they want me around. I also need to be a big brother and help my sister through this terrible time.	NEEDS	I need more attention from you than I'm getting. I feel we're drifting apart. It scares me, and I need to be assured of your commitment to me.
Family responsibilities take precedence over most things.	VALUES	Relationships must be nurtured to grow.
You don't understand the stress I'm under. You're thinking only of yourself.	ASSUMPTIONS	You're using the kids as an excuse to distance yourself from me. Your sister comes before me.
I'm going to be turned off and lose interest in you because you resent what I'm going through.	EXPECTATIONS	We're going to drift apart further and further.

Alice: Oh, too bad. I'm disappointed.

Paul: I know you are, but there's nothing I can do.

Alice: This seems to be happening all the time, lately.

Paul: Look, I can't talk now. I'll call you tomorrow. Maybe we can have lunch.

Alice: Don't bother squeezing me in for lunch. I'm busy anyway.

Okay. Let's dissect this conflict according to the Anatomy of a Conflict guidelines. Paul and Alice should each complete one side of the exercise. They should write in short sentences that describe their feelings. They must be honest—even if it's embarrassing or it hurts. On page 105, you will see how the Anatomy chart might look for Paul and Alice.

After Paul and Alice separately complete the anatomy, it's time for talking. They must discuss their choices with each other. Each will read what the other's written—and ask questions to get more information. Each will confirm each other's position—showing how the other's point of view has truly been *heard*—even if there's disagreement. Listen in:

Alice: I never realized how attached you were to your sister.

Paul: Yes, I am attached to my sister, and it's because our dad wasn't there for us. We were each other's anchor. I remember how sad and lonely I felt then—and I want to see that my nephews have an easier time. I should have taken the time to tell you more about how I feel—this is a really hard time for me.

Alice: You know, we've known each other for two years, and I never knew that your dad had deserted you. I need to know more about that, and I really should have tried to find out more about your past and your family, not just be interested in our present.

Paul: You are part of my family now, one of the most important parts. I've just been so engrossed in my own problems. I see now I haven't made room for you in that family—I've ignored you more than I thought. What have you been going through lately—how have you felt about what's happening?

Paul and Alice are just beginning to understand each other's perspective; each begins to take some responsibility for omissions of communication.

Alice: We haven't been telling each other what was really on our minds, have we? I was sure I knew what was on yours—and I was wrong. My assumption that you were too close to your sister was really off the mark. Frankly, I admire your devotion to those two little boys. You're a real family man—and that's a good thin; it shouldn't threaten me.

Paul: I've felt down about you because I thought you just didn't give a damn about the kids. I always assume you'll try to push me away from the boys so we can be together more—and when I do that, I feel guilty as hell for neglecting these fatherless kids. You know, the other night, I could have come to your house even for a few moments, but I wasn't up for the hassle I assumed you'd give me.

Alice: Hassle? I would have hugged you because your coming even for a few moments would have told me you cared about us. Look—isn't there a way we could see each other almost as regularly as before, and still give you time to see the boys? Can't I be part of the three of you? Why don't you bring them here, for example?

Paul: How come we're so stupid? Of course! It's really so simple. I assumed you didn't want anything to do with my nephews—that they were my responsibility, not yours. We can do lots of things together if you really wouldn't mind.

Alice: I'd love it. I feel so much better. Why don't you bring them over Sunday after church, and we can watch the football game together. Then we can all cook dinner.

So Paul and Alice have used the Anatomy of a Conflict framework to start uncovering the real issues in their relationship. Of course, the issues have been simplified here and they have much more work to do, but they've made a start and begun what will turn into a habit of dialogue; they're digging deeper for the real issues. Once the air is cleared, Alice and Paul will be able to explore even more ways to resolve their differences. As Paul said, "It's really so simple."

Simple when you know how to do it. During a conflict within an intimate relationship, we often put ourselves in a right/wrong box.

RIGHT/WRONG BOX

Alice: I'm right because I want to build our relationship.

Paul: I'm right because I have other responsibilities.

Alice: He's wrong because he cares more about them than me.

Paul: She's wrong because she's selfish and doesn't understand.

This is a BAD box.

Once Alice and Paul learn to use the tools of conflict resolution, they're no longer bad-boxed. Their assumption—that they will drift apart—need not come true once they find common ground.

Complete your own Anatomy of a Conflict making a copy of the blank chart on page 101. This exercise works best if you both complete your portion separately and then come together at the end to discuss the reasons for your choices. Of course, nothing is written in stone, and if you prefer to complete the exercise together, feel free. Whether you complete the exercise alone or with your partner, you must first agree together on the issue that's giving you both grief and condense it to one sentence. Then each of you proceeds to fill in your side, the five elements of your own conflict—your positions, needs, values, assumptions, and expectations—from your own point of view.

Note: If your partner won't cooperate in this exercise, all is not lost: remember, it takes only one person to start making changes. Do this: Try your hardest to empathize, creep into his mind, and fill in his side of the chart as you honestly believe he would respond. If you really don't know *anything* about his side, that's your clue that this exercise is particularly vital for you to do. You *must* discover his side. If you have to do it yourself, it won't be quite the same, but I guarantee that it will give you greater insight into his point of view—and help you uncover the real problems beneath the masks.

Now ask questions of each other based on what's written. Learn anything about the other? Good.

HOT-BUTTON HINT

In order to love more fully, you must learn to value the world of your opposite—especially in moments of confrontation.

Strategy 3: Dig Deeper

This is vital. Although some conflicts are just what they appear to be, most derive from hidden issues—a basic difference in values or a long-simmering hurt that has little to do with the present argument. The only way to get to the real bone of contention is to dig deeper. How? It's as simple as asking the right questions. Here are four charmed questions that have power to dig deeper, if you ask them during the heat of conflict:

1. Can you tell me a little more about . . . ?
2. Is there anything else you want me to know that you haven't yet told me?
3. Can you explain what you mean by that?
4. What do you want to happen?

Strategy 4: The Way You Say It

Anger and frustration can't be buried. They must see the light of day; they must be discussed. How you say what's in your heart is so important. Is your partner going to get more irritated or newly inspired to connect with you? Are you going to turn off communications or open them? It all depends on the way you say it. For example, you may love your partner deeply, you really try to help him, and yet he's always jumping at you! What gets him so angry. What pushes his buttons? Perhaps it's you, even when you think you're only helping.

Consider the following two columns. The first column illustrates the wrong way of saying something—it's a column of button-pushers. The second column illustrates better ways of saying the same thing, ones that will defuse hot buttons.

PUSHERS AND DEFUSERS

Hot-Button Pushers	Hot-Button Defusers
You have to . . .	Are you willing?
You're a controlling person.	Are there any other options we can consider?
You're exactly like your father.	You're an original thinker—and I even see some parts of your dad in you.
You're weak-minded.	Can you explain why you believe that?
You'll feel better in the morning.	I always feel better in the morning—maybe you will also.
You're just trying to get attention.	How can we share the spotlight with others?
You have a problem.	Let's try to solve this problem together.

PUSHERS AND DEFUSERS

Hot-Button Pushers	Hot-Button Defusers
Why don't you just listen to me?	Let me hear everything you have to say on this; then I know you'll hear me out, too.
There's a right way and a wrong way.	Let's see if we can find a win/win solution so we'll both be pleased.

The lesson? Find neutral ways to tell your lover what you want him to know without judging him, calling him names, sermonizing, or winding him up by the way you say it.

Strategy 5: Don't Swallow Anger; Don't Keep Secrets

Lois and David are such a good couple, but they're button-pushers because they haven't learned that boiling inside and keeping secrets are not great sex toys.

The fine thing about lovers' anger is that it can be a gift of energy. When you're angry, you feel your senses spring to life, and you feel passion rising.

So, express the anger or swallow it? Express. But thoughtfully. Repressed anger can wreck intimacy. Even if we don't admit to anger and say instead that we're disappointed, saddened, or hurt by our lovers, we still feel mad. Difficulties turn up when we bury our anger because buried anger is too hot to touch.

Here are two stories about Lois and David. The first story illustrates how they keep their secrets and swallow their anger—and how that almost severs a sweet relationship. Recasting the story, the second version illustrates how they learn to release anger, tell hard secrets—and reclaim their love.

STORY 1: WHY ARE YOU STALLING?

Lois, thirty, and David, thirty-six, have been dating for a year, and they've started to love each other. Lois has been an adventuresome single woman who's led a selective but active and creative sex life. David, formerly married to his high school sweetheart, has been divorced for a year. Although he is less sexually experienced than Lois, he has wonderful vitality and intelligence that she admires. David has begun to press Lois to move in with him. She hesitates because she knows it's a prelude to marriage. Although David is stellar in every other respect, sex means a lot to Lois—and the bells are just not ringing in that department. Worse, she's embarrassed to tell David, and she doesn't want to hurt him.

Lately, the atmosphere has been tense. The anger is building, and neither is really sure why. One day:

David says: I've been suggesting we live together for three months, and I get answers like let's wait and see, I'm not ready, I haven't the time to discuss this right now. Lois, I'm losing my patience. I'm really sorry, but if we don't settle this soon, I'm out of here.

> ***David assumes:*** She's biding her time until she meets someone better. She's using me.

Lois says: You're bullying and threatening me, David. Just lower your voice. If you weren't such an insecure baby, you'd be sensitive to my needs—and what I need is more time.

> ***Lois assumes:*** If I bring up the sex thing, he'll be crushed. No man can take criticism of his macho power.

David says: How much time do you need—why are you stalling? I love you, but our relationship's got to go forward or end. I feel so damn frustrated!

> ***David assumes:*** She's stalling because she's definitely keeping something from me. I have to act strong and firm—that's what women want.

Lois says: Well, do you think our relationship's perfect the way it is?

> ***Lois assumes:*** This is an issue of control—he's trying to control the relationship. Oh, I'll never be able to tell him about the sex thing. We're doomed. I've never seen him so full of heat, so animated.

David says: No, I don't think it's perfect, but I do think there's a wrong way and a right way to deal with issues, and your subterfuge, your keeping secrets is the wrong way. You're a spoiled child.

> ***David assumes:*** She's trying to control the relationship, and she definitely has another guy. I'm sick about it, but I'm also starting to boil. From a failed marriage to this—I don't need it!

HOT-BUTTON ANALYSIS

This much is clear: David loves Lois. Lois, as it happens, also loves David. They're trying to express their feelings but will never manage to do it if they continue to wrongly assume so much. There may indeed be issues of control and procrastination, but Lois has masked the big problem—the sex is boring. David simply doesn't know her spots. He is clueless about sexual experimentation. Lois has had lovers who turned her on with their tongues, with their fingers, with ice cubes. Ice cubes? Yes. Passion matters to her.

She's embarrassed and shy about telling him this, even though she knows she could never marry anyone unless she felt sexually fulfilled. She hopes that in time the sex will improve all by itself. She stalls about moving in with David, and she never confronts him with her dissatisfaction.

But now, crisis time: Both their hot buttons have been pressed. In frustration and despair, he preaches to her (there's a right way and a wrong way), makes judgments (she's spoiled), and threatens to end the relationship. That makes her feel angry, abandoned, and unloved. She's accused him of being a bully and an insecure baby. That kind of name-calling and pseudopsychology make him feel furious, insulted, and disrespected. Both suspect the other of trying to control the relationship, when each is really desperately trying to find a way back to each other.

Let's recast this story into one where each stops swallowing anger and keeping secrets.

STORY 2: LET IT ALL HANG OUT

The heat of David's anger can be a catalyst for change in this relationship, but keeping secrets and burying the anger are terribly destructive.

Lois says: I can understand why you're upset and why you think I've not been totally honest, and you're right. I have been less than forthcoming. But I have to tell you that when you threaten to leave me, I see red. That's no way to discuss stuff.

David says: Well, I'm sorry. But I do feel hurt. I think you've been toying with me. You know what? I'm not just hurt, I'm mad. Is there something you're hiding?

Lois says: Maybe so. But it's difficult for me to talk about, and I don't want to hurt you.

David says: I knew it! Listen, I can handle it. Is there someone else?

Lois says: No, no, not at all. It's about sex, if you must know.

David says: Sex? Our sex? Why have you been keeping it a mystery all this time?

Lois says: Because everything else was so good, I didn't want to ruin it. Look, honey, this is very difficult for me to say. I've led you to believe that things are great in bed for me, but they're not. Frankly, I don't feel fulfilled, and it's not because I don't love you.

David says: I'm so sorry that you've been feeling that way. You deserve more. I know it must have been really hard for you to share this. But you know what? I really want to make it better for you, Lois. Tell me, what do you need? What can I do?

Lois says: I need you not to be in such a hurry. I need you to touch me more, and I don't mean just hugs. I want to try new things with you. Our sex is so . . . bland.

David says: And this is something you've been hiding? I needed to know it. I may not be Tom Cruise, but I want to learn. Tapes, videos, could we do that? Look, I'm not saying my feelings aren't hurt a little, but I know something you don't know: I'm a fast learner. I love you, Lois. First lesson—now or after dinner?

And they lived happily ever after.

HOT-BUTTON HINT

It takes two to speak the truth.
One to speak and the other to hear.
—HENRY DAVID THOREAU

Strategy 6: Acceptance

Acceptance Therapy is an approach to conflict resolution put forth in a book called *Reconcilable Differences* by Dr. Andrew Christensen and Dr. Neil Jacobson. It's a new term for a precept I've held dear for years: When all else fails, simply try to accept each other's differences, even the ones that drive you mad. In some situations, simple acceptance of the other's differences can be more productive than striving for change, although I believe the latter is far preferable. Although the authors frequently warn that the approach may backfire, they contend that acceptance of a partner's irritating traits and behaviours often leads to compassion. Compassionate partners are more willing to be productive about conflict. The theory? When partners feel pressured to change, they often become defensive, say the psychologists, but when they feel accepted and understood, they tend to make changes willingly. Even if no change occurs, acceptance and compassion tend to bring a couple closer together. It's a worthwhile strategy.

Change

Listen: Couples who thrive have changing relationships. The greatest enemy of intimacy is apathy and stagnation. Learning how to turn off hot buttons with your lover depends on your ability to communicate in new ways—ways you're reading about in this book. Do it, and the possibilities for closeness grow infinite.

Be patient. Your conflict style has been part of you forever, and it won't be easy to turn off the rages when they happen. Remember, incredible results come from change and not from the following:

- **Going for the jugular:** The hot button lies there. Even if he looks like a bully and you feel like a victim, don't bring up the thing that hurts him most (you know what that is—the fact that he's sometimes impotent, or that he never graduated from college, or that he was fired). Retaliating by attacking the other's most vulnerable point is not fighting fair and is never productive.
- **Stockpiling:** Extinguish anger blazes when they happen by immediately trying to get to the real issues rather than swallowing all the resentments and having them grow into an enormous stockpile, just waiting to be ignited by one last spark.
- **Saying mean things:** Don't push buttons by using guilt or sarcasm, yelling, or blaming. That never works to turn off the anger.

You can do this. Believe it.

6

Hot Buttons and the Family

Happy families are all alike;
every unhappy family is unhappy in its own way.
—Tolstoy

Think of the myriad possibilities for unhappiness in family life! There's the critical mother-in-law and father-in-law, not to mention your own often irritating parents; there's the judgmental sister-in-law, and your ditzy brother, cousins, and uncles—and wait, you've also got the relationships from your first marriage, and from his (about 75 percent of divorced persons eventually remarry). We've talked about the anger inherent within children, but we grownups also have our clan minefields everywhere. Have you talked to your own sister since the Big Fight a year ago? What about your brother-in-law who's never liked you? How will your husband feel if there's a permanent rift between you, and would it break your heart to see your husband so sad?

The opportunities for conflagrations are awesome. Family feuds and sibling rivalry and in-law pressures create exposed and tantalizing hot buttons. Sometimes it seems you're got to be a saint to resist those beckoning buttons.

It's true that some rare families seem to have sprung

from Pollyanna genes. They have few arguments, hardly any discernible tension, and when there is a problem, they manage to talk it out before tempers flare. Most kinfolk are not so lucky. These volatile relatives seem incapable of holding back any harsh judgments. Their positions are fixed in stone, and they can see no side of the conflict but their own. They require apologies. They can never be the first to make the first gesture of peace.

Well, why not just drop family members as we do acquaintances who tick us off? Why bother working on relationships with those in your family who own short tempers?

Consider the Consequences

You've got history with these people. What will happen to you and the rest of the family if you don't work it out? Imagine what will happen. Be very specific.

For example:

- If my sister-in-law and I don't finally resolve our differences, I'll miss my nephews' entire growing up—and I'd hate that.
- If I don't work out my fury with my brother, we'll never be able to have a full family Thanksgiving—and how will I be able to explain that to my small kids? Won't I be setting an example for them and their future relationships?
- My ex-husband—sure, it would be great to just get him out of my life, but how would that affect our son and also my relationship with his mum, whom I love?

History counts.

Three Rules

Here, for starters, are three of my most potent principles in the art of gentling conflict within family groups:

1. *This is not about your sister (brother, mother . . .); it's about how you react to that person in moments of anger.* If you plan to change your cousin or get everyone around you to agree that he's the bad guy, you haven't a hope of turning off his hot buttons. Instead, remember that it takes only one person to make a cosmic change—you. Start with pulling back, cooling down, and checking *his* perspective—make sure he feels heard.

   Then think: Why are your hot buttons being pressed so hard (a private fear, something in your past that still hurts, a blow to your dignity, an insult to your friends or lifestyle) Take a risk—share these thoughts with your cousin. Changing your own reaction often leads you to common ground where both your needs can be reasonably met.
2. *Know thine own hot buttons—then figure out your next move in advance.* If you know where your buttons lie, you can practically write the script for your next encounter with the family member who also knows the location of your buttons—and will press them, rest assured. What does make you angry? If you don't already know, here's a simple way to figure out the issues that most tick you off.

   Privately, make a short list of people who bug you, and in ten words or less, write what you can't stand about those persons. For example:

My sister Linda: exaggerates, thinks she knows everything

My mother: infantilizes me

My ex-husband: lazy, untrustworthy

My cousin Mary: constantly complains—her life sucks and everyone else owes her

My uncle Sherman: sarcastic; belittles my opinions and politics

My mother-in-law: tries to control me

My daughter-in-law: tries to control me

Now you've identified some of your own most sensitive buttons. Anyone who acts superior, treats you like a baby, lies, whines, involves you in a power struggle, or implies that you're a no-nothing probably makes you nuts. These are the qualities that always are red flags for you. Now that you know what pushes your buttons, you can anticipate stress situations, figure out your moves, and actually choose your reactions when you next see the irritating person. You're ahead of the game—now you're in a position of control.

For example: You figure that at the Christmas family get-together, Linda will make a joke about you being a gym teacher (she thinks gym teachers are know-nothings) and will also pass on unfair gossip about someone you like a lot. She's done this before—and you've responded with such fury, it ruined the whole party for everyone. When it happens again, as it surely will, decide in advance what you would like to happen this time. In order to achieve that goal, anticipate the dialogue. Think about what Linda will say to you, and have your lines ready for a response that is not defensive, not angry, simply informational. You might also try to figure out what Linda will say to your response and what you will answer.

Chances are you've averted a pushed hot button. Peace reigns, even if Linda's still not your favourite person.

3. *What do I really want?* In moments of anger, ask yourself the question, What do I really want? Answer it in one or two sentences. If you can be clear and focused about what you really want, you can shift the conflict from hurt feelings to real issues and a plan to achieve what you really want. This technique instantly calms you and helps others to cool down.

   In the midst of a conflict with your brother, for example, you might say to yourself, What do I really want?

- **I want my brother to respect me.** Therefore, I won't be a Slash-and-Burner, and I won't bring up his divorce or his business failure to get back at him for his nasty remark. Instead, I'll shift the conversation to something interesting I'm doing—and ask his advice about it. That way he'll be hearing about the work I know he'll respect—but he'll also be flattered that I asked his opinion. It will cool the whole atmosphere.
- **I want my mother to honour my decisions without trying to change my mind.** Therefore, I won't avoid her—shut her out of my life—but I also

won't allow my anger to flood and rage through our relationship. Instead, I'll use the energy of my anger to check her perspectives and then teach her how to step into my shoes and see things from my view. I'll try to establish a level playing field.

- **I want to have a real conversation with my uncle Sherman without his scoffing at me or riding loudly over my thoughts.** Therefore, I won't withdraw as usual (a Peace at All Costs manoeuvre) when he starts to embarrass or blame me. Instead, I'll use the Five-Step Formula: I'll step back to see the situation more clearly, confirm if, get more information about his views, and then quietly assert my own thoughts. Eventually, we will reach common ground. I'm determined to break our pattern of faulty communication. I'll no longer feel shame or blame if I don't deserve shame and blame.

Shame and Blame

The shame/blame game is played endlessly in family situations. It starts in your earliest years and it doesn't stop. When you are thirty-six and hurting because you're newly divorced, expect that at the next gathering, Uncle John will bring up the time when you were sixteen and dated the boy who ended up in jail.

"You always did pick losers," says Uncle John. Whoa—hot button pushed!

In the heat of arguments, families dredge up the same old stories and feelings—because they know your history. The same shame and blame you felt when you were little and couldn't defend yourself are destined to be part of your present and your future—as long as you have family. It's not that your kin are terrible people—it's just that they're . . . well, family. In addition to the good things they do, they also push buttons.

When someone in your family shames or blames you, it sounds like this:

THE SHAME/BLAME BOX

- You don't show good judgment in men.
- You'll never understand.
- It's your fault.
- You don't show the slightest respect for me.
- You've misinterpreted me entirely.
- You don't care about me.
- You're always talking down to me.
- You never tell me you appreciate what I do.
- Is that the way you bring up your children?

Those cutting, unfair words—nothing gets you more wound up, right?

So, how do you get out of the shame/blame box and make such irritating comments work for you and for the relationship? First, don't get defensive, don't start attacking back, and don't even try to explain why the statement is absolutely a lie. Try humour—if you're funny—but never the sarcastic brand, and never make jokes at the button-pusher's expense.

Then cool 'em down.

Cool 'Em Down

THE COOL 'EM DOWN BOX

- I don't show good judgment in men? Thank goodness there's always another guy to practice on.
- You think I never understand? Tell me more about that so I can understand.
- It's my fault? What have I done that makes you feel that way?
- You feel I don't respect you? What can we do together to make it better?
- You feel I misinterpret what you say? I want to change that. How can I start?
- You're feeling unloved; let's think of ways I *have* showed you that I care very much.
- You feel I talk down to you? Let's both work on being more sensitive to each other.
- You feel I never express my appreciation? Perhaps you're right. Tell me what you think I need to do in the future.
- You disagree with the way I'm bringing up my kids? Give me some examples of when this happens so I can understand what makes you worried.

These cool-off statements work because they're meant to disarm someone who's intent on pushing your buttons. Your relative may push your buttons simply out of habit, not because she wants to hurt you. She may push your buttons because she's mischievous. Or she may want to push your buttons because, frankly, she's a little mean. For whatever reason they do it, button-pushers can anticipate that you'll get defensive and angry because you always have in the past.

Instead, using cool-off statements gives you power. You won't take the bait. Instead, you answer the button-pusher calmly, with respect, and maybe even with humor—and that defuses his need to set you off. You seem to want to know what he thinks, and you're interested in starting a dialogue. That's flattering to the button-pusher.

Try the following at the next family gathering when someone tries to shame or blame you:

Button Turnoffs

Say you're sorry—and mean it!

Take a breath and listen.

Speak quietly.

Take a break.

Use humour.

Acknowledge anger.

Ask a question.

Try to get her to explain.

Ask what's important to her.

A Brother, a Sister, a Mother

Let's talk about a specific situation creating huge distress in the adult segment of families—siblings and the question of elder care.

More than half of all Americans say they believe it's likely that they will be responsible for the care of an elderly parent—and they're right because nearly one-fourth of the US's elderly do require assistance with daily living. Most elderly are not in nursing homes. The responsibility for their care often rests with their adult children. Family dynamics play an important role in these new responsibilities. Will the family pull together as a team in meeting the challenges of elder care? Or will the family dredge up old wounds and get fixed in positions of stone in their differences about how to reach out to their beloved elders? Check out the following scenario involving two adult siblings.

Sam's the Favourite

Sam is forty and his sister, Arlene, is forty-three. Sam's a national sales director, and his job requires a substantial amount of travel. Arlene's a homemaker and takes care of her husband and two daughters. Both brother and sister live near their mum, a seventy-four-year-old widow who's been diagnosed with Alzheimer's disease. Her neediness has required Arlene's constant supervision. Arlene and Sam haven't been particularly close for the last few years, but their mum's heartbreaking memory losses have brought the two of them in contact more frequently. Here is the situation from each of their perspectives.

Sam's Perspective	**Arlene's Perspective**
My mum needs Arlene. It looks like this is going to be an ongoing problem. I just don't have the time to deal with it, even though God knows, I love Mum so much. I was always her favourite.	My mum needs both of us, and her problems are not going away. We both simply have to make time for her.
Arlene's a woman. Women know how to do this better. I'll be responsible for most of the financial burden. She'll give most of the hands-on care. That sounds fair.	Sam assumes that because I'm a woman, I'll do 90 percent of the dirty work. What a nerve. It takes more than money to deal with a mum who's always been there for us. This time, I'm not going to be taken advantage of.
I respect Arlene and always tell her to use her good judgment on decisions about Mum.	Sam tells me to use my good judgment, then criticizes me later if he doesn't like what I decide to do.

Look—Arlene can make Mum more comfortable than I can—what takes me an hour takes her ten minutes. It's a waste of time for me to get involved with that stuff—I have a business to run. Also, I get embarrassed seeing Mum in intimate ways I never saw her before—on the toilet, getting dressed.

Think I like to see Mum on the toilet? She's our mother—deal with it. Mum needs holding and hugging and physical nurturing—especially from Sam because he's always been her favourite. But Mum always treated him like a prince—and now he believes he is one.

HOT-BUTTON ANALYSIS

Often in heated conflicts, there *is* more than one goal. In this conflict, each party is arguing about his or her own problem. Arlene and Sam are like two trains going in the same direction but on different tracks. In order to resolve their problems, they both need to identify *what* it is that they're arguing about—their clashing goals.

Sam's prime goal is to find the quickest and easiest way to have his mother, Kate, taken care of. He feels he can fulfill his goal by spending his money on professional nursing care. Sam, like many men, is task-oriented: Get the task done—that's his goal.

Arlene's prime goal is to get Sam to have a hands-on relationship with their mum because she is relationship-oriented. Arlene thinks she knows what Mum wants—and that is Sam's touch, Sam's presence, along with her own.

There are other goals as well. Arlene needs Sam to confirm what a good hands-on daughter she is and that her caretaking work is as important as his. She feels that Sam devalues her because she is a stay-at-home wife. Sam feels that Arlene devalues his business pressures and also his offer to be responsible for most of their mum's financial needs. Both have had their buttons pressed by each other.

What needs to happen between this adult brother and sister?

Both must have a conversation in which their goals are clearly expressed. They must agree with each other that both goals are different, but both are valid. Then they must find a mutually satisfactory solution.

Reframe!

A marvellous way to develop a conversation that heals is by reframing—a hot-button technique that will be invaluable once you learn it. We'll see how Arlene reframes their disagreement so each can achieve goals. But first, what *is* reframing?

Visualize this: You have a lovely painting, but you've had it for many years, and you're getting tired of it. Throw it out? You can't bring yourself to do that. In an inspired moment, you have it reframed. Suddenly the painting takes on new nuances. You look at it more positively, more affectionately. It's the same old painting—but reframing has made it somehow fresh, new, and more congenial.

When you reframe what someone has said, you do exactly the same thing: You take the essence of that person's words, pick up his cues, and then translate those words in a fresh way that gives the dialogue a new direction. Reframing points you to problem-solving. Here's why: No conflict can be solved until everyone feels heard, and reframing shows you've heard the other person. An added bonus is that the sting of a sharp remark is removed. Here are some general examples:

Statement	Reframed Statement
The fact is, I'm totally right on this issue, and face it, you're dead wrong.	You may well be totally right—and I want to understand your perspective, so I'll listen hard to you—and then, you can listen to me.
I can never get through that dense head of yours.	Tell me what you want to happen and what you want. Let's understand what's in each other's minds.
You upset Aunt Betty so much—and she was so hurt.	I probably was a factor in Betty's unhappiness, but instead of finding fault with each other, let's figure out a way we can fix it.
You've never trusted me—I know that.	Maybe we need to talk about what trust means to each of us, so we can figure out how to change the situation.
I told you my Jimmy hates mayonnaise—why do you persist in making him salad dressing with mayonnaise?	There must have been a miscommunication somewhere. I want to be very clear about what Jimmy likes in the future. Tell me again what he prefers (sometimes, you just have to take the high ground even though you know Jimmy *loves* mayonnaise).

A vital principle of reframing: Don't try to echo the exact words of the other—translate what he says into your own words, when possible.

Here's how Sam and Arlene worked out their elder care problem by reframing:

Sam's Statement	Arlene Reframes It
Look—I'm so clear about this—what's the problem? We divide up our obligations—I take over the financial burdens, and you do the day-to-day stuff. Don't you get it?	I can tell you see it clearly, and sure, I'm willing to check in on Mum daily. You feel you'll have done enough if you pay for everything, and I can understand

Sam's Statement	Arlene Reframes It
	that feeling—it's very hard to help her on the toilet or in her bath. Can you also visualize times when we may have to do things differently?
Well, I guess I'd have to be there if you and Artie took a vacation—but that won't happen too often.	You're right—a vacation would be just once in a while. There's another issue with Mum, though. I don't know how to respond to her when she says, "Where's Sam? I want him." What do you suggest I do?
Tell her the truth—tell her I'm busy.	I do tell her of your commitments, Sam, all the time—I also tell her that you travel a lot. Can we figure out a way that you might stop over at her house on your way back from trips or on weekends—maybe only for forty-five minutes at a time—so Mum can hug you? That's what she craves.

As Arlene reframes Sam's statements, one by one, he reluctantly comes to see that care involves more than cash. The brother and sister continue to discuss specific dates when he might manage to stop in at Mum's for a short time, *short* being the operative word for Sam. Sam has felt guilty about not spending time with his mother, and this conversation gives him permission to assuage his guilt by finding ways to fit in limited but meaningful visits with his mum.

The brother and sister also begin a dialogue about additional care their mum will need. This directly addresses one of Sam's greatest worries—that of being responsible for helping his mum to the bathroom. They start to work together on decisions that might need to be made now, as well as in the future. The two agree to hire a permanent health care worker who is experienced with Alzheimer's patients. To avoid unspoken hard feelings, Arlene insists on paying something toward this even though Sam will pay much more. Sam concedes that it won't kill him if he has to occasionally help their mum with intimate care. He also tells Arlene how proud he's always been of her. And she says the same thing back to him.

The unspoken anger and tension between Sam and Arlene finally begin to abate. Their mother's problems will probably bring them closer together.

HOT-BUTTON HINT

Men respond much better when they are seen not as the problem but as the solution.

—John Gray, Ph.D.

Sibling Rivalry

Grown-up sisters are lucky to have each other: Who else can so totally share history, genes, and memories? They're lucky, that is, if they're not torn apart by the rages that divide sisters who have not resolved their sibling issues.

The Story of the Stay-at-Home Sister

As our new century begins, intelligent, aspiring women have different goals. Some choose to stay at home nurturing a family, some choose a career, others choose both—or another variation. Ruth is married with three school-age children. Her older sister, Audrey, who lives in the same town, is a high-powered marketing director in the clothing industry. She's married, with one son in college. They both do volunteer work at their local church.

RUTH

They all call me a "stay-at-home mum." I really resent it. Do they think I sit around all day watching talk shows? I work as hard as they do. I manage my children and take care of a whole household. My sister, Audrey, doesn't appreciate how hard I work. She jokes with me, but I think she secretly envies me for my happier family life. She's harbored resentment for me since we were kids. Now we're both active in our community church group and work together on our annual fund-raiser. All the members of the committee keep saying, "Ruth can do this. Ruth can do that." They dump the dirty work on me because they think I have all the time in the world. What really agitated me last night was when my sister practically ordered me to make more phone calls. I almost blew my cork. Well, I flat-out told her, "You've a nerve to ask again. Get someone else."

AUDREY

This fund-raising event is vital because of our new scholarship programme, so we all have to work harder this year to make it a success. I give my all—and not only because my boss likes that kind of thing. Still, to be honest, putting in time at church fund-raisers is a step up to a promotion.

My sister, Ruth, has never worked under deadlines or real pressure, and every time a job is assigned, she balks. I'm on a very strict time schedule, and there are certain chores that I absolutely cannot do. If I can't count on Ruth, on whom can I count? She keeps carrying on about how hard she works with three kids, but she just doesn't know how to budget her time. Also, she doesn't have a boss breathing down her neck. Last night she shouted out, "No, I won't. Get someone else," after I gave her new phone calls to make. I was shocked and embarrassed in front of the others. She's spoiled and self-centered, just as she always was.

But the next day Audrey calls Ruth and says that they really need to talk about what happened the night before. She tells Ruth about a new tool that she'd heard of called Anatomy of a Conflict and asks if she could stop by Ruth's house on the way home from work. Because they care about each other, they would spend some time working on the exercise and, for the first time, talk through their situation. Ruth agrees.

As Audrey and Ruth work through the model, a dialogue develops. It is just what these sisters need to soften their anger. They go into more depth about long-held assumptions and dredge up old issues like who was the favourite in the family and who was expected to succeed. In between shared tears, they even are able to joke about the old days and how faulty their assumptions have been about each other for such a long time. They decide that these issues have always clouded their relationship—and their rancour came to a head at the meeting for the church fund-raiser.

Ruth: It's clear that much of my thinking about the church event was wrapped up in our sibling stuff. We've been mad at each other for many things without understanding why.

Audrey: Sometimes I see you as the spoiled brat you used to be.

Ruth: And I see you as the controlling older sister.

Audrey: I have been controlling—and hard on you and so wrapped up in my own work stress that I haven't thought about what a stretch it is for you to juggle *your* schedule so you can do volunteer work in the evening.

Ruth: I really needed to hear you say that.

Audrey: From now on, the committee needs to divide up the last-minute work among all the members—not pile the work onto you.

The Underlying Elements

The Anatomy of a Conflict helped these two sisters have a meaningful discussion that began to lift their long-standing anger at each other. As they dug deep, they discovered powerful underlying elements—Ruth's need for her sister to value her lifestyle and Audrey's hidden dependence on Ruth—that couldn't be verbalized without dissecting their relationship. Ruth and Audrey were able to excavate the landscape of their connection to find out what was really troubling them. These sisters were lucky.

Are You Getting Good at All This?

If you are, you'll know what set off Linda's hot buttons in the following exercise.

Cousins

Linda and Roberta are cousins. Linda's a single mum in her late thirties. Her son, Louis, is thirteen. Roberta is single and in her early thirties.

Linda: Did I tell you the great news about Louis? He just made the debating team, and he got the honour by competing against a hundred other students from schools all over the country. He's finally coming around and getting serious about his education. My hard work is paying off.

Roberta: That's so good. You know the guy I'm dating—Ron? Well, he's a lawyer and he won a lot of awards in college for debating—you should just hear him in court.

Linda (furious): Hellooooo? What does that have to do with Louis?

Roberta: Not much, really, just thought you'd want to know.

- What happened here? What pushed Linda's hot button? Roberta isn't listening—she's too wound up in her own news.
- What should Linda say after Roberta's last remark? Linda might say: "Well, I would want to know about Ron if we were talking about Ron, but we were talking about my son. I feel sad that you're giving such short shrift to his news."
- What will that accomplish? You've given an "I" message that will cause Roberta to rethink her impulsive, self-centered response without feeling rage at you.
- Is there anything Roberta can do to turn off Linda's hot button? Sure there is: She can acknowledge her cousin's pain and irritation, apologize for being thoughtless, and tell Linda how truly proud she is of Louis.

You *are* getting good at this. See how you do with the next scenario.

Sisters-in-Law

Lorraine and Sandra are sisters-in-law. Sandra's husband is a successful stockbroker. Lorraine's husband has recently been downsized and is trying to start his own computer business.

Lorraine: Want to know the truth? I'm getting tired of endlessly hearing about your exotic trips with Harold and what a wonderful marriage you have. Why are you so insensitive about what's happening in my life?

Sandra: I'm not insensitive, and I'm quite aware of your situation. Does that prohibit me from ever sharing anything about my family? After all, the guys are brothers.

What pushed Lorraine's button?

Lorraine is feeling a little jealous at Sandra's luck but, even more, insulted that her sister-in-law doesn't seem to be aware of her problems. Let's continue this conversation, starting with what Lorraine says in response to Sandra.

Lorraine: I didn't think I stopped you from sharing good news about your family. I would just like you to be aware that I'm feeling quite vulnerable right now. Perhaps I did come on too strong a moment ago.

Sandra: Next time, rest assured that I'll listen more to your cues. You're a good friend to me, and I want to be there for you. Tell me about the new computer business—I really want to know.

What happened here?

Both sisters-in-law feel much better. They've both expressed their feelings, and both have listened well to each other. Hot buttons have been deactivated.

Mothers-in-Law

Certain family relationships are almost a cliché: So many people have found them sources of anger that they've become a common joke, a joke that's not so funny. Mothers-in-law and daughters-in-law, for example, are often involved in pushing one another's buttons. Here are some comments guaranteed to irritate.

The Mother-in-Law Pushes a Button

I'd never do that when I had young children.

Don't you think you should spend more time with the kids and work less?

I asked my doctor what he thought about Johnny's temperature and he said . . .

You'll scare the kids.

Do you really need a new house? Can't you make do with this beautiful home?

You're so irritable. Why don't I take the kids to my house?

Don't yell at me. I'm not your husband.

Don't tell me what to do—I wasn't born yesterday.

Bob's looking awfully thin.

Bob loves his vegetables steamed.

Haven't you put on a little weight, darling?

The Daughter-in-Law Pushes a Button

You clearly haven't read the latest studies.

Take it from me, your son loves corn soup—my corn soup.

We do things differently in my generation.

Why do you always have to be in control of everything?

Stop preaching to me.

Hold the baby's hand when you cross the street.

Ask my permission before you move anything in my house.

You're living in the Dark Ages.

Is that what you're wearing to the wedding?

Haven't you put on a little weight, Mum?

In the following scenario, the mother-in-law and the daughter-in-law are wildly pushing buttons—even if it's only in their thoughts.

Another Sunday Dinner

Edna's thoughts on the way to dinner at her son's house . . .

I'm thrilled I'm going to see my two beautiful grandchildren whom I just adore, but the minute I open my mouth, I know I'm going to have to deal with Rita's disapproving looks. She acts as if she's the only one who's ever brought up kids. I wish she would listen to my advice just once—I wasn't born yesterday, you know.

I think she secretly wants to drive a wedge between me and my son.

She does a particularly patronizing thing—agrees with me and then sneakily does things her own way. And she's so obdurate about simple health issues—all that fried food in that house! When I quietly suggested that she go light on the frying, she blew her stack.

I'm going to give the kids these magic lollipop rings when she's not around. I know she has a thing with sweets, but the kids love them so, and what she doesn't know won't hurt her. She just wants control over everything.

Rita's thoughts as she prepares dinner . . .

Another Sunday dinner I've got to get through—steamed everything, ad nauseum—just to please her. Paul hates steamed veggies. My mother-in-law is a piece of work. She knows everything and has a comment on whatever I do. Even when she doesn't have a comment, there's that look. She wants to control our lives. If she only wouldn't keep comparing me with her own daughter all the time. And she's so hypocritical. She complains that I cook fried foods, yet she brings candy to the kids even after I tell her that I don't want the kids to get hooked on junk food.

She wants to make me look bad with my own kids.

Edna and Rita continue to make negative assumptions about the other's motives. They already have a history of pushing each other's hot buttons—for years they've been expressing their thoughts in oblique but painfully clear jabs.

This is what Edna and Rita need to do:

1. Acknowledge that each somehow taunts the other with irritating comments.

2. Take turns giving examples that have made each of them feel hurt and devalued.
3. Listen to each other without interrupting.
4. Don't try to win. Each feels right from her perspective—the point is to try to understand the other's position and get to a win/win situation.
5. Make an agreement that if either repeats the hurtful behaviour, they'll both take "time out" and discuss it on the spot instead of harbouring resentment.

Here's how their conversation might sound. (Listen for the "I" messages—*and* the "you" messages. See which are more effective.)

Rita says . . .

I know that we both do and say things that bother each other—push each other's hot buttons. Sparks fly when we're together. I'll give you an example of what I mean—and then you give me one, too.

When you tell me how your own daughter does things—like how she entertains so beautifully—it hurts me because I feel you're putting down my style of entertaining. I feel incompetent when you do that. Then I get angry and don't want to listen to you anymore. It seems to me as if you want to control the way I entertain my friends. So I defend myself by saying something unkind to you. Also, you had your turn with kids. Now it's my turn, and I don't appreciate your constant criticism. And I hate them to get hooked on junk food. I need you to respect my feelings about that.

Edna says . . .

I can understand how you feel when I talk about my daughter. Now that I think of it, my mother-in-law did the same thing—and I hated it. The truth? Maybe I do think she's better than you in certain areas, but I also think you're better with your kids than she is. I guess I don't tell you the good parts, though—only the bad.

But here's my side: I also feel incompetent when you say things like, "Don't tell me what to do." Rita, I want the best for you, Paul, and the kids. And then you turn it around as if I'm preaching to you. I really don't mean to do harm, and maybe I have to find another way of saying things that doesn't upset you so much. Can we figure out a way that I can say what's in my heart so that it won't come out the wrong way? And can we figure out a way I can bring my grandchildren treats and you won't kill me for it?

Consider How You Look to the Other Person

When someone pushes your buttons, she becomes a monster in your eyes:

- How can she talk to me like that?
- What a bitch!
- Dumb and dumber.
- She appreciates nothing I do for her.

Step back and reflect: How do you look to the button-pusher?

In heated conversations we view ourselves as all-worthy and our opponents as all-willful. Think about how you look to each other:

How You Look to Yourself	How the Other Sees You
I give good advice.	You're a busybody.
I'm assertive.	You're aggressive.
I like to get things done right.	You're a control freak.
I tell it like it is.	You're so blunt; you're mean.
I'm sensitive.	You're too thin-skinned.
I'm bold and lusty.	You're crude.

The Ex-Wife and Her Ex-Husband—Still Family?

You bet. They have Jamie to consider.

Think of Jamie

You may think you're severing family ties when you divorce, but as long as you have a child between you, there's an implicit family relationship that persists. During the throes and aftermath of divorce, hot buttons are particularly vulnerable. Some of us feel so angry at ex-spouses that everything they do irritates. Even worse, some of us are never finished getting revenge for the hurts we sustained during the terrible battles. The children caught between the grownups' need for retribution are horribly damaged.

US tabloid headlines continue to tell us of the ongoing hostilities of cosmetics tycoon Ron Perelman and his ex-wife who was suing Perelman, months after their divorce, for an additional amount of money for child support. The ex-Mrs. Perelman pointed out that their tiny daughter needed many thousands of dollars a month more than the divorce judge originally awarded her so that the child wouldn't feel inferior to Perelman's daughter by another marriage. Ruling against the second Mrs. Perelman, the judge pointed out that what children need is very different from many thousands of dollars a month.

Does anyone out there think that Perelman's small daughter was not adversely affected by her parents' litigious, acrimonious, and hysterically public split? These parents are still carrying on their personal battles. The feelings of the littlest Perelman seem to come in a distant second.

Many other children of divorce are swamped in a tidal wave of anger over finances. My workshop participants tell me that the number one battle of a divided family is always about money. No matter who wins the best financial deal—the husband or the wife—the children lose the most during the combat. Rather than alimony, child support is usually the explosive hot button and the chosen battleground. The child is not only the victim of the divorce, but the victim of continual wrangling over money.

I know. I was once a child torn apart by divorce and arguments over money.

Ned and Wendy have been divorced for two years. Their nine-year-old son, Jamie, is in the fourth grade. Here's the situation from Ned's and Wendy's perspectives:

Ned's Perspective	Wendy's Perspective
She's taking my hard-earned money and spending it foolishly.	He makes me nag him about money for his own child—it's demeaning.
She thinks I'm a money machine and doesn't give a damn that I have to pay my own rent, too.	He doesn't even consider the hours I spend tutoring Jamie—that time spent is worth money, too.

Ned's Perspective	Wendy's Perspective
It wasn't in the agreement, so she'll have to spring for Jamie's school trip.	He won't acknowledge that everything couldn't be written down—there are so many hidden expenses, I couldn't think of them all. It's his child, too.

Before Jamie goes to school one day, this conversation takes place:

Wendy: When you see your dad after school, remind him I haven't gotten the cheque yet.

Jamie: Okay.

When Jamie comes home . . .

Wendy: So what did your dad say when you asked him about the cheque?

Jamie: He says the cheque's in the mail.

Wendy: Sure it is.

What's happening here? When ex-spouses are in a state of fury, they fail to see the situation from their child's perspective and are not attuned to their child's needs. What is the impact of his parents' relationship on Jamie? What is Jamie's perspective? What are Jamie's needs? I'm not a psychologist, but I do know what Jamie went through.

If Ned and Wendy were to sit down either separately or together to make an honest list of how their battles look to their son, it would be the start of a dialogue that could change Jamie's emotional life for the better. Here is one all-important rule for such list-making: Neither parent may blame the other.

Here's what such a list might look like.

Through Jamie's Eyes

Jamie's Perspective	Jamie's Needs
They're fighting because of me, so it's my fault.	I need to be loved by both of them.
They're always going to keep fighting.	I need there to be peace.
	I need to be secure.
They put me in the middle, and I don't want to take sides.	I need them to accept me.
They make me feel like I'm a pain in the neck to have around.	I need them to be happy.
They're too busy quarrelling and don't pay attention to me.	I need to not take their messages back and forth.
	I need to not be scared anymore.

Making such a list helps Ned and Wendy understand that Jamie is the one who is really being hurt in this family battle. They begin to think about how important it is to fulfill Jamie's needs as well as to balance their own needs. They've got to create solutions to minimize ex-spousal difficulties and promote harmony.

Creative Solutions

This is what Ned and Wendy *might* do:

1. Arrange time when Jamie is not around to talk about the issues so as not to involve the child in their differences (including sending messages through him).

"Let's either meet for coffee periodically or talk on the phone after Jamie is asleep."

2. Exchange information about Jamie's progress. Compare notes about Jamie's feelings.

   "Jamie was very excited when you showed him how to use the new computer game, and he told me it really helped him in school. He also mentioned that a kid in his class was bullying him. Have you heard about this?"

3. Be flexible about time and financial commitments.

   "The insurance and car payments are coming at the same time this month—what can we do about this?"

   "I have a late meeting, and I can't pick up Jamie next week. Can you do it?"

4. Acknowledge each other for his/her commitment.

   "I never realized what you have to go through just to buy Jamie some shoes. I nearly stepped on ten children who were playing on the floor in the store."

5. Brainstorm ideas and do problem-solving.

   "The price of painting the house is unreasonable. Why don't I come over and paint it, and we can use the money somewhere else?"

6. Select a neutral event that you can attend with your ex-spouse and child.

   "Why not go to Jamie's school play together and have dinner afterwards, so Jamie can see that his parents, while apart, are not enemies?"

HOT-BUTTON HINT

The overall purpose of human communication is—or should be—reconciliation.
—M. Scott Peck

HOT-BUTTON HINT

How come my parents know the location of every one of my hot buttons? That's easy—they installed them.
—GRAFFITI ON A WALL

Adult Children and Their Parents

Dialogue is the only way to turn those buttons off. Do you know what stops dialogue between adult children and their parents? Dialogue-killers. Dialogue-killers do it every time—push those buttons until they implode.

How to Kill a Conversation (check as many as apply to you)

Dialogue-Killers	Dialogue-Enhancers
Do you often. . . .	*Do you often . . .*
Finish your mum's sentences?	Listen for feelings to emerge—even if they're not stated in words?
Interrupt your grown son when you have a great idea you can't hold in?	Eliminate wandering attention (talking to yourself in your mind when listening to someone else)?
Give unsolicited advice?	

Dialogue-Killers	**Dialogue-Enhancers**
Do you often. . . .	*Do you often . . .*
Compare others' situations with those of your own children?	Ask questions to clarify the other's views?
Try to reassure your adult children as if you have secret knowledge (it will all work out; you have nothing to worry about)?	Ask the other to repeat information that's not clear to you (even if you worry you'll be thought dumb for not understanding)?
Analyze what your son is telling you in terms of your own value system (you can't have an abortion; it's morally wrong)?	Show by body language that you're alert and involved in the other's words (lean in to the speaker, smile, nod)?
Think of what you're going to say next before your dad/mum finishes talking?	Occasionally paraphrase to confirm you're understanding (are you saying that you don't think; you mean that you felt really angry)?
Change the subject so you can get on with your own agenda?	
If you checked four or more dialogue-killers, you DON'T know what stops dialogue dead in its tracks.	*If you checked three or more dialogue-enhancers, you've really got it.*

Parents and their adult children are historically adept at dialogue-killers. If you are a parent of an adult child, or if you're an adult with a parent, and you seem to give each other grief, check out the following.

HOT-BUTTON HINT

A contest between relatives is usually conducted with more acrimony than a dispute with strangers.

—Latin proverb

How Many Hot Buttons Have You Pushed This Week?

Parent to Adult Child	Adult Child to Parent
Why don't you ever call your sister?	Don't tell me how I feel.
You always have excuses.	And don't tell me how you dealt with your husband at my age.
I thought we would be friends when you grew up.	Get a life—don't try to take over mine.
You always have time for your friends but never time for me.	Do you mind if I decorate my own home—I didn't ask for your opinion.
Do you really like that colour green?	I wish you would call before you come over.
What made you choose *her* for a friend?	If I say Johnny can't have chocolate, he can't have chocolate!
You may be thirty, but I'm still your mother.	Join the twenty-first century.

Be Silent. Stay Connected.

When your button is pressed and anger is expressed either openly or obliquely, don't shoot back with your injured response. Certainly, don't cringe. What should you do?

Stay quiet for a moment or so.

Silence is tough for us. We're uncomfortable with it. We're a talky crew, unlike other cultures, where silence is an acknowledged and valued communication tool.

Can you think of the unfortunate remark as the start of a dialogue? Can you stay with the person's anger for a little while? The more silent you are, the more you give that person an opportunity to blow off steam. Your silence should also be reflected in your body language: Your eye and hand movements, even the tilt of your head, should be neutral. Finger-pointing, frowning, and pressing lips tightly together may not make noise, but they're still loud, anger-producing messages. Worst of all, an angry person gets *enraged* when you seem dismissive—when you shrug off his comments as meaningless and unimportant.

Do this: Stay in the picture, silent but connected with the angry person. Listen closely. Nod to acknowledge his fury. When you finally see his voice lowering, his body language relaxing, the set of his angry jaw loosening, you know he's vented.

It's your turn. Quietly give your side.

Mother-and-Daughter Roommates

We seem to have come full circle from the 1960s when any adult still living at home with parents was mightily suspect. Something was wrong if a woman in her early twenties didn't have her own apartment. Today, in the newness of the twenty-first century, dependency issues have given way to rising rents, volatile employment situations, and marriage at later ages. An adult woman living at home with her parents may not be thrilled with the deal, but because it's no longer a stigma, she accepts it—usually at a price.

And so we have here a breeding ground for resentment.

In the following scenario, the roommate arrangement is about to be broken—misunderstanding on its way!

You Think I'm Still a Child

Denise, twenty-six, lives with her fifty-nine-year-old widowed mum in New Jersey. Denise is a sales representative, and she's considering a better-paying, more challenging position with her firm that will require relocating to California. The tension between Denise and her mum is so palpable you could cut it with a knife. It all revolves around the move Denise is considering. They quarrel constantly.

Mum: Are you really considering packing up, leaving all your friends, and moving so far away?

Denise: I'm not sure, but if I know you, you already have objections to it—as you've objected to everything I've ever decided.

Mum: That's not true, and you know it. I just think that often you make hasty decisions, and then you're sorry for them.

Denise: Where did you get that from? When did I ever do that? The truth is that you cut me off at the knees by treating me as though I was still a child—and I've had it. Conversation over. I'm going to my room.

Mum (knocking on daughter's door): Please, Denise . . . forget it. I never said it. You're right. Let's not argue.

Denise (opening door furiously): Listen—I hate when you put me down in your insidious little way.

Mum: I said I don't want to argue.

Denise: You brought it up. You know what else I hate? How you always seem to cave in when we have differences—but you sure still manage to make me feel insecure with what you don't say. Do you do that to hurt me?

Mum: Hurt you? All I want is for things to be good with us.

Denise: You know, you're such a wimp—ever think about that?

Mum: Why are you so cruel to me? (starts to cry) I don't know why I get blamed when I try to do the right thing. So if you have to, take the job in California, and maybe you'll remember to come and visit me once in a while. Maybe you'll remember to come to my funeral.

Denise: You infuriate me! We can't even have a conversation without your crying. I've had it. Just leave me alone—I'm going to the family room to watch TV.

Here are two people who really love each other but are tearing each other apart as they set off each other's buttons. Here's what they should do.

STEP 1: WATCH THE PLAY

Denise steps back for a moment and watches the play unfolding in her home. What does she see? She sees two people at each other's throats.

She sees an angry daughter who depends on her mum and is secretly scared and nervous about taking a new position far from home. She sees a daughter who loves her mother very much but still senses she has to go out on her own, or wither away in her childhood room.

Denise also sees a weeping mother, angry and helpless with fear of losing her daughter and being left alone—a mum who's laying a guilt trip on the daughter.

Denise sees that she needs to repair this relationship, or

forever regret it. She comes back into the living room to face her mum, hard as that is to do.

STEP 2: CONFIRM

Denise: Mum, I'm really sorry that I spoke to you so harshly. You must be so upset to weep like this. Let's talk about it. I'd like to find out about some of the things that are really bothering you—besides your worry that I'll regret a hasty decision.

Mum: Oh, Denise, when you talk the way you did, I feel like a wet rag. And when I think about your going away, my heart stops.

Denise: I never realized you felt so horrible about my moving. Let's find out what's making us pick on each other.

STEP 3: GET MORE INFORMATION

Denise gets her mum to talk about how she might feel if Denise takes the new position. She probes some of her mum's concerns. She asks open-ended questions like: "What's the worst thing about my moving? What do you think will happen to our relationship if I take the position in California? What do you want to happen in *your* life?"

Her mum responds that she'll have nothing to do without Denise to take care of, and that she also worries about what will happen if she gets sick. She thinks that if Denise is far away, they'll grow further and further apart.

Denise listens carefully until her mother seems finished. She acknowledges all of her mum's feelings by saying things like, "I can see how my going so far away might make you feel alone and fearful. After all, you're used to seeing me every day."

Then, she says, "I'd like you to see the situation from my side."

STEP 4: ASSERT YOUR OWN INTERESTS AND NEEDS

Denise now goes into more detail about the job opportunity. She gives some of the big plusses—it's a promotion; she'll get a raise; the company will pay for relocation and help find an apartment; the workforce is young and dynamic. She talks about the drawbacks—she'll have to work out of two offices on new and unfamiliar projects; she's a little fearful of the challenge and scared about being away from home.

She finally says to her mum, "It's so important to me that you support me in whatever decision I make."

STEP 5: FIND COMMON GROUND

Denise and her mum come to realize that they both have issues of dependence and a fear of separating from each other. Denise and her mum talk about some of the pros and cons if Denise takes the new position. They also talk about some interesting new possibilities for mum's future. Then, finally:

Denise: You know what? I'm inclined to do it. After all, it's time to go out on my own. I'm feeling really excited—what do you think?

Mum: Honestly? It's going to be very hard for me at first if you do go. But if you make the big move, maybe it'll get me going, too. I can get a job. I need to get off my backside and out of the house. You know, we've really been living in each other's pockets—maybe it's time to make a change. And we can talk on the phone as much as we want—right?—and now I'm determined to join the twenty-first century and get e-mail.

Denise: The good news is that the job requires a lot of travel to New Jersey, so I'll get to see you a lot. But one more thing. In the future, when we have a discussion and we differ, don't cave in so quickly. You need to speak your mind. Otherwise, I won't know what's griping you.

Mum: I'll try. And you, my love, shouldn't walk away from an argument. We both need to work on the way we handle problems.

HOT-BUTTON ANALYSIS

With the Five-Step Formula, Denise and her mum have identified their differing conflict styles. Her mum is the typical Peace at All Costs fighter. The minute peacemakers smell an argument, they back down. Denise is an Avoider—make it go away!—and she walks out on arguments. These conflict styles keep people from having a lively disagreement—one where all the issues are out on the table.

Each is encouraged to drop the old carved-in-stone patterns of anger and avoidance, a good start to a new relationship.

Consider the following as you decide to work on some of the hot-button issues within your family. See if these help.

Recapture the Good Stuff

Look back to the times when you and your angry family member were close. Try to recapture those good feelings. Remember specific events when she shared with you, expressed love to you, touched you in affection. Now open your heart. Forgive.

Clean Up

Recall recent problems that you've had with your sibling, mum, or sister-in-law that you never really addressed. Review the issues from your point of view, by yourself. Be objective. Now think about them from both sides, and look for the things that really bothered you and the things that might have bothered the other person.

Next, try to find a quiet moment when you can discuss these conflicts with the other person as if you two were "watching the play." Clean up the emotional detritus! Often people are not ready to look for a solution until the old stuff is faced and retired.

Change Course

Go in a new direction and leave behind the old ways you dealt with anger.

7

Hot Buttons and Children

Wild Things

More than three decades ago, the prescient children's book writer Maurice Sendak wrote a book called *Where the Wild Things Are*—a story of a really angry kid named Max. Reviewers jumped on it, saying that Max and his rage were out of line, that the book would terrorize little ones who were not privy to Max's destructive adult emotions. Parents weren't crazy about *Wild Things* either, fearing Max would put nasty and disturbing thoughts into their own children's minds. Teachers wouldn't touch *Wild Things* with a ten-foot pole. The only ones who loved the book were the kids. Loved it, ate it up, couldn't hear it enough times. Here was someone who heard their rage. *Where the Wild Things Are* became an instant classic.

It's taken awhile for the experts to catch up to what the kids have been telling them, but last November, a *New York Times* headline read, PRIMAL SCREAM: TEACHING KIDS TO GET A GRIP. The article highlighted the cutting-edge theme of the National Association for the Education of Young Children: anger management.

Anger management may seem more suited to adults in adult relationships, but in these days of widely publicized school ambushes, hot-button control is an emerging theme in the education of kids from three to seventeen. Sendak was right. Children do feel anger to a degree we never imagined. And they're getting madder.

The Changing Family

Divorce

How come kids are so wound up? Experts point to the changing family. For example, in America in 1950, for every hundred children born, twelve entered a family torn by divorce. In the year 2000, of those hundred kids, it's estimated that a whopping sixty will be born to a divided family. And let's face it: Anger is a predictable and typical reaction of many children of divorced parents. Although it is true that adults are becoming more tolerant of divorce, partly because many people who are starting families may be products of divorce themselves, a family divided always hurts, and the littlest ones hurt most.

Depending on their ages, children react differently to the trauma associated with a family upheaval, but sadly, many remain angry for most of their growing-up years. Even if they know other kids whose parents have divorced, children still struggle with a sense of being different or unworthy when parents split. And they translate their sadness and worry into anger.

New Kinds of Family Structures

Families are changing in other ways that push kids' buttons. Single parents, same-sex parents, grandparents raising kids—all may be wonderfully loving and intelligent, but complicated family structures often create unbearable stress. Every child raised in a "different" family will not necessarily feel anger, but chances are that if his family looks different from most of his friends' families, and the adults in his family don't figure out ways to make him comfortable with the differences, he's going to have extra pressures.

Workplace Strains

The workplace has also been responsible for drastic changes for children since the early 1990s. Perhaps one reason kids in this new century are so ticked off is because of new expectations placed upon them. With their mums and dads at work, children today are asked to assume burdens that were never before theirs. Many have larger responsibilities for younger siblings. Some even seem to have taken on the responsibility of comforting stressed-out parents who return after a hard day at the office—a significant role reversal from earlier decades.

A Sense of Control

Finally, children of all ages want structure and stability in their days. When they sense that the adults in their lives are the least bit shaky (Does your job require you to move yet again? Does your mother visibly disapprove of your lifestyle—even though you're thirty-six?), they tend to feel that they have no control over their own lives.

Result? Act-Out Time

Whether it's a screaming four-year-old throwing a fit in the supermarket, a furious preteen who won't do homework, or a teenager who's just put another notch in an already well-slammed door, rage runs freely in too many homes. Often it's displaced rage. Kids can get angry at one thing and take it out on the nearest parents, siblings, or friends, who have nothing to do with the anger they feel.

Kids and anger—even displaced anger—are best friends. They have sleepover dates. It's up to the adults in their lives to help them cool down their anger. It's also up to adults to turn off their own incendiary hot buttons, so easily pushed by recalcitrant kids.

I'm here to tell you this is not so hard to do.

Model or Critic?

"Children," wrote the French philosopher Joubert, "have more need of models than of critics." I hate to put the burden on you, friends, but how you handle conflict in your relationship with your partner sends a clear message to your children: The very first step in turning off kids' hot buttons is to be very aware of how you look to them. New research clearly indicates that the way children get along with other kids, including siblings, closely correlates with how their parents get along with each other.

How you disagree carries crucial significance to children, who pick up many of their conflict resolution skills—or nonskills—from watching adult role models. You must be conscious of the fact that you set the standard and that you must rethink your paradigm if you are in the habit of calling your partner names, spewing out harsh criticisms, yelling loudly (even if it's behind closed doors), retreating in silence and anger, or showing disrespect. Resolution of conflict is vital. Conflict is natural in every relationship, but unresolved arguments are the most hurtful and traumatic experiences for children to witness. Parents who walk out on each other in abject fury, even for an hour, strike terror into young hearts.

Words

In the beginning and in the end, it's words, words, words that deflect anger—it's the words that inspire informed choices, that get to the bottom of the feelings behind the anger. If adults can improve useful communication between themselves and the children they love, they have it made.

When your child's been angered, forget fear-inspired approaches to acting out: "Hit Bobby one more time and you're going to get it!" They don't work. Forget permissiveness: "Make up with your sister the best way you know." This rarely works—the kid simply doesn't know.

Forget the kind of communication that makes things worse. For example, certain conversational tactics only get an angry child angrier. Sarcasm may make you feel clever, but it never works with children except to fuel the flame. Disparaging a child is lethal—either telling him bluntly or even implying that you have little respect for him because he's just a kid finishes communication before you start. A mum in one of my workshops, despairing about the relationship she had with her daughter, said things like these:

> I don't know where she got that idea from.
>
> She doesn't have the courage of her convictions, and she won't stand up to her friends.
>
> She's too easily swayed.

Here was a mum who told her daughter in no uncertain terms that she didn't have an original idea in her head and that she was headed for trouble because she didn't have the courage of her (mum's) convictions.

So, let's start. What follows are dialogue-opening tools to help you talk to your child and encourage that child to share frustrations with you so you can help him cool off. These are the very same tools used in the art of any conflict resolution, whether it's in the workplace, the global arena, or the intimacy of the bedroom.

There are no Harry Potter calming salves, no magic bullets—there are only words. Modified to fit circumstances and ages, they work—they always work.

Pay attention.

Small Kids

Starting from the time language is acquired, small kids need to establish themselves as people, separate and apart from parents. It's their job to stake out their own emotional turf, but along with the stakeout comes fury in various forms. The good news is that most school-age children learn early that hitting, temper tantrums, kicking, spitting, and other forms of physical expressions of anger are socially unacceptable. The bad news is that they forget. The same verbal skills your child uses to hurl insults during conflicts with friends and adults can be channeled into dialogue that will calm their anger.

If you happen to be present at such an unleashing of fury between your child and others over an obvious issue (whose turn it is on the swing, who gets to be plant-waterer), the most basic resolution technique coming out of our workshops is one that consists of giving those kids a formula so that they can brainstorm together—because make no mistake, they can come to the point where they'll be able to solve their differences with perhaps only the slightest guidance from you.

First make sure the kids know that rules are to be followed during the process: no interrupting, no hitting, no crying, no kicking, definitely no spitting.

Here's the formula. Each child must have a turn to do the following:

1. *Say what she needs:* In essence, each must verbalize her side of the dispute. (I want to be first on the swing.)

2. *Restate what the other kid says she needs:* This is to make sure that child's views are understood. (I think she wants to be the first to take a turn on the swing.)

3. *Go for the solution together:* Brainstorm various resolutions until they reach one that's mutually satisfactory. (You can take the first turn on the swing, but I'm going to have a little longer turn. You water the plants today, and I'll feed the hamster.)

Encourage your kids to practice this formula, again and again, until conflict resolution becomes second nature.

What if you see signs that your own small child seems to have a volatile temper? Step in and firmly halt the offensive behaviour—No ifs about it, you may not kick Jimmy.

- If you see your child act abusively toward another child who's angered her, act swiftly. Never hit or threaten her physically, which only sends the message that the biggest kid always wins. Instead, teach her that it's okay to feel angry, but violent behaviour always comes with consequences (timeouts or loss of privileges).

- Lavishly praise calm reactions to conflict—whether it's apologizing for a wrong, an attempt at negotiation with a friend, or a whole afternoon of peaceful play.

What happens if you're not present when your small child is attacked in anger? Prepare your child in advance so she'll be armed with good responses:

- Go over possible responses by role-playing. You be the kid who's giving your child grief. It's fun, and it also is a wonderful way to ingrain the art of negotiation in her soul.
- Teach your child to respond to aggressors with firm but calm words like, "I'm not going to let you bully me." Then he should be told to find an adult to help him.
- Give your child frequent talks of encouragement. Help him rehearse the steps he'd take if an older child gets angry and begins to bully him. If your little one is really small, role-play with puppets or dolls.

Sometimes none of this works. The spur that pushed a child's hot button may not be visible. If we're talking about your child, you have to dig deeper to unearth the below-the-surface feelings. We deal directly with the behaviour, but we also must consider the feelings underneath.

Feelings

There's a wonderful, mushy 1970s song called "Feelings." It's wonderful because it's an unashamed ode to the power of simple emotions, the spur to all human behaviour. Little ones have particular trouble expressing their angry feelings in language, and so they act out with antisocial behaviour. Sometimes it's puzzling—what made this kid spit at me or throw a tantrum in the supermarket? What pushed her hot buttons? Look closely for the feelings behind the buttons. It's helpful to keep a chart similar to the one below and try to connect both her feelings and needs to a recent behavioural problem.

WHAT GOT HER WOUND UP?

What Did the Child Do?	How Does She or He Probably Feel?	What Need Isn't Being Met?
Kevin spat at his grandma.	He's **jealous** of the time Grandma spent with the baby.	He needs to be **heard** by Grandma and also **praised.**
Mary Beth is not talking—literally.	Maybe she feels **frightened** and **betrayed** because suddenly Daddy doesn't live here anymore.	She probably needs a greater sense of **security;** she needs to **verbalize her deep fear** that she's responsible for Daddy's loss.
Danielle wouldn't go to sleep. She kept asking for water and another story, and she ended up hysterical.	Perhaps she feels **ignored** because Mummy and Daddy work so hard. Perhaps she's **frustrated** because she's having trouble with her reading at school, and her babysitter doesn't know how to reassure her.	She might need to be **admired more often** for her strengths, and receive more frequent **expressions of love and praise.** She also might need **to be heard** even though she can't find the exact words to express her reading problems.

What Did the Child Do?	How Does She or He Probably Feel?	What Need Isn't Being Met?
Michael told lies when he said he brushed his teeth and did not hit his sister.	Perhaps he feels **guilty.** Perhaps he feels **defensive** because his sister never seems to do wrong things.	Michael needs to be **rewarded** when he acts correctly. Perhaps he needs to be treated more **fairly** even though he's the older, more acting-out child. He yearns for a greater sense of **self-respect.**

Communicating with Children

The Right Questions

Now that you have a better idea of the feelings and the unmet needs behind your child's angry behaviour, you can probably begin meeting those needs. What if you still don't know what she feels or needs? You've got to ask. It may be that you have to ask many times, using different words and different questions until all is revealed. Learning to ask the right questions is a problem-solving technique that's got to work—eventually.

Most child manuals tell you that if your child is feeling angry, question him closely to get to the bottom of his rage. But don't do it with closed-ended questions. We've discussed these earlier, but when it comes to children, the theory bears repeating—it's that important. Closed-ended questions are death to a conversation. They're like true–false questions on a test, asking only for a short, one- or two-word reply. They go nowhere in conversation land. Use closed-ended questions only occasionally because they make kids feel as if the FBI is interrogating them.

These are closed-ended questions:

Are you tired? *No.*

Do you feel sad? *No.*

Did you have a good time? *Yes.*

Do you wish Daddy would come back? *Yes.*

Do you think your friend is going to get in trouble? *No.*

Are you in trouble? *No.*

Did anyone do anything to you? *No.*

OPEN-ENDED QUESTIONS

On the other hand, an open-ended question is more like an essay on the test. It gets a youngster to reveal herself. Often they start with *how, why,* or *tell me about,* and they ask for details, explanations, and elaborations of ideas in a way that makes your child believe her feelings and thoughts are of vital interest to you. Open-ended questions show respect: These are open-ended questions:

Tell me about your new friend Susan.

Why do you think the teacher acted that way?

How do you suppose curfews are handled in other homes?

Tell me how you feel about Daddy living in another house.

A CAVEAT

Don't ask your child too open-ended a question like, "Can you tell me about your feelings?" Where's the kid to start? His feelings when his best friend dissed him? His feelings when he flunked the test? His feelings when you weren't there when he needed you? Chances are he won't answer at all. Also, a cliché question comes under the heading of too open-ended. "How'd it go today, Tommy?" will get you a "Fine."

If your child is acting sullen, irritable, or uptight with a situation you know he hates, get the dialogue going. Start by asking a simple, straightforward, open-ended question in a tone that is accepting and inviting. *Then:*

- SHUT UP AND LISTEN: Give your youngster time to get out his answer. Let him know by your silence that you really want to hear the answer. When he seems to have said all he can for the moment, probe gently for more information.
- DON'T INTERRUPT: Let the answer flow. Don't finish your youngster's sentences or even try to anticipate what he'll say next.
- DON'T JUDGE: Avoid judgmental nonverbal behaviour such as frowning, scowling, pointing, an accusing tone of voice, or shaking your head, all of which send messages of disapproval. Children are masters at picking up voice and body language.
- MAKE A DEAL: Once you understand how your child feels and what needs of his are unmet, you're ready to talk about ways you can change things. Don't make the first suggestion—try to first get it from the child. (What do you want to happen, and how do you think we can make it happen?) Then follow with your suggestions.

HOT-BUTTON HINT

The problem-solving discussions you have with children of any age are basic. These talks are building blocks for negotiation skills later in life. You can't turn off hot buttons without words—just can't be done.

Intent versus Impact

Communication is a two-way street. Have you ever said something you thought was the essence of clarity, only to have it misunderstood by your child? Very often what we say is heard very differently from how we mean it to be heard. Even though we think we're speaking clearly, our kids may receive drastically different messages from our facial expressions, body language, and tone of voice.

Here's a scenario that illustrates a very important conflict resolution tool—being able to distinguish between intent and impact.

Message Sent! Message Received?

Laura, forty-two, and her son Bobby, ten, have been very close to Laura's mum, who lives about an hour from them. Lately, Bobby, who used to jump at an opportunity to spend time with his grandmother, balks when he's supposed to visit her. Listen to their conversation, and see if you can spot how the message the mother wants to send is not the same message the son receives. And then see if you can figure out why the mother is not hearing her child's true message.

Laura: Every time I bring up the subject of spending the weekend with Grandma, you run the other way. What's wrong? I thought you loved sleepovers.

Bobby: It's not the same as sleepovers with my friends.

Laura: You don't love Grandma like you used to when you were a baby?

Bobby: I like her, but it's not the same. Stop nagging me about this.

Laura: I'm not nagging. I'm just trying to tell you that you'll have fun. You have to give it a chance.

Bobby: No, I won't! I hate it there. She's always tired. She goes to sleep early. It's boring. Grandma's disgusting!

HOT-BUTTON ANALYSIS

Bobby's getting a different message from the one Laura wants him to get. Her statements to him have a far different impact from what she intended. By not sending messages that really open up the conversation, Laura is not getting to the deeper issues of Bobby's unease with his grandma.

The fact is, he's worried that Grandma's aging—and that maybe she'll die, like his friend's grandma did, when he's there. Laura needs to hear what he's really thinking.

Intent	Laura Says	Impact on Bobby
Laura would like Bobby to spend time with his grandmother.	What's wrong? I thought you loved sleepovers! You have to give it a chance.	Mummy is unfair and mean. I know she's going to make me go.
Laura would like Bobby to have fun at her mum's house.	I'm just trying to tell you that you'll have fun.	I won't have fun. I'm bored there. Grandma looks so strange when she's sleeping—maybe she won't wake up. I'm not going, I'm NOT going. I hate her!

A SOLUTION FOR LAURA AND BOBBY

Let's redo this scenario by having Laura's real intent heard by Bobby. If she asks her son some open-ended questions, it will encourage Bobby to share his real fear and possibly guilt-ridden feelings. He loves his grandma, but he feels anger at his mum because she's making him do a scary thing. Laura might ask any one, or even all, of the following questions:

- Can you tell me how you feel when you think about going to Grandma's house?
- What did you used to like best when you went to Grandma's house?
- What are some things Grandma might have at her home that would make it fun for you?

When Laura and her mother talked over Bobby's answer, they came to a better understanding of Bobby's fears. Once they understood the child's reluctance, they no longer felt powerless about how to handle the situation. So, what happened?

They both assured Bobby that Grandma was in excellent health and intended to live until he was all grown up. Further, they purchased a computer for Grandma—a stroke of genius because computers were Bobby's passion. Bobby was able to teach Grandma how to use it and also to play computer games with her and by himself when he got bored. He again became eager to spend time with Grandma.

The Literal Approach

There's another important aspect to communication with kids.

Young children from three to ten, notes child psychiatrist Dr. Denis Donovan in his book *What Did I Just Say!?!* (Henry Holt and Co.), are "consummate literalists" and usually hear exactly what is said—not what a parent means. That makes communication very tricky and often opens the door to rage—both on the parent's and the child's part—because the child, misunderstanding his parent, does not comply with the parent's wishes.

Dr. Donovan gives the following examples:

Parent Says	Child Thinks	Parent Meant	Child Does
How many times have I told you to knock it off?	Five, ten, twenty times . . . who knows?	Keep your feet off your brother's chair.	Kicks his brother's chair again.
Don't you want to finish your squash?	No, I hate squash!	Eat the rest of your food.	Continues to stare at his plate.
Can you say thank you?	Yes, I can.	Say "thank you" to the nice lady.	Says nothing.

Busters and Boosters

Sometimes messages are misunderstood because in conversation with children, certain phrases are used that burst the bubble of meaningful communication—even if you have the best of intentions. With a little practice, you can become adept at substituting communication boosters for the busters.

COMMUNICATION BUSTERS

From a Parent	From a Child
That was a stupid thing to do!	I want to ruin my eyes—get out of my room.
I don't want to hear your excuses.	Buy me, bring me, take me . . .
You're getting too big for your britches.	I need it right now!
You're too sensitive—don't worry, I know everything will turn out okay.	You're mean and I hate you!
What did you do to make your teacher so angry?	You never understand and you never will.
Try to be a leader for a change instead of a follower.	Robin's parents said he could!

A SCENARIO WITH COMMUNICATION BUSTERS—SEE HOW THEY WORK!

Jason: The dentist said I have to wear braces for six months—I hate them.

Karen (his mum): Your friends will understand—none of them is perfect either. Think positive. Not one kid will laugh at you. You should be happy we can afford the braces.

Jason: You're dumb—how do you know they'll understand?

Karen: Don't be cheeky—I was just trying to make it better for you. And I know these things because I have more experience.

Jason: Well, you just made it worse. You don't know anything and I really hate you!

What happened here? Karen's not a terrible mother—why did she strike out with eleven-year-old Jason? Well, most mums want to make things better, want to soothe their troubled kids. Karen's intentions are good, but her kid won't be fooled by saccharine messages. The message she wanted to send was not the message Jason received; instead of her good intentions, only the triteness of the message came through—and had a negative impact on her son.

THE SAME SCENARIO—THIS TIME WITH COMMUNICATION BOOSTERS

Jason: The dentist said I'll have to wear braces for six months—I hate them.

Karen: Are you concerned about how you'll look and feel at school? Can you tell me more about that?

Jason: You bet I'm concerned. I'm going to get stared at and laughed at.

Karen: You mean that you think you might feel embarrassed?

Jason: Not think—know. But I guess I'll live. Other kids have them. I'm glad you see what I have to go through.

This time, Karen empathized with her son. She put herself into his shoes instead of telling him what he should think or feel. She stopped her nasty habit of predicting what will happen. He appreciated it.

Listen for the Unspoken Fears

Anger is often the result of camouflaged fear. Naturally, fear takes many forms, resulting from various stressful situations, but the key to conflict resolution in every fear-induced moment of anger is being able to hear the unsaid words: What's making your child feel frightened enough to lash out?

The following scenario involves a stepfamily. A divorced husband has remarried, and a new household is created. The child from the original marriage is asked to blend in with the new family. It's a ubiquitous problem in our time.

Stepfamilies are perhaps the fastest-growing segment of today's population. According to a recent *U.S. News & World Report,* the U.S. government estimates that stepfamilies will outnumber traditional nuclear families by the year 2007. A child suddenly confronting strangers over the holidays—at his dinner table, in his bathroom, when he wakes up frightened from a nightmare—may well experience serious anxiety—and anger is not far behind. There are so many new questions:

- Who's the boss—my dad or stepdad?
- What's my curfew—9:00 P.M. in one house or 10:00 P.M. in the other?
- Who does my laundry—the housekeeper in one family or me in the other house?
- And what do I do about conflicting religions, diets, family finances, and God forbid, the arrival of a new half-sibling?

Stepfamily Blues

Eleanor and Frank have been married for three years. Eleanor has a seven-year-old son, Dennis, and she's expecting a new baby with Frank. Frank's twelve-year-old son, Kyle, lives with Frank's ex-wife, Lucy.

Kyle spends four weeks of the summer and almost every weekend with Frank, Eleanor, and Dennis. This weekend, Eleanor senses that something is wrong. Kyle is withdrawn and sullen. Before he leaves to go back to his mum, the following dialogue takes place:

Eleanor: I hope that you had fun this weekend.

Kyle: It was okay.

Eleanor: You don't sound as if it was so okay.

Kyle (snapping): I don't want to talk about it, and I don't have to. You're not my boss.

Eleanor: Why are you so upset? It makes me nuts when you sound like that—of course I'm not your boss, but I care about you feeling happy.

Kyle: That's not what Dennis said—and here, Dennis rules.

Eleanor: Dennis doesn't rule, but neither do you. I don't know what Dennis said, but I do care about you.

Kyle: Don't lie—you care about no one but Dennis and that stupid baby in your stupid belly. Leave me alone—I want to go home.

Eleanor: What did Dennis say?

Kyle: Ask him—he's your kid. If you must know, he said the reason you take me over the summer is that my own mother doesn't want me around, and you really don't either.

Eleanor: Not true, Kyle—none of it.

Kyle: I don't want you either! And my mum who's always so busy, always going out—I can do without all of you!

Eleanor: It sounds like you feel we don't love you as much as we love Dennis?

Kyle: Yeah. It sucks. But I don't give a damn—soon I'm going to ask Dad if I can go to boarding school.

Eleanor has just realized that the hot-button issues that have arisen go much deeper than Kyle's problems with his stepbrother, Dennis. Indeed, both families are now involved, linked by a common need, Kyle's anger. One thing Eleanor's sure of: This child is afraid of something. She must continue this dialogue to hear his hidden fears.

To continue the dialogue fruitfully, Eleanor must ask

open-ended questions to reveal Kyle's underlying feelings, such as the following four questions:

1. This is your own family. What should I do to make you feel part of it?

   Such a question will probably lead to some of Kyle's unexpressed fears that he's really not part of the family. Once the fear is expressed, the whole family can brainstorm ways (following his lead) to change Kyle's fear.
2. I know how much you love your mum . . . and that's great. You said she's very busy lately—can you tell me how you feel about that?

   This question demonstrates an understanding of Kyle's feelings for his natural parent. It will also give Eleanor more information to work with—like finding out that he's worried about her new boyfriend.
3. Is there anything I've done that you haven't liked? I really want to hear about it.

   This question gives Kyle a chance to tell Eleanor what bothers him—like the time she was on the phone with her friend and said something that hurt him.
4. What would you like to see happen when you come here next weekend?

   This question also can open up conversation and get Kyle to reveal what he wants and needs.

In contrast, here are three ineffective questions that will elicit little information of value and might even hurt Eleanor's relationship with her stepson:

1. Why didn't you tell Dennis how angry you are about what he said?

   This question is an implicit criticism of Kyle for not describing his feelings to Dennis—an act that could embarrass him greatly.

2. Will you talk to your mum about what happened here?

   This question subtly implies that Kyle is a traitor or tattletale if he tells his own mum about the happenings at his father's home.

3. Do you really want to go away to boarding school?

   This is a closed-ended question: A yes or no answer will tell Eleanor very little about Kyle's real feelings.

HOT-BUTTON ANALYSIS

Some of Eleanor's questions sound similar, but when working with children, one question may trigger the answer that the others miss. In the end, it's necessary to ask many questions to get past the "uh-huh's" and "all rights" that tell very little. By watching Kyle's body language and facial expressions as she questions and he answers, Eleanor has found out from Kyle that Lucy has a new boyfriend—and that's what's keeping her so busy.

Now Eleanor, listening hard, has finally heard Kyle's hidden fears. He's terrified that his mum will marry the new man and that the new stepfather won't want Kyle hanging around. Dennis, in a fit of pique, has told Kyle that he's not wanted in Dennis's home either—and the ominously approaching birth of the new baby makes Kyle sure Dennis is correct. So Kyle fears he won't be wanted anyplace—he'll be a homeless eleven-year-old, in effect. And he's frightened and furious.

> Now Eleanor must use some empathic responding statements, which should be utilized every time a child dares to open himself up even a little.
>
> A responding statement is used after someone answers your question. It should affirm or validate the child's sense of worth.

The Responding Statement

Eleanor might respond in these good ways:

I can see how you'd be upset, Kyle.

It was very brave of you to be so honest with me.

Now that you've told me how you feel, I understand so much better.

Eleanor also understands that a resolution of Kyle's anger/fear now involves both families' participation. The grownups must take over because they are the grownups. She and Kyle's dad must speak to Kyle's mum in a non-threatening atmosphere. Everyone who loves Kyle must work together to make him feel more cherished and safe, and thus less angry. Hearing his secret fears makes it all possible.

Blended Families: Three Hot Tips

- Who disciplines the kids—the birth parent or the new spouse or either one? Because discipline is based on appreciation and respect for every child and because discipline is not punishment, either partner should have the authority to insist on thoughtful enforcement of house rules. Such discipline should involve family meetings, frequent discussions to make house rules, and brainstorming to find ways in which everyone's needs may reasonably be met.

- What comes first—the kids' wants or the relationship of the parents? The parental relationship comes first, with the kids' wants a very close second. (I want my own television. I want to stay up later. I want new clothes.) Wants, by the way, are not the same as needs—you define the difference. Creating a chasm in a relationship by putting the wants of the kids first only creates discord in the marital relationship and invites the children to use manipulation skills to play their parent and stepparent against each other. Don't allow it.

  Needs, on the other hand, are not negotiable: Every child needs respect, a sense of dignity, and a feeling of being cherished. Satisfying needs goes hand-in-hand with the marital relationship. Wants can always be negotiated.

- What's the most important feeling a parent and stepparent can encourage? The feeling of belonging—no other emotional need takes precedence. And the feeling of belonging in a new blended family is best instilled when children feel listened to, even when they wish to express their fury, disappointment, or chagrin at being in the blended family. The real trick is for the parents in the new blended family to hear unspoken as well as verbalized feelings.

In the previous scenario involving Kyle and his stepmother, Eleanor, Eleanor heard Kyle's unspoken fears. She was a terrific listener. And you will be also. Here's how.

The Three A's of Listening

All communication depends on listening as much as you talk—and in the case of children, listening much more than you talk. Think for a moment of the two misconceptions most people hold about listening:

- Listening is passive. Wrong. Listening requires an *active* responder. When your child is telling you how furious he feels, you'd better not sit there silent.
- Listening means getting meaning only from words. Wrong. Listening also means listening hard to implied meanings and unspoken feelings.

A good listener is the most popular woman in town. Everyone thinks she's the smartest, the nicest, the funniest—all because they feel heard. This is how a good listener listens.

ATTENTIVELY

She demonstrates her interest by giving her full attention to the speaker, makes direct eye contact, even leans slightly forward. She acknowledges the other person with smiles, nods, and other nonverbal cues of approval. Listening attentively doesn't have to mean you agree with what the other is saying, but it should show you care that he's saying it to you. If you listen attentively, even if he's been feeling mad as hell, he will calm down.

ACTIVELY

She continues to show interest, but now she responds in a number of ways:

- She may summarize or restate what the other has said. (So you believe that . . . It sounds like you were . . . Did you mean that . . .)
- She may ask clarifying questions. (Where do you suppose that will lead? How might this affect the others? Who was around when he did that?)
- She may ask for elaboration or for more detail. (What other choices did you have? What else did he say?)

AFFIRMATIVELY

In a confirming and positive manner, she is now listening for the other's emotions and feelings—and commenting on them. (You seem very concerned about . . . I really appreciate that you're talking to me about this . . . It sounds like you're very proud of . . . It must be very satisfying when he . . .) By affirmative listening, she demonstrates caring, empathy, and respect. Listening in this way almost always turns off the other's hot buttons—and ironically, yours as well. Paying deep attention to someone else's point of view silently encourages him to do the same for you.

One Cool Listening Strategy

Throw "why" questions out the window. These put a child on the defensive:

- Why did you miss your curfew?
- Why haven't you done your homework?
- Why are you so rude?

Instead, to soften the interaction, try:

- What were the reasons you missed your curfew?
- What are the reasons you're late with your homework?
- How did you feel when Dennis said the mean thing?

The Chinese Way

Discussing the art of listening in a recent workshop, a young man asked if he could write the phrase *to listen* in Chinese for me. The words are composed of the three characters that stand for *eyes, ears,* and *heart.* Exactly. Listen with eyes, ears, and heart.

Behaviour Modification

Daniel Is Driving His Mum Mad

Six-year-old Daniel was driving his parents mad. He swore like a truck driver, used four letter words freely, mouthed off at his parents, and called his grandmother, *his grammy,* a motherf—. Where did he get those words? No one had the foggiest. His parents, Teri and Bob, were frantic. No amount of careful questioning and listening seemed to work.

One day Teri was shopping with three-year-old Elise tucked into a supermarket child seat and Daniel trailing behind her. First he plucked the box of Mutant Ninja Turtles Cookies from the store shelf and Teri told him to put it back. “Nooooo,” he wailed, “I want it!” In short order he proceeded to lift a box of animal crackers, a can of Coke, a box of crayons, and a jar of pickles. Each time, loudly protesting, he was told to put the item back. Finally, in a rage, he threw the pickle jar against a wall, and amidst shattering glass, he began to stamp his feet and scream obscenities. The baby chose that moment to drop the jar of jam she'd been playing with; naturally, it also shattered. She screamed in terror.

Teri felt like running away, abandoning both kids to the kindness of strangers.

It was Daniel's third public temper tantrum that week. What to do?

Wish Lists and Other Negotiations

Child analysts report that 99 percent of most aggressive, angry behaviour reflects troubling things that are going on in the child's life, and getting to the bottom of the trouble is usually the best approach. Still, when the child is quite young, a favourite anger-defusing technique of those same analysts is behaviour modification—treating the behaviour instead of the cause of the behaviour. Here are some suggestions:

- Don't be frightened by a tantrum, which is basically a way for a child to exert some control over his life. This too shall pass.
- The very simplest means of warding off anger tantrums: Don't go to the supermarket (or anywhere else) if Daniel is hungry or tired.
- Adopt the word *consequences,* as in, “If you continue to throw things, call Grammy bad words, kick your sister—there will be consequences, and we'll have to

leave the supermarket, go to your room, give up dessert, etc." Specific consequences are different from threats, which are scary and usually don't deliver. (You're going to be sorry if you don't stop!) Make sure the consequences are clear and are delivered. If, from previous experience, Daniel knows that promised consequences never happen, he'll ignore you. But if he knows you won't fold, he may turn off his furies just like that.

- Never give in on an issue just to quiet a screaming child. If Daniel knows he wins by screaming, that's the method of negotiation he'll employ from then on. If you think you might give in, do it *before* the situation reaches meltdown. "Okay, I'm going to change my mind and let you have the Yankee Doodles because you used the *please* word so nicely."
- A psychologist friend suggests a *wish list*—a staple of behaviour modification. Each day on pretty, coloured index cards, Daniel and his mum were to list two things each wished would be different at home, then two things each wished to have.

Daniel would wish for another ten minutes before bedtime and then one thing he could choose and keep on every supermarket trip with Teri. Teri would wish that Daniel not use bad words, and she might also wish that he would never scream at the supermarket. Each week, different lists. As each wish came true, it would be crossed off their lists with a feeling of accomplishment.

In only two weeks, the temper tantrums faded away, and Daniel's vocabulary resembled a six-year-old's more than it did a truck driver's. Is it bribery? No, consider it a negotiating session, not bribery. Friends, husbands, and wives negotiate their conflicts all the time, whether they call those sessions wish lists or not. You still see it as bribery? It works. This kind of behaviour modification technique promotes self-control and problem-solving. A big theory behind this kind of anger management is you do for me, I'll do for you. Not a bad thing to learn.

- Other behaviour modification techniques might include family meetings at which the whole family regularly discusses issues that inflame tempers, including household chores and limits on television viewing. Along with the discussions could go other kinds of incentive reward systems—star charts, for example, a star granted when a child doesn't explode with anger. The youngster can cash in his stars at the end of the week for a material reward (a box of coloured pencils) or a social reward (a game of checkers after his usual bedtime).
- Behaviour modification can even include gentle punishments—three minutes in a "timeout" chair upon returning home from an anger explosion in the supermarket.
- Finally, the very best way to help a small child turn off his hot buttons is to give him language. Teach him to say it in words—no fighting, no biting. What a gift. Toddlers to ten-year-olds who have words to express their ire rarely resort to violence or acting out in any way. Taking the time to show children how to express their emotions with words is a vital

key to turning off the anger that leads to screaming, cursing, hitting, or worse.

- Could we share? Could we take turns?
- I feel angry because . . .
- I need you to listen to me right now.
- I'm so mad, I can't hold it in.

Teenagers

Oh God, does he have to talk back on every issue? Does he have to challenge my very existence? Yes. There's a reason why some of us refer to them in exasperation as smart-mouths: Our teens are smart and getting smarter every day, and testing us to see if we're keeping up—testing our patience, our intelligence, our very sanity. Teenagers are the most secretive, hard-to-reach, spaced-out group in society, but they're ours—and we love them and have to keep them, even when we don't feel so loving. How to deal with their anger?

Stressful Times

First of all, understand that we live in times of special stress for teens. A recent *New York Times* poll found, for example, that just over half of American teens believe a murderous rampage could erupt in their schools, and just under half of those teens say they know someone their age who's tried to commit suicide. With more money to spend and more choices to make, today's teenagers constantly face hard decisions and frustration.

We certainly expect more from our teens in terms of achievement than our parents expected from us: In 1918, there were about 310,000 high school graduates; in 2018, there will be roughly about 3.2 million high school graduates. And these teen years are a challenge filled with varying layers of rebellion, moodiness, and outright anger.

When the Anger Is Excessive—Get Help

For some kids, the teen years are a time of real crisis, with out-of-control anger escalating and resulting in substance abuse, inappropriate sex, hurting others, and even self-mutilation. This has given us national angst. Every Columbine diminishes us as humans. Extreme teen anger—the kind that's connected to violence—is the result of kids never being heard at home or at school. So, what's excessive anger? You ought to get some professional help if your child often

- gets into fights.
- breaks rules.
- loses his temper.
- steals.
- lies.
- hits.
- threatens friends or strangers verbally as well as via the Internet or by letter.
- harms animals.

Even if your child is generally sweet and mild-mannered, if there's a history of his being taunted or teased at school, or a pattern of drug or alcohol abuse, or even if you notice your child excessively involved in violent video games—ask for help.

This section addresses the rage that's part of the normal stress of adolescent life—not the kind responsible for wiping out communities. Be vigilant to see what kind of anger lives in your house.

What Are They Thinking? We Haven't a Clue

Most of us will get through our children's teen years using our own common sense to help us turn off their hot buttons. Knowing this, we should now really admit we haven't a clue as to what those adolescents are really thinking—and that makes it difficult to help quiet their angers.

In this age of the Walkman, Nintendo, and the merry chirp of the Internet, teenagers have discovered almost failproof methods of escaping the human voice. This won't be a problem in twenty years. Experts predict radical new therapies to control teenage anger that will rely on virtual-reality simulators. Johnny will be able to practice controlling his aggression in a mock situation, and brain scans will tell his therapist right then and there if Johnny has learned anything about conflict resolution that day. But right now, that's no help. We've got to probe to find out what's fueling their fires—no virtual-reality anger simulators for us.

Again, it all comes down to talk, to communication. We've got to find common ground—at the very least, a common language that doesn't irritate.

Teenage Busters and Boosters

Have you reached an impasse with your child—you're at your wits' end and you're just not getting through to her? Let's revisit the busters and boosters.

Communication Busters	**Communication Boosters**
From Parent to Teen	***From Parent to Teen***
Disparaging: You're just a kid—what do you know about real life?	I know you've had many experiences to help you make judgments, and maybe you can learn from mine as well.
Dictating: I'm the mother—you do it my way.	First see it from my side—and if that doesn't work, we'll look for another way.
Putting down: That essay you wrote was dull.	Your essay was fine. It could be great if you added more descriptions.
Stealing the problem: I feel terrible that this happened to you. I didn't sleep all night. What am I going to do?	I'm sorry it happened and I was worried. I'm confident you'll work it out . . . and if you want help, yell.
Giving hot and cold messages: You're a good debater, but today you were very weak. . . . You once had potential, but . . .	You're a good debater. You may have had a bad day, and you'll learn from your mistakes.
Sarcasm: Oh, Ms. Brilliance strikes again . . .	You're brilliant! You continue to amaze me!
Interrogation: Where were you till ten last night (who were you with, tell me the name of the adult present, what were you thinking)?	I was concerned because I didn't know where you were and with whom until ten last night.
Changing the subject: That's so interesting. Listen—can you help me with the dishes?	That's so interesting—I'm dying to know more about it. Tell me!

I hope your reactions were in the second column. But take heart. You're not the only one who bombards with communication busters. Your adolescent is probably expert at the art. Here's how to counter her busters with some boosters.

Communication Busters	**Communication Boosters**
Furious Teen to Parent	***Parent Defuses the Fury***
Don't tell me how I feel!	You're right. Let me know how you feel.
You'll never understand.	*Never* is a strong word. Maybe I don't understand a lot, but I'm going to try harder.
All you do is criticize.	I don't mean to criticize—tell me when I do it, and I'll rethink what I say.
I hate you—you're ruining my life.	I hear your anger and I know I must pay attention to it—now. Tell me what you need.
You're a control freak.	We may see it in different ways. Please let me know what I do to make you feel that way.
I just do it to spite you.	You really sound upset. I should be quiet and listen to why you feel that way.
Who are you to moralize? Look what you've done in your own life.	You're right—I certainly have made mistakes. That's why I hope I can help you avoid making the same ones.

Next time you get slapped down by a communication buster, stop for a moment before you lash back or retreat into sulky silence—and turn your response into a booster.

Intent versus Impact, Teenage Style

I've said that good intentions don't always deliver good messages. This is painfully true in the teen years. Sixteen-year-old Ellen's boyfriend, Tim, suggests that she forgo the second helping of apple pie. Yesterday, she announced she was on a new diet and playfully asked Tim to help her. But Tim feels baffled and furious when Ellen responds to his suggestion by saying, "Mind your own damn business!"

What happened here? Tim only did as Ellen asked, but she still felt embarrassed and put down. The message she sent was not the message delivered to Tim. When she said to Tim, "Help me," she only meant, "Understand me and be on my side"; she did not mean, "Tell me what to do." Because Tim did not hear her intent, he also became angry. Two tempers flare—and all because two people who like each other weren't paying attention to unstated needs.

In the following exercise, Margaret, a single mum, is talking with her seventeen-year-old daughter, Carla. Margaret is worried because she thinks Carla's friend Joyce may be a bad influence. Joyce has ultrapermissive parents and no curfew, and she is permitted to drink wine and smoke at home. Carla invariably comes in late when she's out with Joyce.

Listen to their conversation and see if you can spot how the message Carla's mother wants to send is not the message Carla receives.

I'm Old Enough

Margaret: Late again? This is when you decided to come home? I've been tearing my hair out with worry.

Carla: Stop being dramatic, and stop worrying. I'm old

enough to take care of myself—I don't need you to tell me when to come home. I hate having a curfew anyway—it's a kid's rule.

Margaret: You act like a kid; you're going to get treated like a kid. I'm still your mother. It's my duty to set limits on how late you stay out, especially on school nights.

Carla: Cut the sermonizing, Mum! You need a soapbox—you just don't understand. I'm seventeen, and I hate when you treat me like I'm four. (starts to cry)

Margaret: I don't mean to preach and you know it.

Carla: No, I don't know it—you do this all the time.

Margaret: Joyce is the worst influence—you follow her like a lamb to the slaughter. And her parents are some pieces of work.

Carla: Joyce does not influence me, and she's not your business. She's my friend. And her parents are enlightened—not like you! (slams door of room—end of conversation)

HOT-BUTTON ANALYSIS

Having a conversation with a teenager is like being on a roller-coaster ride. One moment you're on a high, communicating nicely—you think. The next moment, you dive. You've pressed her hot button and she explodes.

In fact, Margaret pressed Carla's buttons several times even in this short dialogue. The message she intended Carla to hear was not the one Carla received.

Here are just three examples of intent and impact in Margaret's conversation with her teenager, Carla. Carla hears only Margaret's words, not her *intent*, which influence the impact of the messages Carla receives.

Intent	Margaret Says	Impact on Carla
1. Margaret wants Carla to know how much she's loved and how much Margaret worries about her. She also wants Carla to know she's been irresponsible.	I've been tearing my hair out . . .	She doesn't trust me, she's totally unfair, she wants to control me, and I can't stand it anymore.
2. Margaret believes that teens secretly yearn for structure and limits, and she wants Carla to know she's strong and able to provide those limits.	I'm still your mother. It's my duty to set limits on how late you stay out . . .	She's a policeman.
3. Margaret wants to know more about Carla's relationship with Joyce.	Joyce is the worst influence—you follow her . . . her parents are some pieces of work . . .	She won't listen to how other parents are more trusting and modern. She hates Joyce, she doesn't trust me when I'm with Joyce, she believes I don't think for myself. She doesn't see how much I need Joyce. God, I hate my mother.

HOT-BUTTON HINT

If we can choose words more carefully so that intent is aligned with impact, there's a better chance that the message sent will be the one received.

We need to reconstitute this scenario to make sure Margaret's intent is the message Carla receives. If Carla hears what her mum intends, the conversation won't be filled with hot spots. The payoff? Margaret will eventually gain a far deeper understanding of her child's issues, issues she may not be aware of. Understanding more, she'll be able to guide her child through a process of self-discovery and problem-solving. How can Margaret do it? By

- asking open-ended, nonjudgmental questions to get more information.
- making neutral, impartial statements geared to moving the conversation forward, not geared to proving her opinion.

Here's the reconstructed conversation:

Intent	Margaret Says	Impact on Carla
1. Margaret wants Carla to know how much she's loved and how much Margaret worries about her.	I know you don't like it when I worry, but I get concerned when you stay out past your curfew.	I *don't* like it, but I know Mum cares about me—even if I hate that damned curfew!

2. Margaret believes that teens secretly yearn for structure and limits, and she wants Carla to know she's strong and able to provide those limits.	Perhaps we should talk about the curfew and other house rules until we both can agree on what's reasonable. Can you give me an idea of what you think we both could live with?	At least she's giving me choices—I can probably deal with this.
3. Margaret wants to know more about Carla's relationship with Joyce.	Can you tell me more about Joyce's relationship with her parents and why it sounds good to you? I can see the appeal of a friend like Joyce—I used to have someone like that in my life when I was your age.	This is my chance to explain how *interesting* Joyce is. Maybe I can get some ideas of how to handle Joyce and me. Joyce is so cool and wants to be friends, and I don't want her to think I'm a nothing—but frankly, Joyce's parents are really stupid to let her drink and smoke. Not that I'd admit that to Mum.

Have you recently said something to your child that you suspect was not heard as you intended it to be heard? What words or phrases did you use that you now think were conversation-stoppers—phrases which, to your dismay, ended up doing more damage than good? Could the following be among those phrases?

Don't you think it makes you look a little . . . chubby?

You're just like your father.

Is that the colour blue you chose?

Firecrackers

Firecrackers are conversation-stoppers that are guaranteed to enrage your kids and create a chasm wider than the Grand Canyon. They're emotionally charged words or phrases that seem to explode your child's particular hot buttons (what's a firecracker to my kid may not lay a spark on yours). Some of them are obvious, some less so. Listen in on this conversation between Vivian, forty-eight, and her fourteen-year-old son, Michael.

Baggy Pants

Vivian: I can't stand it when you wear those baggy trousers. You look like a mall rat—I didn't bring you up to look that way.

Michael: You have no right to tell me what to wear. You just don't understand, you never will, it's hopeless.

Vivian: You used to look so cute and dress so well, but now I don't even recognize you. Wear those ugly trousers when you're in the house, nowhere else. That's an order.

Michael: Are you crazy? You miss the whole point. You sound like a drill sergeant, but I'm not in the army. I can't wait to leave home.

Vivian: Don't talk back to me—you have a smart mouth, sonny.

Michael: All the other kids wear them. I don't see their mothers complaining. Get with it, Ma!

Vivian: Why do you always compare me to the other mothers?

Michael: Why do you always compare me to wet cousin Phillip?

Vivian: You should be more like him. He would never wear those repulsive, falling-down trousers.

Michael: That's because he's a jerk. Your whole family stinks.

Vivian: We're getting nowhere. Wait till your father comes home—we'll see what he has to say.

In the chart below, check out these eight firecracker words/phrases that either Vivian or Michael used; next to each, notice what the word does.

Firecracker!	**What It Does**
1. Always/never	*Always* and *never* are absolute words that are annoying and can't be proven. Most people hate to be told something is always or never true.
2. Don't talk back to me	This phrase plays a power game: It says, "I'm the ultimate boss" and denies the other's right to speak up.
3. That's an order	A dictatorial phrase that closes down a conversation.
4. You should	A judgmental put-down that says you know better than anyone else.

Firecracker!	What It Does
5. Your family stinks	Grand insult and an ultimate put-down of someone else's loved ones.
6. You just don't understand	This implies the other is either closed-minded or stupid.
7. I can't stand it when	Put-down of the child's needs or desires.
8. You have no right to tell me	Starts a power struggle that has to result in win/lose.

All these firecrackers in one three-minute exchange! If these family members don't change their communication habits, they're going to wipe each other out one day. Later that afternoon, Vivian decided to try again—why make her husband into the ogre? Why shouldn't she take on the responsibility of at least trying to gentle her son's anger? She'd make one more attempt to try to get him to see her side.

But You Definitely Can't Put an Earring in Your Nose

Vivian: Michael, I realize that I may have spoken too quickly and too harshly about your baggy trousers, and I'd like it if we would talk again so I can understand more about how you feel.

Michael: Well, okay—but it's probably useless.

Vivian: Maybe not—let's give it a try. I hear how much wearing these trousers means to you, and I'd like to know more about why.

Michael: It's the style, Mum. Don't you get it? All the kids wear them. If you don't, you're out of it. They may look ugly to you, but to my friends they're happening.

Vivian: I'm trying to get it—I really am. I think I can identify with you. I remember how upset my parents were when I was in high school and wore miniskirts. I didn't hear the end of it.

Michael: So Grandma and Grandpa gave you a hard time? Then understand how it feels!

Vivian: Yes, they did—they had a totally different value system—even then we had generation gaps. When they saw my knees, they thought it looked trampy. To me, the more leg I showed, the cuter I looked. What do you think I see when I look at your baggy pants?

Michael: How do I know?

Vivian: Well . . . I see sloppy, I see unkempt, and I worry that other people think you don't come from a proper family. What do you see when you see baggy pants?

Michael: Well, I see style—the fashion of this decade. A shaved head, baggy pants, ear piercing—they're just styles, Mum. They shouldn't threaten you. I like to show that I know what's happening and that I can look good in the latest style. I don't want to be a nerd. Why do you worry what other people think?

Vivian: I guess I do, I can't help it—but you're probably right. Don't you also worry about what other people think —like your friends? How do you think we can work this out?

Michael: Okay, okay. I do worry a little, I guess. How would you feel if I promised not to wear the pants when your friends were around, or when I have to go somewhere with you?

Vivian: Great! I love you, Michael, even if I don't love your pants. You know, we should try to talk like this all the time so we don't keep fighting about different rules. But could I ask you something? Do you have plans to pierce your nose next?

Did Vivian succeed in cooling down Michael's hot buttons and resolving the conflict? Of course she did. Here are the guidelines she followed.

Guidelines for Parents of Teenagers

1. *Remember.* Think of a time when you were a teenager having clashes with your own parents over differing values—watching TV, going to parties with no parental supervision, wanting your own telephone. Now empathize more with your adolescent.
2. *Respect.* Because values can't be negotiated, you need to demonstrate that you understand and respect the principles your child holds dear. Doing this will create a natural desire for your child to give back—and try to respect your values.
3. *Be there.* Teens have creative approaches to time. They often are ready to talk when you're not. The trick is to be accessible and ready to listen anytime, anywhere. This may sound terrible, but be there to

eavesdrop as well. It's a wonderful way to find out what's making them mad, what's making them glad. Don't actually snoop, but dissolve into the dashboard of the car as they chatter; melt into the kitchen wall as they chew the fat on the phone right in front of you, forgetting you even exist.

4. *Listen—don't judge.* Be a role model for listening deeply to your child. He'll listen back when it's his turn. And don't judge what he says. The words "You should have" and "Why didn't you" should not leave your lips. Just hear him.
5. *Develop options for problem-solving.* When you're certain that each of you understands the other's views, look for ways to solve a particular problem. Periodically revisit that conflict to talk about progress. Look to the future and negotiate "house rules"—when you can have friends over for parties, going away for weekends with the opposite sex, consequences of breaking rules—so that future conflicts can be handled in the same manner.
6. *Touch.* Unless your teenager has a real aversion to being touched (and if she does, find out why!), reach out and make contact often during a conversation. Stroke her face, squeeze his hand in understanding, pat his shoulder. Fathers usually have more difficulty with this than mothers, particularly with their daughters: They may be the warmest, touchingest dads to their little girls, but as soon as those daughters develop breasts, they're hands-off. That's a shame.
7. *Keep your sense of humour.* Even if it hurts to laugh, your teenager will appreciate it.

HOT-BUTTON HINT

When you get to the end of your rope, tie a knot and hang on.

—Franklin Delano Roosevelt

Teen Hot Buttons

In an unofficial survey of high school students across the country on what parents do to push teenage buttons, the following top issues emerged. Alongside you will find some instant resolutions:

Button-Pusher: ***Teens define words differently from you***

Take the word *clean*. "You call that room *clean*?" says a furious mother.

Take the word *early*. "Eleven o'clock on a school night is not *early*," says another angry mum.

Button-Defuser: ***Be specific***

The moment an interpretation is called into question, both parent and teen must stop what they're doing and write down a mutually acceptable definition for the next time. For example:

In the future, we both agree that *clean* means beds made, floors swept, rubbish bins emptied, uneaten food trashed.

In the future, we both agree that *early* means 9:30 on a school night—unless we both agree to change this rule for a specific occasion.

Control of TV controls. Everyone in the family wants to watch something different on the one TV set, and tempers erupt daily.

Negotiate. At the start of the week, each family member "reserves" an equal and agreed-upon number of shows. Reach these decisions by negotiation—I'll give you *The Simpsons* this week if I can watch *Biography* next week.

Telephone addiction. No one can call in or out when Mindy's gossiping for an hour at a time. Mum's not blame-free, either.	Agree on what's reasonable. All agree on a reasonable length for a conversation. Before settling in for a lengthy gossip, each person sets a timer—and sticks to it.
Schoolwork. Parent doesn't want to be responsible for teenager's responsibilities. It turns him into a nag, and teen gets angry. What to do if teacher complains homework is not being done?	Make a contract. Each teenager is responsible for doing homework without parental nagging. The actual contract is drawn up: Parent won't nag; teenager will carry through. If the contract is broken by either, appropriate consequences will be taken (both teen and parent agree on those consequences for a broken contract).

The "I" Message

Which makes you feel less angry?

Someone Who Says	Or Someone Who Says
• You are always late. or someone who says	When I have to wait for you, I feel that you don't value my time.
• Your e-mail was stupid.	I was frustrated because I didn't know how to answer your e-mail.

When you accuse someone using the "you" word, it feels judgmental, it lays blame, and it invites a hostile response. When you say essentially the same thing using an "I" statement, it declares your unhappiness and allows you to describe your feelings regarding the other person's behaviour in a clear and nonthreatening way. (I feel sad, threatened, unhappy when you . . .)

When you use an "I" message, the other becomes less defensive. With "I" messages, eventually there will be room for both people to clarify the issues and their separate needs: Blame or wrongdoing is not attached to the other's actions or statements.

But "you" statements, in contrast to "I" messages, are accusations (*you* always say that, *you* are unfair, *you're* irresponsible, *you're* lazy). They invite the other to angrily defend herself.

HOT-BUTTON HINT

For hot buttons to cool down, feelings must be expressed.

One of my problems is that I internalize everything.
I can't express anger. I grow a tumour.

—Woody Allen

Perspective-Checking

A perspective is one person's point of view. In a quiet, reasoned conversation, people generally listen to others' points of view—and may indeed change their own because they've been convinced in the conversation that the other's perspective has merit or a twist they hadn't thought of. Raise the temperature of the discussion, and different perspectives become a conflict. Points of view now become inflammatory. Suddenly no one listens to anyone else—all we each want to do is make our own perspective known, dominant, and even validated by the other. It won't happen.

Perspectives tend to get fixed in stone. Unless . . . you can stop for a moment and truly check the other's perspective.

To check someone else's perspective, you have to put your own position on hold for a while. It takes empathy—the ability to step into another's shoes to understand his position—and it takes acceptance.

Perspective-checking in conflict resolution also takes something else—the ability to actually verbalize the other's point of view and rephrase it in your own words so that your protagonist feels she's been understood. In a conflict, if you see something from another's perspective, you should then be able to validate the other's feelings, whether they've been stated or not, and most times they haven't.

Mum: Nessa—I know you promised to set the table, but I can see your new yearbook is irresistible. It's okay—don't feel guilty.

Mum: Lucy—I know I embarrassed you in front of your teacher when I said I helped you with your essay. I think you must have felt angry and betrayed. Do I have it right?

Children from four to eighteen have perspectives that are almost 180 degrees apart from their parents. This creates a natural schism. In our heart of hearts we think we know what's on our kids' minds, but the fact is, we're clueless. This gap is a natural hot-button pusher. That is why perspective-checking is a vital conflict resolution tool, especially with teens. Mum sets the table because she understands the excitement of the newly arrived yearbook—and she accepts Nessa's need to give in to it, even though she promised to set the table. What Nessa did was okay even if it was inconvenient.

Consider the following scenario and the art of checking perspectives.

Daddy's Little Girl

Seventeen-year-old Melissa is a high school senior who has ongoing conflicts with her dad, Ronald. When they discuss issues that involve boys, his hot buttons are invariably pushed.

Ronald's perspective: Melissa has made poor choices about friends in the past and is bound to repeat her mistakes. She needs to be protected. And now she's hanging around with a seedy gang of guys from that school across town. Trouble.

Melissa's perspective: Daddy thinks I'm a baby—his little girl. But I'm grown up and I've learned from my mistakes, and he's got to let me make my own choices.

Ronald: I understand you've volunteered to be on the senior trip committee. Isn't there a rule that only seniors from your school can go on the trip—no outsiders allowed?

Melissa: I'm working to see that the rule's going to be changed. Last year's trip was a total disaster because many of our own seniors didn't attend and the school lost a lot of money. We need our friends from other schools.

Ronald: I know why you're on the committee. You want to make sure Kevin and Tom, those guys from across town, can go on the trip.

Melissa: Oh, just stop it! That's just dumb—you're so suspicious, you don't trust anyone I go around with, and I can't stand it.

Ronald: Don't you raise your voice at me.

Melissa: You raise yours, I'll raise mine. All I do is tell you what's happening with the school trip, and you turn the whole thing around and make it seem like a conspiracy.

Ronald: Melissa—be intelligent. I don't trust that gang of two—neither one has a drop of ambition. I've seen them cruising around at night making animal noises. What in the world are you doing with these people? You're naive and gullible—don't you have more sense than to mess around with them?

Melissa: First of all, they're not a gang. They do what all kids do. You find fault with everyone I like. What do you want from me? I have a life! And the way you act, I'm going to live my life somewhere else, very fast.

Ronald: Don't threaten me, young lady, or I'll forbid the trip altogether.

Melissa: You're disgusting.

HOT-BUTTON ANALYSIS

Both Ronald and Melissa are Exploders reacting to each other as if they're set on automatic pilot—it takes just a few remarks to create an impasse of fury. What this father and daughter need to do in order to communicate without exploding is to learn and practice perspective-checking skills.

Recommendations for Perspective-Checking

Communicate to the other that you really want to understand the other's point of view. To do this, you need to follow these three steps:

1. Describe in your own words what you *think* you heard the other person *say*. Do not use his exact words because that sounds as if you're parroting or making fun of him, or even being sarcastic.
2. Give your perception of the other person's *feelings:* by affirming emotions, you open the door to a deeper conversation.
3. Always add, "Have I got it right—is there anything I've left out?" You're checking the accuracy of what you think you heard.

Let's see how we can apply these three perspective-checking steps to Ronald and Melissa. Here's what Ronald actually said, what he could have said, and why that would have worked better.

What Ronald Said	What Ronald Could Have Said	Why It Would Have Worked
I know why you're on the committee. You want to make sure Kevin and Tom, those guys from across town, go on the trip.	It sounds like you were really upset about what happened with the senior trip last year, and you're working under pressure to come up with a new plan. Do I have that right?	It demonstrates to Melissa that Ronald was really listening and understands her. He identifies with her feelings even though they haven't been stated. He gives Melissa an opportunity to fill in other information if necessary.

Now it's Melissa's turn to check her dad's perspective.

What Melissa Said	What Melissa Could Have Said	Why It Would Have Worked
You find fault with everyone I like. What do you want from me?	You seem very concerned about Kevin and Tom, and you think they might be a bad influence on me. Is there anything I've left out?	Even though Melissa doesn't agree at all with her dad, by showing him that she understands his way of thinking, she creates an atmosphere where he will be more willing to hear her point of view.

They continue . . .

What Ronald Said	What Ronald Could Have Said	Why It Would Have Worked
You're naive and gullible.	You feel I don't give you enough credit to make your own judgment about boys—and you're angry with me. What would you like me to know about Kevin and Tom?	Ronald could have narrowed the generation gap by understanding her point of view. By asking for more information, he opens up to discussion instead of insult-flinging.

What Melissa Said	What Melissa Could Have Said	Why It Would Have Worked
I'm going to live my life somewhere else, very fast.	I understand that you've gone through the same stuff and you want to shield me so I don't make the same mistakes. But I'd like to share some nice things I found out about these two guys with you.	Instead of threatening her dad with leaving home, she affirmed to him that he did indeed have life experiences that were worth something and that he loved her and wanted the best. That calmed him.

So where's the solution? What finally happened?

Once both parties are able to check the other's perspectives, the road is open to settling the conflict. The whole atmosphere changes. Many solutions become possible, including the following:

- Ronald takes Melissa up on sharing more about her relationship with Tom and Kevin—and she willingly does.
- Melissa invites Tom and Kevin over to meet her parents—and Ronald's fears are allayed. They're not so bad after all. More important, Melissa's acting so adult, his faith is reinstated.

What Melissa really wanted happened: Ronald reconstituted his image of Daddy's little girl and began to look at her as a young adult.

What Ronald really wanted happened: His daughter shares her life, her friends, and her thoughts with him. She assures him that she understands his fears and respects them—and will keep his concern in mind.

Perspective-checking: It turns off hot buttons.

HOT-BUTTON HINT

Who was it who said that there is no truth, only perception? Perspective-checking is one of the most powerful tools we can use to deepen our communication and build better relationships with our children. It takes practice, and like sex, it gets better with practice.

Finally, ask your teenager to take the following test. You take it, too. Then look over your answers together (if your teen agrees to share). It will tell you just how angry you are and give you an idea of the situations that seriously push both your hot buttons.

What Pushes My Buttons? An Exercise of Irritants

Rate each irritant from 1 to 10.

This Pushes Me over the edge	**Almost Never**	**A Little**	**A Lot**	**I Need Revenge**
	1–3	4–6	7–8	9–10
People pushing in front on a queue				
Failing at something				
Being rejected				
Being blamed for what I didn't do				
Being laughed at				
Being disrespected				
Feeling ignored and unliked				
Losing an argument				
Being told what to do				
Being lied to				
Being manipulated				
Being embarrassed				

If you or your teenager scored anywhere from 1 to 50, this is a reasonable and normal range of anger. If the score is *much* lower, someone's either a saint or lying about his or her feelings. Everyone feels anger occasionally—it's how you dissipate the fury that counts. Consider yourself fortunate in being a parent or a teenager who seems to be coping beautifully with the myriad pressures in the world.

If you or your teenager scored anywhere from 51 to 100, too often you feel humiliated, dominated, or picked on. Still, you usually can respond to each other and to the world without blowing up. If you learn how to cool down hot buttons even moderately well, your angers can lead to creativity and productive resolutions instead of slammed doors. It's interesting to note that many young people who have experienced serious conflicts often turn out to be among the most resourceful adults—if they've discovered how to translate their temper into empathy and cooperation.

If you or your teenager scored anywhere from 101 to 120, you're either a *really* angry parent or a *really* angry teenager. Your hot buttons are quite volatile. Not terrific at all. It's a problem that must take away from your happiness. Understand that it's okay to have opinions and feelings that run counter to those of other people, but find ways to express them productively and nonviolently.

Learn techniques to keep anger from bubbling over. Read the last chapter of this book to discover ways of conquering feelings of being dissed or dismissed. Physical outlets may help—sports or working out in the gym. I know many teens and adults who punch a punching bag, slam a bed with a stuffed sock, or go in the backyard to let out a long and loud yell as an anger release. Meditation and yoga are good things to do. Some young people dissipate rage by listening to music, reading, or watching a movie. If you're a parent, understand this. None of these release techniques are the whole answer—although they work pretty well for the moment.

Finally, perhaps one or both of you need outside help with an anger management program. They're available in most communities.

HOT-BUTTON HINT

Sometimes nothing works—not conversation, not reason, not anything. Sometimes the pot just boils over. What do you do with a seventeen-year-old who blows, who simply loses it, who sets out to leave your house and drive his car with fire in his eyes?

You say no. You quietly, lovingly say no—no setting out. You could get hurt.

The kid will be more angry if you let him go than if you don't. Wouldn't you?

8

Hot Buttons and Friendship

Judith met the man of her dreams, and he asked her to marry him! Out of her mind with excitement, she and her mum planned the engagement party. Soon after the invitations went out, Emma, Judith's closest friend from college, called with regrets. She felt awful, she assured Judith, but she'd also just met a fabulous guy, and he'd asked her to see a Broadway show on the very same day of the party. She knew Judith would understand.

Understand? Judith was livid.

"Where are Emma's priorities?" Judith fumed to her mum. "She's going to blow off the most important day in my life for a date with a new guy? What kind of loyalty is that, not to want to share my happiness? What kind of friend is she?" She said nothing to Emma, but her hot button had been pressed. Hard.

The good news is that Judith somehow got past the initial anger and the friendship persevered. The bad news is that deep inside, she never forgot Emma's slight—and for many years, their friendship never had quite the same intensity or joyfulness.

There is a postscript to this story.

Years afterward, Emma confessed to Judith that the new guy wasn't really the reason she missed the party. The truth was that her family was going through hard times, and she couldn't afford the money for a wonderful engagement present. To save face, she'd concocted the "can't come" story. Emma had been so embarrassed about her financial situation that she felt she had to miss her best friend's party, rather than admit to the truth. When the truth finally did come out, Judith was horrified that she hadn't thought to dig deeper for the underlying issue—what Emma did was so unlike her, there had to be another reason for the insult. Judith cared nothing about a present. All she wanted was her pal at her party. The anger that she'd long felt was unnecessary—and all those years of a strained friendship could have been avoided.

This is a true story. I was Judith.

A Riveting Passion

The power of friendship is immense—no one can make you happier than your best friend, and no one can hurt you more. A need for intense female friendship is one of the most riveting passions in the lives of girls and women. Through friends, we explore new worlds of thought and feeling. We have the power to build up each other's confidence—or tear it down. No matter how much we suffer from some friends who betray, misunderstand, or get furious at us, we still pursue the idea of friendship because having friends gives us our greatest solidarity, our sweetest joys. Most important, it protects us against the most terrible sensation—that of feeling isolated.

Our friends usually outlast our mothers and, in many instances, our lovers and husbands. Even if you have the best marriage in town, chances are that your relationships with your close friends are in many ways more intimate than that with your mate. We use our friends as mirrors to monitor our progress in life, and we learn to make life choices through our friends. Friends are the source of so much emotional and intellectual stimulation that they are an indispensable well of security and happiness.

How many of us have learned the value of self-disclosure from our childhood friends—the willingness to open up and be vulnerable and share the things we somehow cannot even share with our family? How many of us have formed our attitudes on honesty and commitment from what we've experienced with our soul friends?

No wonder we suffer agonies when friends who know our deepest secrets reveal them. With friendship holding such power, it's no surprise that the fallout from betrayal is colossal. One woman told me, "When my friend dumped me, it was like the world ended."

The Goodness of Conflict

It's not conflict, nor betrayal, nor misunderstanding that ends friendships. Sociologist Jan Yager in her book *Friendshifts* (Hannacroix Creek Books) says that "Friendships that last . . . involve friends who know how to effectively handle conflict. Handled well, conflict can actually be positive." The clue to everlasting friendship? It's not a pushed hot button—it's knowing how to defuse anger.

As a conflict resolution specialist, I've learned that some clashes and hostility are a necessary part of every relationship and essential for the growth and changes that must be made by friends within a relationship. Conflict makes us grow, makes us question. Anger is energy. When you're angry, you're fully, intensely alive and present; you're actively engaged in trying to make something different happen. Of course, if you become icy cold and withdrawn from anger, it can make you sick or bitter. When we express our frustration to friends and release it in constructive ways to make good changes in the relationship, then anger's been your advocate, your energy provider. Thank goodness for differences!

Do you believe that the only way to avoid conflict is to choose friends much like yourself? How boring. Not only boring, but wrongheaded to think that all you have to do to understand people is to look in the mirror and understand yourself. Though it's nice to have ideas in common, the truth is that if we feel threatened by opposing points of view or irrevocably angered by an argument with a pal who's had different experiences, we close the doors to change—and it's change that makes life fascinating.

If Conflict's So Good, Why Don't We Welcome It?

The biggest problem is that many women have been taught from the cradle that discord and quarrelling are wrong. Although women have been allowed greater latitude in this society when it comes to expressions of affection and love to their friends, the open expression of fury is almost taboo. We tend to avoid conflict, and then our submerged rage leads to unspoken manipulations that can wreck a friendship. It's clear to me that avoiding conflict is not the solution—in fact, it makes things worse. The truth is that women must learn to confront and work out differences, not turn from them. If anger between friends makes you so frightened you want to run from it, stop. Don't run. Disengaging from relationships because of a fear of conflict results in a lasting loss of self-esteem and a feeling of powerlessness—much worse than a few moments of stress. You can express anger and have the friendship live on.

HOT-BUTTON HINT

I do not wish to treat friendships daintily but with the roughest courage. When they are real they are not glass threads or frost-work, but the solidest thing we know.

—RALPH WALDO EMERSON

Before we go on, I want you to take the following quiz to discover what might be your previously unspoken attitudes about friendship. It would be wonderful if both you and a close friend could each take the quiz, then come together to discuss the results, but in any case, let's see what's on *your* mind about friendship.

Quiz: What Kind of a Friend Are You?

Even the very dearest pals know that friendship doesn't happen *to* people—it happens *between* them. You have to make it happen. And keep making it happen. Sometimes that's not easy: As Samuel Butler wrote, a friend is like money—easier made than kept. Which means you must be very aware of what your priorities are in friendship and what turns on your hot buttons and those of your friends. Knowing how to deal with the anger that's inevitable in powerful relationships depends on how you view friendship—and how you expect your soulmate friends to view it.

After you take the quiz, check the analysis at the end to see what your answers imply.

1. **See if you know the seven top qualities that must be present in a friendship:**

1. Dependability
2. Intelligence
3. Trust
4. Optimism
5. Honesty
6. Faithfulness
7. Being a good listener
8. Sense of humor
9. Loyalty
10. Having ideas in common
11. Energy
12. Tolerance
13. High morality
14. Fun-providing
15. Similar age
16. Compassion

17. Ability to express anger during conflict, then turn it off after dialogue

2. From the above list, check the seven top qualities *you* bring to friendship.

3. You've *never* (check as many as apply):

a. Gossiped about anyone.

b. Secretly wished your friend would fail at something.

c. Revealed someone else's secret.

d. Lied to a friend.

e. Been inconsiderate to a friend.

f. Sabotaged a friend's work.

g. Flirted with a friend's boyfriend (or dated him after they broke up).

4. A friend's new love is your old jerk. You:

a. Warn her. He'll cause her nothing but grief.

b. Say zilch—but feel a little miffed and probably phase out the friendship.

c. Say that he has some lovely qualities (he must, or else why were you wasting *your* time?) and you hope it works for her.

d. Say you couldn't bear him because he's such a nerd, but he may be perfect for her.

e. Lie—say he's terrific.

5. You're in a situation where someone is gossiping (not kindly) about your friend. You'd probably:

a. Say little but report the gossip to your friend.

b. Defend her but refrain from telling her about the incident.

c. Listen, but don't say anything, bad or good.

d. Walk away—you can't stand conflict.

6. In most of your friendships, you:

a. Give too much and often end up feeling victimized.

b. Are the stronger and usually the more interesting person.

c. Get as much as you give.

7. Could you be friends with an intelligent person who is very unpopular because she often blows her stack? (Tell the truth!)

a. Yes.

b. No.

c. Maybe.

8. When was the last time you admitted to a friend that you were wrong?

a. This week.

b. This month.

c. Sometime this year.

d. You're rarely wrong, so you can't remember.

9. Your friend is in minor trouble, and she asks you to tell a little white lie so she can get out of it. You:

a. Say no—you'd never compromise your moral principles.

b. Tell the white lie.

c. Tell her you're going to pretend she didn't ask you to do this—it's beneath her dignity.

10. In your heart of hearts, you believe that most women friends (tell the truth!):

a. Feel a great rivalry with each other, no matter how sweet they are.

b. Will stick by you—as long as it benefits them.

c. Are not as good at friendship as men are.

d. Are capable of enormous generosity and understanding—but watch out if your agenda gets in the way of theirs.

e. None of the above.

11. Answer yes or no:

a. Do you find yourself digging deeper to look for hidden issues when you have a fight with a pal?

b. Can you forgive anything if it concerns a friend?

c. Do you feel more comfortable with friends when their lives are going badly than when they're feeling happy?

d. Do you have a good heart but a hard time keeping a secret?

e. Do you feel slightly sick when good things happen to friends and not you?

f. Do you think that a good friend who betrays you even once shouldn't have another chance?

12. Friendship demands (check as many as apply):

a. A sense of responsibility for the other.

b. Sharing secrets and vulnerabilities.

c. Loyalty.

d. Willingness to lend money, if you have it.

e. Never saying "no" to the other.

f. Hearing the other's side of a story even when you know you're right.

g. Communicating in the same style—"speaking the same language."

13. If there were to be a really major confrontation with your friend, who would break the impasse?

a. You.

b. She.

c. Nobody—the friendship is history.

14. How might you break the impasse?

a. Apologize—no matter who was wrong.

b. Step back—check out the situation as if you were an observer, then start a dialogue.

c. Ask a third person who understands your side of it to help.

d. Get your friend to try to see your side of it first—before any more misunderstanding.

15. Your good friend was terribly unfair and has hurt you deeply. What next?

a. The friendship would be kaput—you expect better from a good pal.

b. You hate what she said or did, but you'd try to forget it.

c. You would insist on—at least hope for—an apology.

d. You'd try to empathize—find out what her reasons were for doing what she did.

16. Your closest friend would describe you as (be scrupulously self-analytical here and check as many as apply):

a. Dependable

b. Touchy

c. Forgiving

d. Inspiring

e. An advice-giver

f. Insecure

g. Jealous

h. Selfish

i. Loyal

j. Disloyal

k. Funny

l. Empathic

m. Out for yourself

n. Generous

17. You love your friends, but you're often too:

a. Suspicious of them.

b. Busy for them.

c. Tired for them.

d. Famous for them.

e. Angry with them.

f. Irritated by them.

g. Put down by them.

h. None of the above.

18. You're dressing for a date with a friend when Mr. Splendid calls and asks what you're doing tonight. You (tell the truth!):

a. Say "Nothing" and cancel with the friend—she'll understand if she's a true friend.

b. Say you're busy.

19. Your attitude about close friends is this:

a. Blood is always thicker than water—even when it comes to close friends.

b. Never completely trust anyone except your mother.

c. Good friends always have your interests at heart.

d. They should love me unconditionally.

e. There is no such thing as a really destructive, controlling friendship. If I feel this about a friend, it must be my own problems with anger—and I can learn to deal with them.

f. When anger really rears its ugly head, I try to ignore it or leave the friendship.

20. Your best friend has bought a new dress for an important business meeting. She looks like a packing crate in it. You:

a. Tell her she looks like a packing crate but that you have some great clothes in your closet that would look terrific on her and you'd love to lend them.

b. Tell her the new dress looks fine—it's her sense of herself that counts.

c. Say nothing.

21. In an argument, it's *most* important that each person be:

a. Heard.

b. Acknowledged.

c. Agreed with.

Answers and Analysis

1. According to studies made by sociologist Jan Yager for her book *Friendshifts*, the top qualities for a friendship are Trust and Honesty, followed closely by Faithfulness, Loyalty, Being a good listener, and Having ideas in common. I'd add to that an Ability to express, then turn off anger after an argument. If you checked at least five out of the seven, *give yourself a 20 score* for this question. If you checked from two to four of the seven, *take 10.*

2. Do you think you bring at least five to seven of these top qualities to friendship? *Take 20.* Do you think you bring from two to four of these top qualities to your friendships? *Take 10.*

3. First of all, *if you checked e, take a –5.* Why? You're not being totally honest here—it's impossible to have never been inconsiderate to a friend. Perhaps you'd better go back and take the whole quiz again, being truly forthcoming, this time—it's the only useful thing to do. Now, if you did *not* check a, b, c, d, f, or g—and you've been honest—*take 20. Subtract 2* for every one checked.

4. *Take 10 for c.* The a, b, and d responses may cause your friend some angst and are not how a truly warm friend ought to respond. *If you answered e, subtract 5:* This is not being straight with your pal.

5. *Take 10 for b*—it's the kindest and most loyal way to respond. Anything else is pretty disloyal—no? And if you retreat from conflict, you need to rethink your anger patterns.

6. *Take 10 for c.* If you answered a, you're not candid about telling your real feelings (a must for friendship), and if you answered b, you're choosing friends you can dominate rather than friends with whom you can feel equal. (Makes you either a bit of a bully *or* pretty insecure, don't you think?)

7. *Take 10 for a* and *5 for c.* You are not frightened off by anger because you value her other fine qualities—and know how to handle the fury.

8. *Take 10 for a or b, 5 for c, and –10 for d*—you need to learn how to empathize with others' points of view more.

9. *Take 10 for b. If you checked a or c, take –5.* (You're so perfect, perhaps you're a tad arrogant? This quality really pushes others' hot buttons.)

10. *If you checked e, take 10. If you checked any of the others, take a –5.* Your basic understanding of women and their instincts is faulty. Perhaps it mirrors your own frustrations, not anyone else's? Think about it.

11. *If you said yes to a , take 10. If you said yes to d, take 5. If you said yes to b, take a –5.* Again, you're not being totally candid. It's hard, I know, but think: Would you really forgive her anything? Do you think forgiveness can be so indiscriminate?

12. *Take 10 each for a, b, c, d, and f. If you chose e, take –5:* you're not getting it. Real friendship allows you to say no, allows you even to have a dramatic difference of opinion, if you then discuss your differences. And friendship doesn't even require that you communicate in the same style (g): You can learn to understand even each other's talking differences, as you will see.
13. *Take 10 for a*—you know why if you've been paying attention to this book.
14. *Take 10 for b*—you've got it. Apologizing when you don't mean it (a) will make you feel resentful. Consulting a third person (c) may create hostility: People in the midst of a conflict usually try to find allies, but when someone takes your side, it makes the other feel even angrier. D is utterly wrong because your job is first to hear her side (see the Five-Step Formula, page 51).
15. *D gets you a 10.*
16. *If you honestly checked at least six of the following—a, d, i, k, l, m, o, and p—take 30. If you checked three to five of them, take 5.*
17. *If you checked h, take 10. Take a –2 for every other one checked.*
18. *Take a 20 for b* and *a –5 if you checked a* (you know why).
19. *Take a 10 for d*—friends should love each other even with faults. *Take a –5 for a or b:* these answers indicate that your expectations of friends are destructively low. C is impossible—when you studied for your high school exams, didn't your teacher tell you nothing is always so? E is quite incorrect: Some friendships are meant to be discarded if they bring more pain than pleasure. F is sad—if you feel this way, it's your inability to put anger to good use that kills the friendship, not the anger itself.
20. *An a answer gets a 10*—it's the only truly helpful one.

The b response is silly and unrealistic—looking like a shopping crate is not going to be helpful to her and you know it, even if her sense of self is excellent.

21. *Take 10 each for a and b—and 20 if you checked both.* It is not important to agree with the friend with whom you're arguing.

Did You Score 240–320?

Friends don't come much better than you. Conflict doesn't paralyze you because anger vibes don't scare you. Although you might feel hurt by a friend's betrayal, you know your friendship doesn't have to collapse, even if you both need a temporary separation to allow time for healing reflection. You seem to have a good idea of your own style of expressing anger, and you rarely go for a friend's jugular. You've learned to deflect the pain of your own hot buttons being pressed—and they rarely explode. Why do friends value you? You're responsive to their pain, you're a great listener, and you're empathic—always searching to hear their side of the story.

Did You Score 160–239?

You're a good but not legendary friend, probably because you often find friendships threatening or disappointing—right? Although you like to have their support, you don't frequently share your own secrets or weaknesses with pals. You try to keep their secrets, but gossiping to others sometimes tempts you.

Still, you're ripe for learning how to be a great friend because you're intelligent and honest. The biggest trouble is that when you feel anger, you don't know how to turn it off. You suffer. You feel helpless. And, if truth be told, you don't *really* trust the hot-button tools you've been reading about in other chapters of this book to work. Trust them, Virginia. Try them.

Did You Score 80–159?

This is a weak score, although it's in you somewhere, that capacity to have and be a great friend. You hardly trust others at all (was it your upbringing or your experience that brought you to this state?), and the level of self-defence you employ could win you a black belt. Worse, you have trouble listening to friends who communicate differently—you can't stand the way one pal roams all over the place when she's telling a story, for example. And you hate it when friends embarrass you, like when they talk too loudly in restaurants or show physical affection.

Still, you show capacity to risk intimacy and be vulnerable—and deep inside, you're longing for a confidante. You have to learn that friendship is magical, but it's not magic. People can't read your mind—forgive them if they make mistakes about what you mean and what you need.

Did You Score 79 or Under?

What happened to hurt you, poor baby? You seem to speak different languages from your friends—and you can't put a finger on what so often irritates you and why others seem to feel annoyed by you too often. You trust almost no one, and conflict makes you so crazy you are either on the attack or on the run from it. Sometimes friends make mistakes or have weaknesses, and sometimes they even tell your secrets—it doesn't mean you have to throw them out the window! Sometimes they ask for your advice, then don't take it—and it gets you furious. But you can learn to put a new face on friendship, one that smiles affectionately on you.

Ten Top Button-Pushers Between Friends

1. Tries to control the choice of a movie or restaurant
2. Is habitually late for appointments
3. Cancels dates indiscriminately
4. Doesn't like your partner—and shows it
5. Becomes scarce when trouble arrives
6. Tells you what to do when she's not asked for advice
7. Betrays confidences
8. Doesn't return calls
9. Carries a grudge—can never forgive
10. Doesn't do what she says she'll do

The Four Big Ones

Okay, let's think about the four big areas that encompass all of the above button-pushers. These are the issues that try friends' souls.

When your anger level rises, one of the following issues is probably involved:

Talking clearly—do you hear what the other is trying to say?

Trust—can you rely on her integrity?

Forgiveness—can you ever stop feeling resentment against a friend who betrayed you?

Friendship testers—can you survive irritations such as husbands who don't get along or chronic lateness for appointments?

Talking Clearly

Talking is friendship's life blood. There is no way to receive the payoffs of empathy, connection, sympathy, and sharing unless we use the currency of words to explore differences and sameness. Intimacy is at its highest between friends when we're talking, whether we're disclosing feelings, communicating ideas on political issues, or even talking about the most mundane of topics. Everywhere in this book, I've been urging you to start a dialogue, to talk during times of conflict.

What I haven't yet told you is that sometimes talk itself is the very source of the conflict.

It is a luxury to be understood, said Ralph Waldo Emerson, and he wasn't thinking about people who spoke Chinese to his English. Sometimes even though we're born and brought up in the same city, we might as well be talking Chinese to our good friends because we have such differing styles of communication. Even the closest and most intimate of friends may have talk-style differences that rise up and grate on each other, and that interfere dramatically with the way they understand each other. It may seem like plain talk to you, but when you say to-may-to and she says to-mah-to, the differences can be a source of anger between friends. These differences in the way we express ourselves can be so tiny that they're hard to detect—and yet they change entire messages we wish to send each other. Even if we can't put our finger on the differences, we just feel something is wrong.

Gloria and Paulette have such communication clashes. They like each other so much, but they can't figure out what often irritates each about the other. Listen to their words and their thoughts.

TALKING IN CIRCLES

Paulette says: I'm so glad I got you on the phone—I know you've been busy. Do you have time to talk?

Gloria says: Sure.

Paulette says: I'm dying to tell you about this new guy I met last week . . . (She proceeds to talk about him, then veers off to mention a newspaper article and then wax lyrical about a summer holiday that she and Gloria took together in Greece.)

Gloria thinks: There she goes again, talking in circles. She doesn't make sense; it's so annoying—do I really have time for this?

Gloria says: I'm not following you, Paulie. First you started talking about the new guy, then an article, then a holiday we took. What's all this got to do with the new guy?

Paulette thinks: Damn it—I wish she would just sit back and listen and not jump down my throat before she hears the whole story—I can't just spit out things like she does.

Paulette says: It's all related—puleeese, just have some patience! (Paulette then fills in information and connects the story of Steve being quoted in a recent newspaper article about his work in Greece—the very place the two women visited!)

Gloria says: Okay. I got it—finally! Listen, let's have lunch when I'm not rushed—how about next Tuesday?

Paulette says: Well, I suppose, maybe it would work. I think it might be possible.

Gloria thinks: I love her, but I can't get a straight yes or no out of her. Drives me nuts.

Gloria says: Well, yes or no? Which day? What's wrong with Tuesday—do you already have something specific planned for Tuesday?

Paulette thinks: There she goes again—I think we could be best friends, but she's always trying to corner me—control me.

Paulette says: Let me get back to you.

What's happened? Paulette and Gloria are very fond of each other, but both feel vaguely unsettled about this conversation and don't really have a clue about what's annoying each of them—and it's happened before! Gloria is irritated because Paulette goes on and on with her story and can't seem to make a simple commitment. Paulette is annoyed that Gloria is too abrupt and controlling.

What has to happen? Both women must become aware of the differences between their communication styles—and not take it personally when one style is diametrically opposed to the other. If you speak in one style and your friend in another, you've got potential button-pushers. Both friends must come to realize that they can bridge the differences, get used to each other's speaking patterns, and not judge each other and each other's messages on the basis of grating differences in diction.

Once you intellectually understand these differences, they almost become lovable. Humour kicks in, and each is able to point out the other's trademark styles with affectionate recognition: "Paulie, you're doing it again—say yes or no, I command it!" And Paulie responds, "Yes, yes, yes, Madame Dictator."

There are four basic pairs of communication styles:

1. Linear or circular

   A linear speaker: I communicate by offering ideas in direct, clear, logical, sequential order that goes from one point to another. "There are two reasons this plan will work. The first is . . . The second is . . ."

   A circular speaker: I speak as I think. When I tell a story and it needs elaboration or examples, I detour. It may seem unfocused, but it all comes together in the end. "The plan will work because—but listen, before we discuss that, I want you to keep another thing in mind . . ."

2. Plain-spoken or vague

   A plain-spoken speaker: I say things as I see them. I say what is on my mind. I am definite in my opinions. If someone asks me a question, I'll answer directly. If someone asks me if I'd like to eat Japanese food tomorrow, I'll say yes or no.

A vague speaker: I am comfortable with language that is not definite. I qualify my language (*maybe, perhaps*). It is more socially acceptable to me than saying a flat no. If someone asks me if I'd like to eat Japanese food tomorrow, I'd say, "Maybe; it depends on my mood."

3. Take-turns or interact

   A take-turns speaker: I wait for the other person to finish before I start to talk. I do not feel that it is appropriate to interrupt when another is talking.

   An interacting speaker: When another person is talking and I have a thought related to what she says, I feel that it is acceptable to chime in. I'm just as attentive as anyone else, but I see interaction as a way of connecting with and listening more carefully to that person. My friend says, "Last week I saw Marilyn . . ."; I say, "Funny that you mention Marilyn—I've just gotten an e-mail from her." My friend continues, "And when I saw her, she told me about her promotion," and I say, "Isn't it fabulous!"

4. Big picture or details

   A big picture speaker: I look at the big picture and deal with broad concepts rather than small and confirming details. I might say, "I see the whole plan on the charity gala—how it should look and its overall theme."

   A details speaker: I like the details that support ideas. I am not comfortable talking about vague ideas. I need evidence that can be used to reach conclusions. I might say, "Tell me the specifics . . . the colour scheme and the entertainment you envision."

Look back at the conversation between Gloria and Paulette. Now you can see that Gloria was a linear and direct speaker, and her friend Paulette was circular and indirect. Also, Gloria was plain-spoken and Paulette was vague.

What's your talk style? Is your method of communication different with your mother from what it is with your friend or your colleague? Most of us are flexible—we overlap and are able to speak in different styles, depending on the circumstances.

WHAT'S THE LESSON?

You hear the talk differences between you and your friend. How can this help you defuse your own hot button when your friend tells a story and meanders all over the place?

Just being aware of talk style differences of friends and colleagues will help you curb frustration or irritation when a person doesn't respond to you just the way you like. Don't assume that even your close friends will have the same thought patterns as you. Listen carefully to the differences.

Don't blame the other person for not understanding or not listening or being rude when in fact they're just saying things the way they've been used to saying them for years. Sometimes geographical differences are at the root of the style differences. For example, people who come from New York are often considered rude because they tend to interrupt. When they interact with people from the Midwest and the South, their conversation patterns are often misinterpreted as being inconsiderate because they don't wait their turn to speak.

Try to adjust your conversation style, just a little. Make it more balanced to meet the other person's style. If you have a direct style, accept someone else's saying "sometimes" and "maybe" because if you insist on direct talk from a circular person, you're bound to make her terribly uncomfortable—and end up pushing her hot button. If you are a circular speaker, make a conscious effort to get to the point more quickly; later on, you can elaborate.

Finally, try this: Sit down with your best friend. Together, look over the communication style pairs. Where do you fit in? Where does she fit in? Where might there be potential for misunderstanding? When did one of you get angry with the other because the other didn't seem to be talking the same language?

You're both on your way to diffusing a major source of anger between pals.

THE ATTENTIVE FRIEND

Earlier in this chapter, you took a quiz called What Kind of a Friend Are You? I hope for communication's sake that you're an attentive friend. An attentive friend listens carefully—she doesn't just wait until the other is finished speaking so she can insert herself into the conversation by giving unasked-for advice or telling her experiences, an anger-maker if I ever saw one. Her responses are empathic, not self-centered. Consider the following examples of communication that feature attentive responses versus anger-making responses:

Your Friend Says	The Attentive Response	The Anger-Making Response
I felt so helpless when Betty got furious with me because I had to cancel our bridge game.	That's such an awful feeling.	Critical response: You do it a lot also—you've done it to me.
Bob was such a bastard—he practically ignored me at the meeting.	You must have felt embarrassed and devalued.	Judgmental response: Bob is very fair—you are overreacting. Maybe you need professional help.
I feel so guilty being angry with my mum for needing me so much, but it seems I don't even have a life.	I can see how painful that must be for you—want to talk about alternatives you can take?	Self-centered response: My mother was an even worse problem. I can remember when . . .
Mary really irritates me and stifles my sympathy—I must be a monster. But, she was divorced a year ago. Can't she just get on with her life? Makes me furious!	You're not a monster—it's an understandable feeling. How do you think we can help her get back to normal?	Unhearing response: Did you get tickets for the symphony? I've forgotten to call the box office.

Trust

For many, trust counts most in friendship, even more than love. Trust makes you feel comfortable and safe with a friend. Imagine being friends with someone you didn't trust. There is no connection without trust. You trust your friend to love you even if your house is dirty, you look a mess, you fail a test or get fired, or you won't lend her your car. You trust that she won't tell what you've confided to her—what hurts and scares you. You trust that you can take off your public face at last—and show your friend your real face, blemishes and all. You trust your friend not to be hurtfully competitive with you. You trust that your friend is not a predator—after your man. And if your friend fails your trust in any of these ways, rage happens.

Let's consider the predator example: Between friends, the "she's after my guy" betrayal is very incendiary.

Many women have been socialized to be competitive about men from their early pubescent years. Try prepubescent. A little prekindergarten girl named Belinda was recently heard saying to her friend Nona in the doll corner, "He's my boyfriend—you go away—go clean the kitchen." When interest in the same man divides women, trust and security between good friends can turn into rivalry and jealousy. Just look at Stephanie and Evelyn.

She Was After Him All the Time

Stephanie and Evelyn have been close friends for many years. Stephanie recently broke up with Ron, her longtime boyfriend.

One night it happened: Stephanie saw Evelyn and Ron coming out of the movies. Before they saw her, she walked the other way, her heart beating furiously. How long had they been dating? Why didn't Evelyn tell her?

Early the next morning, Evelyn happened to call. The floodgates opened. Stephanie blurted out, "I saw you, I saw you both last night—you and Ron! I was so shocked that I couldn't even confront you—you're a hypocrite, and I don't want to hear what you have to say—no explanation could ever fix this." She slammed down the phone and used her answering machine to ward off Evelyn's anguished calls.

But Stephanie couldn't bear it—she had to hear Evelyn's reasoning. Coldly, a week later, she called and told Evelyn to met her at the mall.

Stephanie: This is what hurts the most: Why didn't you tell me you were going out with Ron?

Evelyn: I was clearly wrong—I want you to believe I know that now. This was just our second date, and I didn't even know if there would be a third, so I wanted to wait to see what would happen before I mentioned it.

Stephanie: You mean if you didn't go out with him again, I'd never have known? You would have kept it a secret? After all the intimate stuff I confided in you about Ron and me, how can I trust you anymore? How can we even think about being friends?

How should Evelyn answer? She shouldn't be defensive, and she also shouldn't blame Stephanie for being overly upset. It would be best if she said something like, "I can see how upset you are, and if I were you, I'd feel exactly the same way. Can we talk more about this?" That answer indicates that she knows she's contributed to the problem and that she empathizes with her friend.

Once Stephanie and Evelyn get past the first hurdle and agree to talk about what's made Stephanie furious, perhaps Stephanie will have some questions for Evelyn:

- Why didn't you tell me? How could you not mention it?
- Didn't you know I'd assume you were after Ron all the time I was seeing him?
- Don't you know what this does to our friendship—kills it dead forever!
- What is your definition of trust? I can probably never trust you again.

Evelyn listens to the questions without interrupting. When Stephanie has really finished, Evelyn gives her side of the story, admitting again that she was greatly mistaken about her decision not to tell. She makes sure that she responds to all of Stephanie's assumptions, even though she believes they're wrong assumptions. For example, she says, "I was feeling a little guilty about dating Ron so soon after you'd broken up with him, so I rationalized it by thinking, 'I'd better not tell her until I see if there's a future with him.' But I was so wrong. I didn't know you'd assume that I had designs on Ron when you were dating him—although I can see it probably looks that way now. I know this puts a heavy burden on our friendship, but I don't believe we should end it—it's so valuable to me. Tell me how you feel now and what you want to happen between us."

Once they clear the air with the first pass at dialogue, Stephanie and Evelyn are able to agree on the importance of being up front with each other so that trust can once again thrive in this relationship. They will be talking about the hurts sustained for a long time because bad feelings are going to linger here for a while. Stephanie's powerful sense of betrayal and her red-hot anger are somewhat cooled. This friendship, at least, has a chance. Before the dialogue, it didn't.

If you expect to be able to trust your friends, you yourself have to be trustworthy. How does one get to be seen as trustworthy?

- By curtailing gossip—especially any gossip having to do with friends
- By being reliable
- By always telling the truth

HOT-BUTTON HINT

It is one of the blessings of old friends that you can afford to be stupid with them.

—Ralph Waldo Emerson

FIVE PRINCIPLES FOR DEESCALATING ANGER

So your roommate does something to challenge your trust in her. It's not even such a big deal thing—she forgot to pick up the vegetables for dinner even though she said she'd do it. You trusted her to do it and she didn't, and now your new diet is ruined without vegetables to eat. You feel fury—and you're about to lash out.

Wait just a moment. Can you remember to do just five things that may calm that rage and prevent a terrible blowup.

1. *Avoid the double standard.* We often attribute our own behaviour to a specific situation or at worst an occasional lapse, but we attribute our friend's behaviour to a fixed, personal shortcoming.

   You say about your roommate: Beryl didn't pick up the vegetables for dinner because she's selfish—always thinking about herself and her own problems. She pays no attention to my needs.

   You say about yourself: I didn't get to pick up the dessert for dinner because I got stuck in a traffic jam and the bakery was closed by the time I got there.

   So think to yourself: Did my friend do this thing to betray my trust because she's mean and selfish, or is it possible I could do the same thing, just because I'm a little forgetful or a bit careless?

2. *Be a soul-searcher.* Often when a friend hits your hot button, she becomes a monster in your eyes. You begin to finger-point: *You did this . . . You are a . . . you, you, you.* You see yourself as worthy and your friend as willful. How can she talk to me like this? Is she out of her mind?

   Try stepping back and searching your own soul: Was I . . . ? Did I . . . ? Didn't I . . . ? What am I not doing to cool things down?

   Always remember, there are two sides of the coin. Here's how your friend might see an issue of conflict—and how you might see it.

Point	**Counterpoint**
You were flirting with my boyfriend.	I was being friendly with your boyfriend to please you.
You are a control freak.	I like to get things done.
You were so mean to my other friend.	I'm honest. I cannot tell a lie.
You're so thin-skinned I can't tell you anything.	I am very sensitive—and you should respect that.
I think you're a busybody—who asked you for advice?	You should be grateful for my advice. It means I care about you.
You told my secret because you're cruel.	I told your secret because I was sure the other person could help you.

3. *Walk out and start again.* You and your friend are in the thick of it—furious and hurt.

   You say, "We're headed for serious trouble here,

and we've got to stop before we really do damage to our friendship. Please bear with me—let's take a break. I'd like to walk out of this room and come right back again in a minute. Okay?"

Now, do it. The very surprise of the act seems always to change the nature of the heated conversation. This principle is similar to Watching the Play in the Five-Step Formula (page 51), but we've got a physical distancing here, not just a mental one. Taking a break from the heat, even for two minutes often works wonders. When you return, you pick up the conflict, but something about the break tones down the anger.

You only can do this once. If you get in the habit of walking out during a conflict, it will surely begin to irritate your friend.

4. *Use brainstorming techniques.* Assume there is a solution to the thing that's ticked you off, even if you both still feel terribly angry. Agree that you'll each try to throw out a couple of ideas to solve the problem—and that you will not judge each other's ideas, and that no idea will be arbitrarily discarded unless you both agree it's unworkable.
5. *Acknowledge that you're sorry. Admit that you know you added to the problem in some way.*

   Acknowledging that we ourselves are imperfect people eventually leads to button turnoffs, and finally to solutions.

HOT-BUTTON HINT

The definition of righteous indignation? Your own wrath as opposed to the shocking bad temper of others.
—ELBERT HUBBARD

Imperfections shouldn't brand us as traitors and failures, unworthy of respect or love, which brings us to the third big one.

Forgiveness

To err is human; to forgive, divine. (maybe)
Forgive and forget. (NOT)
Love means never having to say you're sorry. (NOT)

The clichés come easily, but the truth remains: Though the ability to forgive may be divine, no one can forgive and forget unless she's a Mother Teresa clone. In fact, trying to repress the hurt by forgetting it can make you angrier. There's no way that Stephanie is going to forget that image of Evelyn and Ron leaving the movies together, but it's all right. The memory will be softened if she's able to forgive, even without forgetting, and she'll feel good about herself and get a lot of credit from Evelyn for the forgiving part—if she can swing it.

And whoever wrote, "Love means never having to say you're sorry," was wrong. Saying you're sorry counts. Even groveling counts when you're wrong—if you can bring yourself to grovel.

Look: A forgiving nature is essential to maintaining

friendship. I believe that the ultimate therapeutic task of our lives is forgiving the wrongs that have been done to us.

I also believe that there are certain kinds of betrayal and violence that are unforgivable. I've been dealing with conflict resolution almost all my life, but if you have an affair with my husband or abuse a child or run over my brother with a truck, I'm history—you can forget forgiveness, pal. It seems to me that in certain rare instances, when our comfort zone has been totally destroyed, we can forgive ourselves for not forgiving. It would take a higher form of saintliness than I possess to forgive everything.

Even if we're talking about selective forgiveness, we ought to try awfully hard. Why? Why should we forgive when a friendship gets challenged by a pal who's done something crummy?

First, not forgiving can make you physically ill. Holding on to anger can also make you cranky and resentful. We should forgive because the very act of forgiveness is described by many experts as a letting go of anger, a release of your pain. When you hold a grudge against your friend, you yourself remain wounded.

Second, it often comes down to the fact that no one's perfect, and real life requires choices. Is a blemished relationship with an imperfect friend better than no relationship at all? Usually, yes.

HOT-BUTTON HINT

She who seeks revenge should dig two graves.

—Old Chinese Proverb

Many scenarios illustrate a conflict between friends that calls for forgiveness, but there's one situation that unfailingly comes up again and again: What happens when a friend tells your secret? Listen to the story of Veronica and Harriet.

How Could You Do That?

Veronica and Harriet are buddies, and so close that they both look forward to vacationing together every year. This year, though, Veronica changed her plans, and she was quite evasive about her reasons. Harriet was not happy.

Finally Veronica told Harriet something she'd kept secret for all ten years of their friendship: She was the sole financial support of a father with a history of alcohol abuse. This year, he was trying to beat his addiction at an expensive clinic, and he needed Veronica—and her money—more than ever. No vacation for Veronica. She asked Harriet to keep it confidential—and of course Harriet agreed.

A month later, a mutual friend asked Harriet if she and Veronica would be returning to their favourite vacation place and Harriet said, "Veronica is having some financial problems and is going to pass on vacation this year."

The mutual friend went back to Veronica and asked if she needed a loan.

Veronica was mortified. She called Harriet and shouted over the telephone, "I told you to keep my secret. How could you open your mouth and tell the world? I'm humiliated and horrified!"

Harriet was shocked. She tried to explain, but Veronica slammed down the telephone. After repeated e-mails and calls, Veronica grudgingly heard her out.

It sounded something like this.

Harriet: I can't understand why you are so hurt and angry. What terrible thing did I do?

Veronica: You've got to be really dumb or totally insensitive if you don't know. You betrayed me; you told a secret that I asked you to keep confidential. Now the whole world knows. I'm sorry I ever confided in you.

Harriet: Look, I told Sheila that you weren't going on vacation because of financial problems. That's all I said—I said nothing about your father!

Veronica: I told you to keep it absolutely confidential. All of it! Do I have to spell everything out to you? If I do, it's not worth the effort.

Harriet: I can't help it if you're so secretive. A lot of people have problems with finances and even with alcohol—it's not shameful anymore. Join the twenty-first century. Okay, I'm sorry, don't jump down my throat.

Veronica: You have no respect for other people's sensitivities. Who are you to judge what I should feel uncomfortable about revealing? This isn't the first time that you've talked with others about my secrets. As my mother once said, you have loose lips.

Harriet: Look, I never thought that you would react this strongly. I'm terribly sorry. I can't undo what I said. What can I do? Will you ever forgive me?

HOT-BUTTON ANALYSIS

Self-disclosure is a very personal thing. Some people find it easy to reveal the most personal secrets about their lives, and others keep their secrets close to the vest. Revealing certain aspects of our past is very painful for some: Raw nerves are exposed, and we become agonizingly vulnerable.

Veronica, the daughter of an alcoholic, carries the financial and emotional burden of his condition. Her memories of being taunted by schoolmates for her father's problems are still vivid. For the outside world, she'd constructed an elaborate fiction about a happy and prosperous family. She finally told Harriet the truth because she trusted her and no longer wished to cover up the real reasons for her financial difficulties. It was an exquisite relief to stop pretending. At least with Harriet, she could be truthful about the reason for not being able to go on their vacation. She felt as if she'd come many miles.

When Harriet passed on her confidence, Veronica felt betrayal of the first order. Could she ever forgive her friend, who asked for that forgiveness? Could they ever restore their relationship?

Veronica must reflect on the following questions. (If you are currently furious with a friend, substitute that friend's name for Harriet.)

- What would happen if I were to forgive Harriet?
- What would happen if I were not to forgive Harriet?
- Am I ready to forgive?

If you suspect you're ready to forgive, and if not forgiving her would make you sadder than forgiving her, it's time for the last question:

What do I need to do to forgive?

First, talk to other people you love about what happened. Sometimes we can draw strength from others who genuinely wish for our well-being. They might help you with ideas on how to approach forgiveness, what words to use. It bears saying that you should avoid those people who seem to thrive on conflict. They will always encourage you to beef up the argument.

Then talk to each other about the dangers of miscommunication. Harriet and Veronica interpreted the meaning of the word "secret" in different ways—and so their communication was faulty. Harriet went for a looser interpretation of the word. She felt that as long as she didn't mention Veronica's dad's alcoholism, she wasn't giving a secret away. After all, everyone understands financial burdens. But to Veronica, every word she disclosed to Harriet was part of the secret—and sacrosanct.

Be clear and precise to avoid miscommunication. For example: I cannot ask my friend Eileen to keep a secret from her husband to whom she cheerfully admits she tells everything. She doesn't even count that as "telling." But I do. If I don't want Robert to know my secret, I won't share it with Eileen. On the other hand, if you tell me a secret, I won't tell anyone—even my husband. Know your friend's habits and be precise about what you need from her.

When the two women discussed this, Veronica vowed to be totally clear in the future about what Harriet might and might not reveal about her. And Harriet vowed to listen carefully to avoid miscommunication. Because both valued the friendship, forgiveness happened.

When you do manage to forgive, be specific about what

you're forgiving. Do not say, "All is forgiven," or "Don't worry about it anymore." Do focus your forgiveness on the issue at hand: "I hate that you told my secret, but I understand now that you were not doing it just to gossip, so I forgive you. Let's get on with our lives."

Don't wait until you cease to feel resentment. Forgiveness begins as a conscious decision, not a feeling. Choose to forgive—and then, gradually, one comes to feel forgiving. Anger is the last feeling to go, but it does.

Lose the "but" word. "I forgive you, but . . ." never feels good for either of you. If you've decided to forgive, do it without the qualifiers.

If you've brought yourself to forgive, put the past behind you. Though you can't forget the wrong, you should not bring up the crime every other month—"Remember when you told the secret about my father?" only pushes buttons all over again.

Don't wait for the "I'm sorry." Forgiveness is not about fairness or about making the other humble herself. If the apology happens, it's nice. If you just feel that your friend would give anything to take it all back, that's almost as nice.

About apologies: If you're the one who's transgressed, do try to say you're sorry. Although forgiveness shouldn't depend on your getting the "sorry" word out, it helps. Not surprisingly, men tend to have more trouble with apologies than women.

Don't be a habitual apologizer—that's more obnoxious than never apologizing. A friend who keeps doing the same lousy things and expects to be forgiven just because she says "I'm sorry" every time uses up her forgiveness credits.

If you've managed to forgive, be happy with yourself. You've done a hard but useful thing. By forgiving, you've taken control of the way you want your life to go instead of letting anger direct your life path.

HOT-BUTTON HINT

Forgiving is not forgetting; it's remembering and letting go.

Friendship Testers

There are many things that can test a friendship. Do you feel cranky when your pal asks to borrow money, or is too dependent, or has something you can't have—like a baby? You have a friend who constantly keeps you waiting when you make a date to meet—is there anything more hostile and annoying? Well, maybe even more irritating is the friend who cancels all the time—at the last moment. Or the friend whose husband can't bear your husband. Or even the friend who puts you in the middle of an argument with another friend and asks you to take sides.

The whole wonder of being really good friends is when you discover you're survivors. There's not much that could cause you to end the friendship, even if tempers do flare when the friendship is tested. Confronting the weaknesses of any relationship makes you both stronger, assuming you feel affection and respect for each other. The friend who's always late needs a serious talk. Perhaps a gift of a snappy new watch will make your point with love. Ditto for the friend who cancels all the time. You've got to start a dialogue with her, get her to stand in your shoes for a moment to understand why she should never make appointments that will probably have to be cancelled. And the friend who is always asking you to take sides? Well, another dialogue is called for here. We all love allies, but being caught in a three-friend triangle as an ally to one and not the other can be murderous to all involved.

HOT-BUTTON HINT

When two of your friends fight, don't get caught in the middle. Stay out of the line of fire, and stay loyal to both.

In the end, it's always talking—dialogue—that turns off the hot buttons.

Let's consider one of the most ubiquitous friendship testers—and see how two women strengthened a friendship that could have been shattered.

When the Husbands Hate Each Other

Cindy and Kate have been good friends since elementary school. Cindy has been married to Tom, a high school English teacher, for eight years, and Kate has been married to Neil, a political consultant, for six months.

They have to face it: Their husbands have never hit it off. Neil is a high-powered, golf-playing, sports-loving guy, and Tom is a contemplative, music- and art-loving guy. When both couples get home from a date, the husbands inevitably say, "Must we go through this ordeal over and over?" Cindy and Kate are not happy about this situation. They're always trying to devise things to help, but nothing works.

Eventually, tension begins to build between the women, each thinking that the other's husband is the "culprit"—the one responsible for pushing them apart. Their regular phone calls diminish with each passing month.

After a year of increasing coolness, the couples try again for a fun night out. Disaster.

Cindy meets Kate for lunch the next day to see if anything in this once tight friendship is salvageable.

Cindy: Why don't you tell Neil to stop talking about Washington politics all the time? Doesn't he know that it doesn't interest Tom in the least?

Kate: Since when does Tom have to be entertained?

Cindy: You know, that's really a lousy thing to say. What are you implying about Tom? I love our friendship, Kate, but I resent your words.

Kate: Well, why are you laying this all on Neil, as if he's to blame for this problem? Tom just sits there puffing on his pipe, adding nothing to the conversation—Neil tries so hard.

Cindy: Tom can't get a word in edgewise! Neil is so involved in his work, he doesn't act as if there's anyone else around with other interests. How can anyone deal with that?

Kate: That's a low blow, and you know what? I do detect a bit of envy in your comments.

Cindy: Envy? Envy of what? Are you out of your mind?

It doesn't take a brain surgeon to see where this conversation is heading: more insults, more defensiveness—until blowup time. Actually, the tension had been building for months, and now it's all pouring out.

Cindy and Kate may have had a good relationship before both were married, but they now have a serious problem. In her heart of hearts, each woman hates to lose the other, but they don't know how to get out of this escalating mess with each friend accusing and attacking the other. Something big is testing their childhood friendship—and it happens to be their husbands. Where should their loyalties lie?

They're about to learn a critical conflict resolution skill that doesn't require them to choose husband over friend.

Social Feedback: Ask the Right Questions

Feedback is a vital skill used in personal relationships to elicit more information. With friends, it usually consists of getting and giving reactions to their behaviour and how it has affected you or appeared to you. When you're willing to give and receive feedback, it tells your friend you're interested in what she thinks and feels—that's very seductive. The most important benefit of feedback? It allows each friend to find out more about what the other is really thinking, so together they can search for common ground and solutions.

The best feedback is obtained by a question—but a friendly, not a hostile, question. A question that accuses in tone or content makes a situation worse rather than better. This, for example, is *not* a friendly question: Do you really expect that Neil's attempts to act superior are going to make Tom admire him?

This *is* a friendly question: How did you feel when Tom and Neil seemed so bored with each other?

Asked for correctly, feedback does not elicit a judgmental or defensive reaction. It encourages a sharing of knowledge and emotions that can be helpful in solving a problem: How do you think our meeting last night went? Was there something I could have done differently?

It appears that there hasn't been a history of feedback between Cindy and Kate even in their long relationship, so at the first sign of serious tension, they're in trouble. Here's how Cindy and Kate can practice feedback in an effort to repair their friendship.

Ask Questions That Elicit Information

- Did anything work last night?
- What could we have done to build on some of those positives?
- Is there anything either of us has done in the past to keep our guys from communicating better?
- Is there anything more I should know about Neil's (or Tom's) interests that I can pass on to my husband?

Come Up with Creative Solutions

Cindy and Kate discover from their feedback session that they were both concentrating on their husbands' differences and not listening for the possibility that there might be something in common between them. They came up with three possibilities:

- Cindy told Kate that Tom was involved in the Senior Internship Project at school. One of his best students wanted to apply for an internship in Washington as an aide to a senator. Cindy saw this as an excellent opening for a conversation and a possible project that would use Neil's expertise and even some of his contacts.
- Kate told Cindy about one of Neil's clients who had expressed an interest in developing a mentoring program—perhaps a "speaker in the classroom" program. Perfect for Tom to help here!
- The two women, listening to each other's feedback, decide that marriage doesn't mean they're tied at the hip to their husbands. They plan to schedule more time alone with each other—perhaps go away to a spa as they did in the pre-husband days—and they feel good about this decision.

HOT-BUTTON HINT

No one wants advice—only corroboration.

—JOHN STEINBECK

Divorcing the Friend

Sometimes it's just too painful. You or your friend senses that the friendship isn't going to work. After too many conflicts, you no longer feel completely safe being honest about your personal life, or you are tired of reminiscing about the past because there's no current history between you, or you just don't look forward to being with her.

It's time to call it quits. You're allowed to call it quits—really, you are—and you haven't failed at conflict resolution when it's not just a question of conflict, but also about huge differences in values or interests.

Don't divorce your friend by not returning phone calls, cancelling dates, or just drifting away. Do it with dignity, talk it out, and agree to take a timeout from friendship.

Make sure that you really want the divorce. Letty Cottin Pogrebin, author of *Among Friends* (McGraw-Hill, 1987), suggests that if you're the one ending the relationship after a fight, first ask yourself these questions:

- Have I been fair? Have I given my friend the benefit of the doubt? Never dissolve a friendship on hearsay evidence.
- Am I fed up with what she did or with what she is?

If you're the friend being dumped after a serious conflict and you want to fight for the friendship, think about this:

- Can I acknowledge the errors I've made without meanness or being defensive?
- Should I do it by phone, by letter, via e-mail, or in person? On my turf, on hers, or on neutral territory?
- If I think I want to change and I promise that, can I keep my promise?

- Can we learn to disagree and still get along, or is it just a matter of time until the next explosion?

If the breakup is final, forgive your friend for not forgiving you. And forgive yourself for not being able to turn off the hot buttons—yours or hers. Onward.

9

Hot Buttons and the Workplace

There's not a working person who hasn't experienced anger at work.

Perhaps it was because your manager gave you a low performance rating, perhaps because someone expected what you couldn't deliver, or someone misunderstood what you said, or someone unfairly chewed you out, or someone in the next cubicle talked loudly on personal calls all day . . . whatever the reason, when your buttons are pressed at work, it's different from anywhere else. Feel real rage with a lover, a friend—even a child—and it's terrible, but it's the relationship alone that suffers. Rage in the workplace also threatens the bread you put on your table.

Lately the tensions at work seem to be escalating, and everyone is operating on a short fuse. You say one little thing—and someone jumps down your throat. How come? It's because, as Dickens says, we do live in . . .

The Best of Times and the Worst of Times

The Best of Times

Let's look at the larger picture at work. Your workplace is not your father's office. In so many ways, as we enter the new millennium, it's a whole lot better.

Whether you work for a huge publishing company or a pocketbook manufacturing company, the numbers are probably flourishing, and the economy continues to grow at a dizzying pace. This is also the era of merger mania: Exxon and Mobil, Pfizer and Warner-Lambert, General Accident and Commercial Union, Time Warner and America Online—there's hardly a business that hasn't connected with another business for increased profits. There also have been spectacular boons on Wall Street, the US is at an all-time low unemployment rate, and the business atmosphere is expectant. There's been a globalization of markets, a worldwide spread of information, and rapid technological innovation. We connect with the world. So that's a sign of the best of times.

THE GENDER AND ETHNIC GOOD NEWS

There's more. Increasingly, men are no longer the only or even the primary source of family income. For example, 80 percent of American mothers return to the workforce when their youngest child enters school and half of UK women returners have a child under five years. And a whopping 64 percent of all married women with children under six years of age are in the workforce—in contrast with only 18.6 percent in the workplace in 1960. Women now comprise about 47 percent of the entire workforce in America, and 44 percent in the UK. That gives us power. Athough women are still not being paid the same salary for the same work as their male counterparts, we're in there, we're pushing for change, we're seeing results—more slowly than we'd like, but results.

The ethnic composition of the workplace has also changed in extraordinary ways. As the world has become more of a global community, the workplace has become increasingly diverse with men and women of many ethnic groups working side by side. That's great news: For many, the workplace is the only place where people of different races or ethnicities mingle—it's a fine leveler. So there are immense and exciting changes in the workplace.

The Worst of Times

Prosperity brings pressures.

The negative impact of changes, even good changes, in the workforce is alarming. Almost everyone has been touched directly or indirectly by downsizing, reorganization, and reengineering. The new fighting words are "cut close to the bone," "trim away," "lean and mean." Translated, that means that companies are reducing many layers of middle management in order to compete in the global economy and beef up the bottom-line figures.

Merger and acquisition mania may be great for business, but change makes individuals nervous. It's not uncommon to read in the paper about wide corporate layoffs. For example, the Exxon/Mobil merger is expected to cut 14,000 jobs (12 percent of its workforce) over the next three years—a fact of life that's going to raise some hefty tension in the Exxon/Mobil offices.

Even if you've survived a merger, you're nervous and testy—on edge. Workers who have had to find other jobs or relocate have had a shell-shocking, cynical effect on their colleagues, the workplace survivors who think:

- Will I be able to learn the new computer system?
- Will I get a despotic manager from the other company with whom we've merged?

- I know someone with a great performance appraisal rating—and he was fired.
- Who is going to be next? When am I going to be let go?

Workplace stress is enormous. Tempers flare.

JUGGLING MORE BALLS IN THE AIR

Labour shortages have drawn more family members into the workplace. Satisfying special needs is becoming urgent for those men and now, of course, women, too, who are concerned about family life. Watching one's kid be a tree in the kindergarten production suddenly has taken on greater importance. Flexible hours, job sharing, and telecommuting are options increasingly desired by many, but it places enormous strain on workers who are trying to balance home demands from their children and their parents with the challenges of the workplace. Bosses tend to get cranky because they're forced to acknowledge that workers have lives outside the office. It also makes co-workers cranky. Those who are required to take over the slack—do the job of the person who was downsized—feel threatened and exhausted. Even if I'm a very understanding person, if I have to juggle more and more balls in the air, I'm going to be ripe for conflict.

We always thought that it was the Japanese who were the ultimate "workabees." But studies have shown an increase in working hours in most nations including the US and Britain. Many Americans are clocking sixty-hour weeks. For most of us, a forty-hour week is a distant memory.

In a recent survey of 400,000 workers, most say that workloads are chokingly excessive, and the increased pressures of uncertainty are creating havoc in many workplaces. Tensions are rife. Hot buttons are being pressed all over the workplace.

Turning off those buttons is necessary for survival.

Where Do You Hang Your Hat?

If you are in the workforce, you've heard about "the enlightened organization." This is a workplace where CEOs and managers strive to be on annual lists called "Best Places to Work." It's a workplace that encourages an environment in which people are listened to, empathized with, trusted, and valued. When conflict occurs, there are things to do to fix it.

Where do you hang your hat—in an environment that is rife with buttons being pressed, or one that promotes a respectful work environment? It's easy to discover by taking the following survey.

IS YOUR ORGANIZATION HOT-BUTTON-PRONE OR HOT-BUTTON-PROOF?

Rate the following statements according to the scale below:

(1) Strongly Disagree (2) Disagree (3) Undecided or Neutral (4) Agree (5) Strongly Agree

1. My manager respects me as an individual—I'm more than a cog in the wheel.
2. My manager recognizes my contributions—telling me when I've done well.

3. Most of my co-workers cooperate with each other.
4. My manager is fair in giving out special assignments.
5. My co-workers respect my opinion.
6. Even if I disagree with my manager, I'm confident that there won't be retaliation.
7. I trust that my manager will be my advocate.
8. My manager evaluates my performance fairly.
9. My manager asks for my input when making changes.
10. Most of my co-workers value people from diverse backgrounds.
11. Most of my co-workers respect each other.
12. My manager is sensitive to work/life needs.
13. My manager is helpful in resolving conflicts and tension between co-workers.
14. I can't remember having my stomach tied up in knots from work conflict this week.

Add your scores.

DID YOU SCORE 60–75?

Your organization is hot-button-proof, and it is a workplace in which you should feel pride. You appear to be a valued member of the organization, and management seems to have made a clear commitment to your well-being. There also seems to be a sincere effort on everyone's part to create a work atmosphere that is harmonious and savvy about constructively resolving conflicts. Trust, respect, and fairness are evident in every department. Collaboration is more than a dream here—it's a reality. Feedback is sought and freely given without fear of retribution. When problems arise, anger is managed with help from management. You've got a great job!

DID YOU SCORE 45–59?

Your organization gets points for trying. Although it's far from a perfect place to be, management still seems to recognize that problems exist and is probably in the process of implementing changes toward a conflict-resolving environment. Difficult behaviours happen in any workplace—and an organization trying to soften hostile attitudes and distrust among workers is a place ripe for transformation.

This actually could be a very reasonable workplace with a little more effort. The key is to avoid being locked into attitudes and behaviour that trigger feelings of powerlessness. The organization—from management up—needs practice in listening to the interests of its employees.

DID YOU SCORE 30–44?

Too low. **Your organization is hot-button-prone.** There are many problems in this work environment as I don't have to tell you. Communication is guarded and creativity stifled because people don't often listen to each other. Respect for differences seems limited as well.

Workers don't trust each other and are confrontational. They don't feel as though they're treated fairly, and their individual needs are discounted. Managers either micromanage or have a totally laissez-faire attitude—both approaches leading to frequent misunderstanding.

If the organization can improve communication, the

atmosphere can change dramatically. But don't hold your breath.

DID YOU SCORE BELOW 30?

Is Genghis Khan your employer? This score is redolent of a workplace where power plays, bitter hierarchies, and political game-playing rule the atmosphere. Yes-men abound, and original thinking and challenges to the party line spell disaster for the thinker. Worst of all, when tension in your marketplace grows, hot buttons explode willy-nilly. Everybody's shooting daggers at everyone else—not terrifically fun for a worker.

If you can't get management to listen to suggestions for change and the resolution of conflict, think about changing jobs. There actually seems to be a trend toward leaving large organizations to enter midsize and small businesses that leave more room for self-expression: They seem to be less toxic and more open to collaborative relationships.

The Collaborative Process

Central to a hot-button-proof organization is the theme of collaboration. When individual employees join forces to work together in a united fashion, everyone feels a sense of satisfaction, and there is nothing better for profits. If the collaborative process is to work, certain basic tenets of teaming up must be followed.

I want to show you how the collaborative process can work using a scenario that illustrates a common cause of conflict in today's business world—the whole issue of mergers and acquisitions. Although the bottom line usually gains during a merger, there are many headaches in the blending of two firms into one. People get fired or reassigned, new bosses emerge, and conflicts erupt over how the different companies can work together effectively. It's a nervous time for the workers.

The acquired companies feel the greatest resentment—especially if they're smaller than the acquiring company. Employees and managers are often made to feel they don't know how to solve their own problems. In most cases, managers and subordinates of the smaller company are not consulted about the changes that might ripple through their lives, even though they'll be directly affected. The atmosphere is ripe for misunderstanding and anger. Collaboration can fly out the window.

The following story is timely and happening in one form or another in thousands of businesses across the country. Are you part of this story? Is it coming your way?

It's a Whole New Ball Game

Arthur James is a manager working for a pharmaceutical company in New Jersey that recently acquired a smaller firm in Florida. Now Arthur has been temporarily assigned to the smaller Florida firm to make sure it adapts its payroll and accounting policies to echo those of the acquiring New Jersey firm.

Maureen Avery is Arthur's counterpart at the Florida location. She has mixed feelings about the acquisition. Her beloved boss was replaced, and her staff is feeling very insecure about its future. She has never even met the new boss in New Jersey. She's ready to hate the person who's her equal in the larger firm and who is coming to Florida to give her orders, which is what Arthur is about to do.

Arthur: I'm expecting you to comply with the new policies in time for our next corporate meeting.

Maureen: Don't hold your breath. You expect us to change our whole computer system overnight? Are you nuts? It'll even take time to notify our customers about the changes—look, you're simply not being realistic about the time frame here.

Arthur: Sorry, we don't have the luxury of time. It's a whole new ball game. Our goals must be met next month. We need to involve your people in a new research project, but we can't do it until the systems are in order. We're one company now, so you better get used to it.

Maureen: You're not even listening to me. I want to cooperate, but we've been made to feel like stepchildren in the new company, and we're all stressed-out and . . . (Arthur interrupts)

Arthur: Stop with the complaints. Complete my agenda—then iron out our differences.

Maureen: Your agenda, your timetable. Well, it can't be done. I've spoken to my colleagues, and they want me to take this whole mess to the next corporate meeting. I'm going to tell the big honchos they're shoving all this down our throats too quickly—and I'll also mention that I don't appreciate your paternalistic attitude.

Arthur: You're making a major mistake, major.

Maureen: I'll take my chances. Frankly, I resent your coming in and acting so bossy. You're not my supervisor—yet.

HOT-BUTTON ANALYSIS

Maureen pressed the very vulnerable hot buttons of Arthur James.

She challenged his competence by threatening to take the issues to his boss. Bang—a direct hit!

Although they threatened each other, Arthur attacked Maureen's hot buttons differently. By not listening to her, by not acknowledging her concerns, he made her feel invalidated and powerless.

Arthur better act quickly before this conflict escalates out of control.

Why Arthur? It's his job to initiate the hot-button cooldown. Arthur wants something from Maureen, and so he must be responsible for initiating a peaceful solution.

This is what he has to do to repair the breakdown, resolve the conflict, and make their relationship work. He has to adopt the collaborative process, a way to approach problems nonconfrontationally. Resolution occurs when people share their worries and brainstorm to find ways to work toward common ground. Even if your company is not in the throes of an acquisition, the collaborative process is a great hot-button technique to use in any rancorous dispute.

No matter whether the dispute is a result of mergermania or simply the collision of two strong egos, these steps of the collaborative process can point the way.

1. Show a Willingness to Listen

Arthur will try to defuse Maureen's anger by showing strong interest and listening with care. He might now say: "I realize that before, I didn't give you a chance to tell me what problems you're having. Can we talk now? Can you be specific about what you see as the most serious issues?"

He explores those issues and personal feelings as he questions, and he listens attentively to the answers: "What is it specifically that's keeping your staff from meeting the deadlines for the changes in the computer system? What can I do to help this process along?"

2. Stress Collaboration

Arthur needs to stress the theme "We're in this together." That's true collaboration. He should now also take some responsibility for the problem—something that has not yet occurred to him. He might say: "I should have been able to anticipate your problems and communicate with you before this visit." Also, he might say, "Now that I see the problem, I also see that we need to help you adapt our systems, and if that means providing more resources, we'll have to do it because this is an emergency."

3. Share Your Own Vulnerabilities and Concerns

The aim is to make yourself more human to the other and give the other permission to allow herself to be vulnerable as well. Arthur might say: "You know what really bothers me personally? I'm pretty uptight because I'm being carefully scrutinized—all corporate eyes are on me. If I don't produce harmony here, my job's out the window. What do you say we start all over again and help each other without blame or criticism?"

4. Brainstorm New Ideas and Develop Options

This is a great step in the collaborative process because when each person generates ideas, other creative ideas seem to jump out. Arthur and Maureen agree to exchange a lot of thoughts about how to work out the problem.

5. Find Solutions

Once many ideas are generated, Arthur and Maureen select the best ones. Maureen concedes that she would probably even be able to meet the present deadline if

1. Arthur could stay at the location for a while longer to assist the staff.
2. Arthur could arrange a videoconference among Maureen, her staff, and the computer people at the New Jersey location to iron out any remaining differences.

Bottom line? Arthur agreed to Maureen's request. He stayed on, got to know the people in Florida, and developed a good working relationship with them. The collaborative process worked. The goals of both were met.

HOT-BUTTON WORKSHEET

If you think you'd like to try the collaborative process, ask a colleague with whom you're experiencing conflict to reflect with you on the following questions:

How did our conflict start?

What hot buttons were pressed? Yours? Mine?

What needs of yours are not being met?

What do I need?

What are your goals?

What am I doing or saying to thwart your goals?

What are the costs of not solving the problem? Be specific.

What are the benefits of resolving the problem? Be specific.

What are you willing to do to resolve the problem? What can I do?

How can we start?

Truthful answers will expedite the process and begin a dialogue between you and your colleague. You're on your way to collaboration!

The Butterfly Effect

You have power to make things different. All it takes is one reasonable person to bring even a small change, and that can alter the atmosphere of a hot-button-prone organization. And then extraordinary things can happen. Change catches on. One person starts listening more, starts giving useful feedback, starts showing an interest in her colleagues, and quietly, morale grows. Mutual trust builds. A more relaxed workplace takes shape.

I've seen it happen time and time again. I call it the *butterfly effect.* Did you know that the flapping of the wings of one golden butterfly in the Amazon jungle can alter wind currents in such infinitesimal but absolute ways that a sandstorm will eventually develop in Topeka, Kansas, or a hurricane will happen in Miami? The wings of one butterfly—imagine it!

You can be the butterfly. You can instigate change. It may take awhile, but if you hang in there, it will happen.

For starters, if you're in a managerial position, nurture

down—don't be so tough-guy professional. Share some of your power—it'll come back tenfold. Delegate responsibilities to show trust. Provide support and an atmosphere that recognizes individual styles. Show interest in your employees' off-the-job lives—personalize, but don't impose on privacy. You'll soften the burgeoning frustrations of the workers who answer to you and also develop a work staff who will fight to the death for you and your ideas.

If you're not in a managerial position, don't be afraid to nurture sideways—your colleagues need attention; everyone does. And don't hesitate to nurture up. The art of honest flattery—when specific and pegged to small details—is an essential lubricant in every business on every level. People need to think well of themselves, and if you help them do that, they tend to view you positively as well. Write a generous note to someone who's done a good thing for the company. Give a compliment when it's deserved. Tough guys become pussycats when they're stroked—but, more important, nurturing up sets a precedent that bosses often follow. They're not dumb; that's why they're bosses.

Whether you are a manager or an employee, try to involve your co-workers in things you do that will affect them. Somehow it satisfies the need we all have for power and control over our lives, and when colleagues help make decisions, they're less likely to criticize you.

No matter what position in the workplace you occupy, share, listen, and respect differences in ethnicity, religion, politics, and work aims instead of looking over your shoulder to see who's gaining. Take someone under your wing to mentor. Network. Confide in and give your best tips to colleagues. You'll cut the anger level in the office to smithereens. Stress cooperation—you don't have to love your co-workers, but don't pit one against the other.

If you're in an organization where tempers are hot, be the butterfly's wings.

How Conflicts Escalate

Conflicts that are not resolved to everybody's satisfaction linger on. Small misunderstandings fester, take on a life of their own, and grow into big trouble. They never just get better. People either ignore them or rush to get them out of the way when they're only partially resolved, and then the underlying issues reappear in even more menacing ways. People dig in their heels, and negative attitudes get fixed. The adversary becomes demonized. Allies—people to stick up for you—are sought. Soon we've got an armed camp here. Resentments turn into desire for revenge or retaliation. A self-perpetuating vicious cycle appears. Rage happens.

Workplace conflicts can be solved if they are faced openly and collaboratively. Management is the key.

The Heart of the Organization

The manager/employee relationship is at the very heart of the workplace. It's the key ingredient in promoting or inhibiting a hot-button-free work environment. Congenial and empathic relationships can make pressures bearable, while adversarial relationships make the atmosphere toxic. Everyone should know this, right? And yet, in a 1999 survey of 500 professionals, 95 percent of the people who left jobs did so because of poor relationships with their immediate bosses.

A great relationship between managers and the people

they manage ultimately comes down to only four issues that build employee commitment and restore loyalty:

Trust: Trust is a two-way street. Do managers and employees express confidence in each other?

Respect: Everyone needs to be recognized for competence. Does the manager, either in conversation or in a note, offer regard and appreciation for an employee's work?

Inclusion: Does the manager include an employee's opinions and welfare in decisions that will affect her?

Fairness: Fairness is giving everyone an equal opportunity to be successful. Does the manager create an atmosphere that is impartial, even-handed, and objective in judging her contribution?

See if you think these four issues were considered in the following scenario.

Annie and Joe

Joe Hunt has been the general manager of a health food company for twenty years. A year ago, at his suggestion, the CEO installed a team approach to manufacturing. Joe appointed one of his employees, Annie Parker, as one of the team leaders. The company is launching a new product line, and the due date is very soon.

Annie: Those production goals that you set are really inhuman. We just can't work that fast!

Joe: That's what we put teams in for—to speed up the process.

Annie: No one asked us if we thought teams were a good idea. Frankly, it's not working—some people work slower than others. Some on the team don't have the required skills—they never got the proper training. They can only do one task at a time, and you know that being on a team requires several skills at once. And there are safety issues as well. The team members are starting to snipe at each other.

Joe: Don't argue with me. That's what you're there for—to lead the others. If you were a stronger leader, maybe they'd listen to you better. This team approach must work. My job's on the line—I wonder if you were the right choice for team leader.

Annie: You've switched one of my best people to second shift, and it affected the numbers—we couldn't get as much work done. You know, you didn't even give her a chance to make day care arrangements. That sends a terrible message to the others. Why did you do that?

Joe: They needed someone good in that shift. They're even further behind in the numbers.

Annie: Well, thanks for telling me in advance about the switch.

Joe: Cut the sarcasm. I have to make quick decisions. I'm the one who's accountable—if this doesn't please you, Annie, you know what to do.

Annie: Okay, okay, you're right. You're the boss. I'm sorry I brought it up. I'll get back to work. I'll deal with it.

HOT-BUTTON ANALYSIS

WHAT'S HAPPENED HERE?

Trust, respect, fairness, and inclusion have not even entered the picture.

Annie and Joe are having two separate conversations. Annie's conversation is about the quality of life at the facility. After a few exchanges with Joe, she begins to feel that voicing objections or complaining is useless.

Joe is concerned with meeting goals. He wants everything done—yesterday! He shows neither empathy nor respect for Annie's position. He never asked her—or the other members—how everyone would feel about the team approach, and now he feels he has to act tough—rather than admit he wasn't quite fair.

A situation like this develops into a fortress mentality. The management and the employee camps seem to be working side by side, but they're at loggerheads.

Remember the Five-Step Formula (page 51). It's helpful to step back for a moment, put yourself in someone else's shoes, and "watch the play." What do you see here? If you're "getting" this, you'll see the separate perspectives of Joe, the manager, and his employee, Annie.

Perspectives

Joe

- Why don't they understand the pressures I'm under?
- They have no *get-up-and-go!*

Annie

- Why doesn't he understand he's asking me for the impossible?
- He callously took away my best worker—and expects us to double *my* work? Now everyone is mad at ME.

Joe

- Don't they know that I have their interests at heart?
- They make me the bad guy. It's not my fault. I have to answer to the CEO.
- I do what I can to make it better for them—this team approach was supposed to raise productivity.

Annie

- I'll tell him what he wants to hear—that's the only way out.
- What's the use? No matter what I say, nothing will change. He doesn't give a damn about us—just the bottom line.
- Who needed this? We could have told him that teams would fail without proper resources.

The rest of the story of Annie and Joe—except now it's called Annie and Bryan.

Annie and Bryan

Joe retires—he's tired of dealing with frustrations and he doesn't know how to get rid of them. He's out of there.

Bryan replaces him. Bryan sees power differently from Joe. He sees power to persuade, not to control—he doesn't use sarcasm or threats to get his way. When Bryan entered the picture, he knew he had to work differently with the team originally managed by Joe because he sensed hostility and distrust at every turn. His first move: Over a period of two weeks, he asked these questions of Annie, the woman he knew he needed to make his ally:

- What is the biggest problem we face here?
- Do you have any ideas about how to fix it?
- What do you want me to do to help fix the problem?
- How can we involve the other team members?
- To what extent would your team agree or disagree with your point of view?
- What have you done with the team you're most proud of?

HOT-BUTTON HINT

Conflict is about control: Who's got it? Who wants it?

HOT-BUTTON ANALYSIS

By asking good questions, Bryan has gotten Annie to identify the big problem. Not enough is being done to help the poor performers, and the good workers, having to work twice as hard, feel resentful. He's given Annie the feeling that he cares about her opinion and that he will do the right thing in terms of fairness and inclusion. They begin to work together to come up with a solution without judging, without acrimony, and without blaming.

They agree that the biggest problem is the need to improve employees' skills. Bryan and Annie agree to work together to

- sponsor a "lunch and learn" series to bring people's skills up-to-date.
- start an informal mentoring program.
- develop a videotape of a new packaging procedure that will help bring their product in on schedule.

Bryan can now go back to the CEO of the organization and report that, for minimal cost, solutions to getting the product out on time appear to have been found. In addition, solutions to the workplace friction that was threatening to sabotage production are at hand. This makes the CEO sleep better.

The Happy Ending

As a result of the collaboration between Annie and Bryan, Annie's team had the highest productivity and quality rate in the last quarter and won the grand prize offered by the organization at the yearly banquet. Annie and Bryan were invited to represent the team as they accepted the award.

This is a true story.

Who Holds a Laser Beam Directed at Your Hot Button?

The colleagues, managers, and subordinates who most tick you off at work have particular conflict personalities, just as you do—as you discovered in the quiz "Do You Know Your Conflict Style?" (page 61). These styles may mirror your own, or they may be entirely different. If you can pinpoint your colleagues' fighting styles, you can learn how to manage your connections with them by defusing the hot beams aimed at your most vulnerable spots.

Here's what to do: Give it some thought when you are alone—who really bugs you at work? List the qualities that are most grating. Now, read the following so you can prepare strategies in advance to calm or put them off guard so they can't dominate your work environment. *Note:* There are as many male button-pushers as female, of course, but we've identified the button-pushers as female for ease of writing.

The Ruler of the World

The Ruler of the World lives to dominate. She's afraid of nothing—and is usually loud and aggressive. Best of all, she loves to play Boss, even when she's no higher than you in rank. At team meetings, she tries to rule—she has an answer to every problem and a put-down for every solution that's not her solution. The Ruler of the World pushes buttons because she's obnoxious and controlling.

Here's what not to do: Don't slash back—she loves that, and rest assured, she can talk louder and more forcefully, probably even more persuasively, than you because the Ruler's often quite intelligent. Don't back off.

Here's what to do: Stay calm and reasonable, and remember what you want to accomplish. Acknowledge her and her concerns. Tell her you want to do the best by the company, and you're sure she feels similarly, but it's impossible for you to share the floor with her unless she agrees not to interrupt. Don't criticize, blame, or call her names. Act as though you expect the Ruler to be reasonable. Sometimes it's a self-fulfilling prophecy.

When expected to act well, people usually do.

The Gossip

She really gets your goat. She is spreading rumors, telling your secrets—all behind your back. Why is she saying all these terrible things about you? The Gossip is often someone who pretends to be your friend, then pumps you for information she uses to undercut you.

There's only one way to deal with a gossip, and that's directly.

First, see if you can find out from a trusted friend exactly what the Gossip has been saying about you; having such information gives you a position of strength.

In a quiet, private time, take the Gossip aside, and in a

friendly way tell her exactly what you've learned. "Beverly, I want to be frank about something that's troubling me. Several people have told me what you have been saying—about me." Right away, you're going to have the upper hand. Gossips hate to be confronted, and she'll probably lie and say it's not true. The conversation can segue in this way: "I'm certainly relieved to hear it's not true, and I want to tell you that if any part of what I've heard is true, and it's happened because of a misunderstanding between us, then I want to talk to you about it."

You've given the Gossip an escape hatch, a face-saving opportunity, and a way to address a hurt or oversight she feels you've done her. You've turned off her hot button.

The Appeaser

Similar to the Peace at All Costs personality, she's so easy, so agreeable that she'll agree to anything, but watch out—you can't trust that she'll keep her promises. More than anything else, the Appeaser fears rejection.

Why is she so irritating? She makes you feel furious because she's so damned slippery and untrustworthy.

Here's what to do. Pin her down, gently but firmly. "Susan—can you get me that report by six?" "Beryl, I'd really appreciate your giving me your recommendations for the next staff meeting." "Lucy, I see something good fulminating in your head (she'll never volunteer it): Tell me your idea and how you think we should implement it."

Appeasers do better when they're affirmed and validated in advance for the work they're about to do. "Lynne, I know that the CEO is going to be out of his mind with happiness when he sees your report—it's that important."

The Spouter

Workplace Spouters need to vent. Let them. Even if she doesn't listen to you, you listen attentively to the yelling, whining, and criticizing. Hear her out, even if her spouting is starting to destroy collaboration. Let her know you're listening by your body language—leaning forward, nodding. Affirm that you've heard what she's spouted to you and to the group. While not agreeing with her, acknowledge that you respect her position and understand why she feels so vehemently.

Then ask the Spouter, "What do you want to see happen?" Move her from explosions and complaints to advocating a plan. Acknowledge her ideas and ask if she minds if you and the others add to her plan.

What to do if the Spouter's truly impossible and refuses to be positive about anything? Quietly state what makes her actions hurtful for office morale. Try to do this with witnesses—it makes your position stronger when people agree with you. Spouters need to know there that there are consequences to their annoying behaviour.

The Sidestepper

Here's someone who won't involve herself in the workplace politics because she has decided that the less she's involved, the less trouble she'll get into. She pushes buttons because she acts so irritatingly passive. She avoids you when you ask her to take a stand, doesn't say yes, and doesn't say no. Sidesteppers usually lack respect even for themselves and probably don't feel liked or even likable. They rarely pull their share of the workplace load. When she does partake in a decision, she invariably upholds the negative side. She'll say, "This can't work," or "Even if it works, it'll only bring more problems."

If you're her manager or have to work side by side with her, give her choices—neither of which allow her to sidestep entirely ("Which job do you want, writing to the customer or dealing with invoices?"). At meetings, instead of allowing her negativity and avoidance to push your buttons, wait her out. Ask her a question and be silent when she doesn't answer immediately. Try to draw her into an energy contest, gradually increasing your own participation and positive force of personality. It's amazing to see how overtly passive people often can't help mirroring a stronger person.

Finally, try confronting her with niceness: "What is important to you about this project? How can we accomplish this?" It's hard to sidestep someone who's smiling directly at you.

Tell Me the Truth: Business Feedback

Business feedback is any manager's secret weapon and a fundamental business tool. Constructive feedback turns off more hot buttons than you can imagine—in a subtle way. Feedback gives a manager access to what the employees need and think, and it also gives an employee a sense of how she's doing. When a manager tells me specifically how she thinks I'm doing on a particular project, I get information, I see how she sees my work, it gives me incentive to do better, and it makes me feel surer of the ground I stand on. Feedback can encourage and spur me on, it can cause me to rethink what I've done, or, in the case of non-constructive feedback, it can utterly discourage me from trying. That's when I feel anger.

Researchers have discovered that truly inept people are usually supremely confident of their abilities—more so, in fact, than people who do things well. The inept have few "self-monitoring skills." This happens because of the lack of critical feedback. Social norms prevent most people from telling other people, "You stink at this," and even the worst jokes are usually met with polite chuckling. No one tells them the truth. No one wants to hurt feelings, so they don't get honest feedback. How can they monitor themselves?

Still, the giving of specific feedback is a thorny issue, creating the most anger-filled moments in management/employee relations. Because it's so closely tied to the need for achievement, recognition, and self-esteem, if done poorly, feedback pushes buttons. Many managers simply don't know how important it is, so they don't give it at all. Others give feedback that's cruel and thus ineffective. Poor or no feedback has the potential of escalating conflict because people feel as though they're working in a great void and their individual contributions are not even noticed. Lousy feedback is a form of disrespect—and disrespect maddens people.

Constructive feedback, in contrast, can offer the greatest promise of achieving the goals of the workplace—not to mention trust, respect, and fairness. It's enormously important in identifying potential trouble spots and nipping angry feelings in the bud.

Listen to Kevin talk about his boss, Melinda, who gives lousy feedback.

Specifics, Please!

I'm an Information Systems Manager, and out of three possible ratings—*Meets Expectations, Exceeds Expectations,* and *Below Expectations*—my boss gave me an annual rating of *Meets Expectations.*

I want to get a higher rating next time, so I asked Melinda for feedback in three areas—technical skills, ability to handle and motivate my staff, and customer service.

Her response? She told me that to get a higher rating I would have to do better in all three areas.

What did that really mean? I asked her very tactfully for specifics.

Her eyes glazed over. She looked like she wanted to get this meeting over with as soon as possible. She told me to consult the company manual. Finally, reluctantly, she gave me a specific (she thought). She said I had good rapport with salespeople.

That's it? What should I think? Is she reluctant to confront me with my drawbacks? This is not the first time this has happened. I have the right to know *how* I can improve. I want to advance in this company, but from her I hear nothing—not good, not bad. I'm getting nowhere with this company, and it's making me nuts. I've been taking my frustration out on the people I manage—I realize that—but I feel so angry.

What to Do?

If you're a manager, give good feedback. It's so important. There are three kinds of feedback.

SUPPORTIVE FEEDBACK

Supportive feedback is simple praise telling you that what you did was fine. It affirms your performance and behaviour. People can't get enough praise. It's a big motivator, and many employee surveys tell me that supportive feedback is worth its weight in gold. Why are they so stingy with compliments? complain employees. It's like pulling teeth to tell someone she's done well!

Make sure your praise of an employee is specific. Kevin's manager told him he had good rapport with salespeople. That meant nothing. Instead, the manager could have said, "You really communicate well with the salespeople. The way you ask questions shows your interest in their progress. I like how you get them to state their specific targets." This feedback is something tangible that Kevin can use to build his strengths and leverage with his own staff.

SPECIFIC FEEDBACK

This tells you where you need improvement or where you missed your goals.

Just as employees complain that organizations are stingy with their praise, they also complain that managers are vague in their criticisms. We all want to know specifically what we need to do to improve. Employees want truth.

Feedback is a very personal thing and must be handled diplomatically, being sensitive to the employee's vulnerabilities as well as strengths. Managers tend to be uptight about giving specific feedback for fear that it will be misinterpreted—most of us don't like to give bad news. A good manager knows how to use a velvet glove but still give honest feedback.

Melinda should have given concrete information. She might have said, "Kevin, at a meeting when people brainstorm their ideas, don't expect everyone to jump in. Leo is not as quick as others to come up with ideas—he requires more time to contemplate. The idea is to value everyone's different kinds of contributions. How can you set it up so that can happen?"

Kevin also wanted feedback on his technical skills. Melinda might respond, "You need to learn about the newest Web-based tools so you can understand the codes."

PERSONAL BEHAVIOUR FEEDBACK

Feedback is not just about performance—it's important to give information to employees on their behaviour in general. Misunderstandings and resentment about a worker's behaviour can take on a life of their own and pop everyone's hot buttons. Good managers never let unacceptable behaviour slip by: "Well, that's just the way Tom is. He may sound bigoted, but he's harmless." That kind of thinking will do you in. I guarantee you, Tom will push someone's buttons hard—and then you'll have serious problems.

Problems can be avoided by offering personal behaviour feedback in staff and team meetings and in private conversations with colleagues. If you happen to notice an older man putting his arm around the shoulders of a younger woman—a man who grew up in a world when sexual harassment was not yet defined—help him avoid a furious accusation by giving him feedback that explains the new rules.

HOT-BUTTON HINT

Give me good news, give me bad news, but give me news.

Power

There are two kinds of power in business: control power and persuasive power. Control power is far inferior to persuasive power.

Control Power

Many companies are run like an army command. In this kind of workplace, managers often do not have decision-making powers—they are just following commands themselves, and in the pecking order, they give commands to the next person down the line. They seem like they're uncaring bosses because as they exert what little power they have, they don't want to be questioned—questioning might reveal that they have no real power. Managers who use their power to control overemphasize rules. That makes employees feel like robots who have to beat the system in order to succeed. Controlling power also bestows special favors to a chosen few in exchange for support.

Here are some examples of control power and how it's wielded:

> Mastering: I will be your master no matter how unhappy you are. I'll yell at you, threaten you, and back you down when you question my decisions.
>
> Ignoring: When you don't do as I tell you to do, I'll treat you as though you don't exist, as if you're lower than dirt. When you make a suggestion, I'll discount it as if I didn't even hear it.
>
> Carping: I'll find fault with your every decision, every act. I'll nitpick you to death. I'll make fun of you in

front of colleagues and blame you for everything that goes wrong.

Sabotaging: I'll wear away your confidence by going behind your back to demean you. I won't answer your calls, and I'll forget to do what I promised I'd do.

It doesn't take a brain surgeon to see that conflicts in a control-power workplace have a greater potential for escalation as overburdened, insecure bosses wield callous authority over employees. Collaboration? These managers never heard of the word.

Not a great place to work.

Persuasive Power

Enlightened organizations teach their managers to use persuasive power—a far more positive way of managing. These managers are given greater power even as they're encouraged to share it. Persuasive power involves influencing others by involving them in the decisionmaking process. The employee is encouraged to be a self-starter. The manager asks questions that get others to express themselves, give information, feel valued, and solve problems. A persuasive manager who shares power and displays faith in her employees engenders respect.

The Manager's Lament

Middle managers sometimes feel like cogs in a wheel also. Top management often doesn't give them any credit for being able to think for themselves. There's a cynicism in the workplace, and it's often passed down from the bosses and up from the employees.

Top management pacifies middle managers, often giving them big bonuses just to keep them in place. What top management really should be doing is giving middle managers the opportunity to make decisions—that's true power. What follows are some ubiquitous complaints of the middle manager:

1. *Manager overload:* They want me to do more with less. Two years ago I managed twenty-four employees. Today, I manage forty-one. How much help can I give these employees?
2. *Finished-at-forty syndrome:* I'm worried about being replaced by a younger, cheaper worker. I have grave concerns about a midlife stall in my career.
3. *More demanding expectations for global travel and global linkage:* I live out of a suitcase and even when I'm home, I'm on twenty-four-hour call through mobile, e-mail, and fax.

No question about it, managers do have legitimate gripes. It's easy to see how their anger is fed and how it escalates. There's so much you can't control—so much that's just out of your hands. If you are a manager, it's important to keep the peace in the workplace, for your own psyche as well as for your subordinates. Here are some of the ways you can either violate or promote the trust of your subordinates.

KEEPING THE PEACE WITH WORKERS

Trust-Busters	Trust-Boosters
What managers do to violate workers' trust	*What managers do to boost workers' trust*
They . . .	**They . . .**
• Fail to deliver on promises • Ask for input and then ignore it • Hold employees to standards they don't follow • Show partiality to other employees • Act as if employees are cogs in a wheel • Game-play—keep employees guessing about what employees are doing wrong or right • Are sarcastic, judgmental, belittling	• Provide specific feedback on strengths and how well the employees are doing • Provide feedback on problems—help employees correct mistakes before it's too late • Involve people in decisions that affect them • Make expectations of performance clear • Resolve conflicts in a timely fashion—step in when they see grudges building or anger flaming between employees

Diversity: Challenges and Promises

Diverse workplaces—that is, workplaces with people who are different in terms of gender, age, race, ethnicity, religion, class, education, disability, sexual orientation, values, work styles, and background—tend to attract and retain the best and the brightest of talents. They have been proven to be more productive on the factory floor as well as in the boardroom because the variety of opinions and work styles invariably makes for more creative decisions. These are the companies that always show up on "Best Places to Work" lists.

But diversity has a downside. As companies ask very different types of people to collaborate, friction happens. People tend to shut out information that doesn't mesh with their own beliefs. They respond to others' perspectives with knee-jerk reactions. The differences in their cultural and educational backgrounds may put up stone walls between them, and miscommunication and misunderstanding become lightning rods for conflict.

Even people with good intentions may unconsciously harbour and perpetuate subtle racism, sexism, or ethnocentrism—judging people of other cultures according to the values of their own culture. They may be uneasy in intergroup situations and try to avoid them. They may unintentionally say or do things that are offensive to others. One racist or sexist slight may be insignificant, but a pattern of slips or oversights does press hot buttons and escalates conflict, resulting in submerged anger, there and waiting to explode.

This can't be you? Test yourself.

A white male manager bangs his fist on the table and demands that deadlines be met. He is seen as a no-nonsense leader. But tell the truth: Could you be guilty of even an unconscious bias by seeing

- a female who does the same thing as a controlling bitch?
- a black male who does the same thing as threatening?
- a Generation X-er who does the same thing as a know-nothing upstart?
- a gay person who does the same thing as temperamental?

- an older person who does the same thing as an ineffective blowhard?

One of the biggest tools for turning off hot buttons in yourself and in others is simple awareness. Whether you are a manager or an employee, you need to be mindful about how each person's hot button can be pushed. Have you ever seen any of the following (or similar) situations in your workplace? Here are the issues—and some possible solutions.

DIVERSITY HOT BUTTONS: HOW TO DEAL WITH THEM

The Hot-Button Issue	The Complaint	What Can Be Done
Challenge to competence	*A black woman says:* I was told I'm not ready for a promotion while a white colleague with the same experience got moved up.	Speak to your manager and ask what specific skills you need to develop to get that promotion. Ask for a timetable and frequent feedback. Be persistent.
Size discrimination	*A heavy woman says:* Why did I get passed over for a receptionist's job I know I'm qualified for? Why am I kept filing in the back office?	Go to the human resources manager and explain you think you were passed over because of your weight. The manager should be your ally, question the decision, and ask for specifics.
Privileged power to white males	*A white woman says:* When I go on a sales call with a colleague who is a man, the client looks only at him and disregards what I say.	Arrange with your colleague that in future calls, you will divide up the presentation so each is responsible for different areas.

Contributions overlooked	*A Filipino nursing supervisor says:* They seem to gloss over my comments at staff meetings—I think it's just because I have an accent.	Talk to the person who leads the meeting in advance. Tell her you believe it would be in the best interests of the team if you're able to contribute your ideas for improvements more effectively. Ask her if she has any suggestions how you might best accomplish this.
Being a token	*An Asian woman says:* I am uncomfortable because I was chosen to go with a team to make an advertising presentation just because I'm Asian. Advertising is not my area of expertise—research is.	Offer to consult with the team on any issues that might help with the Asian market, and then tell the manager your expertise would be better put to use in the research department.
Set up for failure	*A Latino male says:* My organization was under pressure to have minority managers. I was appointed but given no staff and no resources, and I'm expected to perform miracles.	Help your superiors see it's in their best interest for you to succeed in the job, and state specifically what resources and staff you need to get the job done.
Limited expectations	*A black male says:* They offered me a dead-end job in community relations because they assume I can relate to the black community. But they know my background is in finance.	Tell your manager you will gladly pitch in and assist in community affairs but that you want to contribute in finance where you know you can make a huge difference to the organization.

The Hot-Button Issue	The Complaint	What Can Be Done
Breaking the mould	*A Hispanic woman says:* My colleagues always act so surprised to hear I got an MBA from Harvard.	The next time it happens, gently ask why they're so surprised at your accomplishments. Just as gently, challenge their wrong assumptions and point out other high-achieving Hispanics.
Acting on stereotypes	*An over-fifty man says:* Why do I always get the easiest jobs to do? Just because I'm fifty-two doesn't mean that I can't learn new technology—and they always overlook me when an opportunity that requires advanced technology training comes along.	Point out your superior technological skills with specific accomplishments. Ask when the next tech training will occur, and demonstrate your motivation to take part.
Talking down to you—literally	*A wheelchair-bound woman says:* My boss thinks that because I'm in this chair, I don't have what it takes to succeed. She gets me furious because she compliments me on the most trivial things, as if I were a slow-witted child.	Thank her for the compliment the next time it happens, but explain that you want her to have higher expectations for you so that you might prove your capabilities to her.

If you want to help create a harmonious environment and be a champion of diversity in your workplace, here are some steps you can take.

ACTION STEPS

1. Go out of your way to acknowledge someone of a different race, culture, or education level for his/her accomplishments.

2. Accept responsibility for something that went wrong in a diverse group.
3. Listen attentively to someone of a different cultural group with whom you were in complete disagreement.
4. Demonstrate respect for people who speak English less fluently than you and hold as praiseworthy their ability to speak more than one language.
5. Respectfully disagree with those around you who make prejudicial comments.

What's the payoff of being tuned in to diversity issues? More productivity, more peace, and more profits for everyone.

HOT-BUTTON HINT

Think of differences between people not as deficits, but as assets.

What a Difference a Decade Makes

Here's another diversity issue that often creates conflict in the workplace: When people born in different decades have to work side by side, serious conflict may result, often because their thinking about work style and values is so different. It becomes difficult to spend great amounts of time in what should be collaborative connections, because people of different generations often do not understand each other's attitudes and approaches to their jobs. The contrasts in the way generations look at the workplace can become fertile ground for miscommunication.

In today's work arena, adults born before 1945 (often called *veterans*) share their workdays with those born between 1945 and 1964 (*baby boomers*) and the youngest, born after 1964 (the Generation X crowd). Here's just one example of what it sounds like:

The Boomer and the Generation X-er

Paul is forty-six and works with Louise, who is twenty-eight, in the corporate training department of a retail chain. Paul calls Louise at home to tell her that she has to come into work on Saturday to complete a company training manual because they are behind on a deadline date.

Paul: We're really in a crunch here, so come in at eight on Saturday. George and Sally will be here, too. We'll work until noon and have the rest of the day free.

Louise: No way! It is totally not necessary. I can work on the project at home, e-mail you all the materials, and then we can all teleconference. That's the most efficient way.

Paul: Well, that just won't work. We have problems to solve on the spot. Louise, you have your priorities all wrong.

Louise: No, I don't. You see things only your way. You've never even listened to my ideas about using all the new technology in training.

Paul: That's beside the point. Let's not argue anymore. Let's get the job done on Saturday.

Louise: Why should I waste time on the thruway for forty-five minutes when I can get the work done just as well here, even faster? I will call you at the office on Saturday. Paul, you can stand on your head, but I'm just not coming in.

HOT-BUTTON ANALYSIS

Paul and Louise are operating within a generational gap and looking at each other from distorted lenses. They interpret each other's comments in a negative way, so along with the comments, they trade jabs and innuendos.

Paul sees Louise as not carrying her share of the work. He feels that she doesn't understand that there's a real emergency. She's more committed to her personal life and not as loyal to the company as he.

Louise sees Paul as a control freak, trying to run the show. He presents things to her as a done deal and is not a team player. She sees him as stubborn and inflexible, with tunnel vision.

After their phone conversation, both are literally shaking with anger.

Their clash stems from two sources: a values conflict and a work style conflict, both formed in the times in which they grew up.

The Values Conflict

Paul, a baby boomer, believes in a more traditional approach to doing work. It's time put in on the job that counts. He values different types of *personalized* meetings to share information and accomplish business goals. He believes that these meetings are the most efficient way to make effective decisions. He far prefers face-to-face interactions with specific agendas to phone conferences.

Louise, a Generation X-er, believes that people should be

judged by the results of their work, not by the amount of time they put in the office. She believes that effective decisions can be made on the spot at informal gatherings and by teleconferencing. She shuns workplace meetings unless required, because she feels that they are just a rubber stamp for decisions already made, and that they are a waste of time.

The Work Style Conflict

Paul doesn't exactly live in the Dark Ages, but he uses technology mainly for e-mail and Web searches and is not acquainted with the newer multimedia approaches to training programs. Paul is resistant to the newer technologies not only because he doesn't understand them, but because he doesn't see their advantages over the existing company materials. These materials have been rated well by participants, so he feels, "Why fix something that's not broken?"

Louise, the Generation X-er, was raised on computers and uses technology with great ease. She knows that work can be accomplished faster with technology. New training technologies are beneficial because people can learn at their desks at home as well as in the classroom, and they should be integrated with the existing company training programs.

How should the Boomer and the Generation X-er handle this problem that threatens their work atmosphere?

For starters, Paul should have an open mind and be more flexible in his requests. He must first listen to Louise's ideas without judging them. Then he should find out specifically how Louise can meet the deadline by using her technology expertise.

Louise ought to listen to all of Paul's objections to her plan and respond to each of them. She should talk about the added benefits of completing the task by e-mail and teleconferencing. Finally, she should express her willingness to come in on Saturday if any of his objections are not satisfied.

They decide to try to hear each other's views without judging them in order to come up with a plan for the completion of the training program. Paul agrees to have Louise use her teleconferencing idea. Louise agrees to come in early Monday morning in case they have to iron out any last-minute issues. Finally, Louise suggests that Paul attend a conference with her on managing in a digital age. He accepts and invites another boomer along for the ride.

HOT-BUTTON HINT

Conflict, dealt with carefully, offers people an opportunity to create new and innovative solutions that cross generational lines.

What Do You Say or Do When Someone Pushes Your Button?

Sometimes you're associated with an organization that just doesn't get it—a hot-button-prone workplace. Perhaps some people ridicule or publicly undermine your performance or get you in trouble by not doing their part of the work. Perhaps you feel that excessive work gets dumped on you and you'd get punished if you complained. Your emotions have undoubtedly led to one or more of the following responses:

Feelings of

Fear	has led to	I better keep my mouth shut
Anger	has led to	I feel like I'm a time bomb
Frustration	has led to	I'm gonna scream!
Irritation	has led to	Stay away from me—just deal with it—leave me alone!
Helplessness	has led to	Nothing I can do
Alienation	has led to	I'm out of it—not a soul knows I'm alive
Worthlessness	has led to	I don't count—I'm stupid and klutzy
Exploitation	has led to	I'm a cog in a wheel—used and abused

But you like most of your colleagues, you like your work, and you even like your pay. What you don't like is the behaviour of some of your colleagues or managers. Bottom line? You want to stay and try to make a difference while keeping your dignity.

I think the very best form of help sometimes comes in suggesting specific responses to people who push your buttons. See if you can find your own recurrent button-pusher or one similar in the following examples.

When conflict does arise, here are the general principles and the mind-sets that begin to turn off the buttons.

Stay calm—don't lose your temper.

Don't fall into a trap and become defensive.

Deal with the task at hand, not on whose fault the conflict was.

State the issues as differences, not as who was right and who was wrong.

Be persistent in stating your case.

Be constructive and focus on a solution.

Now try these responses on for size, with the following conflicts divided into manager/employee problems and conflicts that frequently occur between employees.

Manager-Generated Conflicts

Manager: You are the only one to complain about the new instructions for the payroll system. You make too much trouble.

Your response: I meant to be helpful and I do respect you. Perhaps no one else has commented because they haven't yet read the new instructions. I viewed my comment as a suggestion, not a complaint. *(Your answer doesn't always have to respond to every negative point. Remain strong and dignified.)*

Manager: You've made a billing mistake, and it's not the first time this has happened—your thinking is foggy! You seem to try to screw up.

Your response: First, show me exactly what went wrong and I'll correct it immediately. Then let's look at the records so I can review past problems. In the future, I would appreciate frequent feedback so we can avoid problems. *(Ignore sarcasm unless it's excessive and abusive, in which case, give an "I" message: "I'm upset that you believe I don't think clearly. Tell me why you have this belief.")*

Manager: You're spending too much time with some customers, and you're keeping the others waiting. You're rude.

Your response: I know we both think that certain customers need more personal attention. This way we establish a good relationship with the client and get repeat business. I'll certainly be more aware of waiting customers, as you suggest. *(Don't be defensive—you know you're doing the right thing—but still, be open to his concern about the other customers.)*

Manager: Don't you know we have to get that shipment out right away? You're too slow and we are all suffering from it.

Your response: I'm aware of the emergency. I remember that when you divided up the tasks, you gave me more to do than the others, and you said it was because you felt I was fast. Now, is there another way we can work out this situation? *(Stress the importance of cooperative problem-solving while you gently assert the truth.)*

Manager: I am tempted to tell the vice president that you're responsible for the mix-up in the memo. You could be in deep trouble.

Your response: We have differences about who's responsible here. Let's figure out how we can correct the problem, and then clear up the misunderstanding we had so it won't happen in the future. *(Don't be part of the blaming contest; don't respond to threats—focus on the future.)*

Conflicts Among Employees

You and a colleague have applied for the same promotion. Now she's acting like an adversary and won't sit with you at lunch anymore.

You say: I realize we both want the same job, and I don't want it to affect our relationship and make us into opponents because I like you too much and have too much respect for your work. Can we have lunch sometime together again?

A colleague comes to your desk and hands you a memo, saying, "The boss put this on my desk by mistake—it's your responsibility to handle it."

You say: Perhaps there *was* a miscommunication. Tell you what—just to make sure, let's check it with the boss so we can get the task done most efficiently.

A teaching colleague is very nosy about your private life, gives you unasked-for advice, and implies that she knows better than you about raising kids.

You say: Some of the things you advise me do make sense, and I know you've had a lot more experience than I with kids. Yet my situation is different from yours, and I'm confident I'm going to work it out myself. Thanks so much, though, for your interest.

A colleague takes too many smoking breaks, and you've had to answer her phone too many times.

You say: I respect your need for smoking breaks, but taking your messages has been pulling me away from my own work too often. Can we figure out together how to deal with the situation?

A colleague goes over your head to complain to the boss about your work.

You say: I heard you complained about me to the boss—true? Listen, you may have some valid reasons for dissatisfaction, but it would have been a much happier situation if you talked with me first. Next time, perhaps you'll do that, and I'll surely listen and make corrections that are necessary.

A colleague always has emergencies and always asks you to do part of her work to help her out.

You say: Look, we all work under lots of deadlines, don't we? I'm really sorry I can't help you this time because I promised my family I won't be late for dinner again. I hope you'll understand.

A Note to the CEO, the Big Cheese, the Top Kahuna . . .

Studies during the past five years show that workers put the highest priorities not on pay and fringe benefits, but on the "softer" elements of their work: being treated with respect as an individual, getting honest recognition, and being "in" on changes. When a CEO shows trust through communication, sharing, asking for help, admitting errors, and eliminating status and hierarchical differences, he creates one of those "best companies to work for" that appear in the magazines.

You should know the costs of *not* resolving conflict in the workplace. We have discovered that about one-quarter of senior-level management time is taken up with interpersonal job-related problems, many of them stemming from miscommunication, misunderstanding, personality clashes, and anger about performance issues. The higher up the ladder a conflict moves, the more confrontational it becomes. Sides are chosen, and management and employees develop an adversarial instead of a connected relationship. Productive work time is thwarted. Conflicts in organizations that are ignored or shifted around tend to take on a life of their own.

> **HOT-BUTTON HINT**
>
> A company, like any relationship, should thrive on conflict and come away from differences refreshed and renewed. Resolving conflicts productively brings a new sense of commitment and vitality to an organization.

It Ain't Rocket Science

In fiscal years 1996–1998, there were over 311,000 discrimination cases settled in the US. Awards and litigation costs totalled more than $700 million. The employment cases involved included those relating to race, colour, age, religion, sex, national origin, and disability and in areas such as hiring, promotion, firing, pay, and privileges. There was a lot of anger in those lawsuits.

In addition to visible and crippling costs of litigation and out-of-court settlements, there are hidden costs of conflict adding up and chipping away at the bottom line.

Here's what a CEO needs to do:

1. Pay attention. Demonstrate that you want real information—the good news and the bad news. Dispel the "happy family" myth.

2. Listen seriously. Listen to different points of view—from all levels of your organization. Walk around the workplace, and make it clear that you want people to tell the truth about what's wrong. Be a conflict-collector—sounds bad, but it is good.
3. Act to remedy the problem. You will start to hear themes about what's going on or what's wrong. Fix it as soon as you can, and hold people responsible for their actions.
4. Inform your employees when you've remedied the problem. Let everyone know that you are taking their comments seriously and what you are doing to fix things. Keep the information flowing.

HOT-BUTTON HINT

Whenever I ask my workshop participants who most pushes their hot buttons at work, three kinds of hot-button-pushers always dominate

- people who don't listen to me
- people who don't respect me
- people who try to control me

Ask the Conflict Coach ™

Temper, Temper

Easing our way into this new millennium, we meet with tense faces. Anger management classes are springing up everywhere. Every workplace has its share of furious people, even the entertainment workplaces where the rich, famous, and beautiful are, are on the edge as much as you. When Sean (Puffy) Combs was arrested for assaulting a record company executive, he was ordered to participate in a day of anger management. Obviously, he needed more than a day: At this writing, Mr. Combs is now facing more serious charges relating to his hot buttons. Latrell Sprewell has been required to take a similar course, as have Courtney Love, Mike Tyson, Tommy Lee, and, reportedly, Naomi Campbell. Anger management doesn't stop at two legs. There's a Brooklyn, New York, organization of dog owners called FIDO that holds seminars on conflict resolution for dogs and owners who just cannot get along.

For many years, my own workshop participants have been calling me the *Conflict Coach*, a title that at first made me laugh but that I've now grown to love and claim as my very own. As part of most workshops, we usually set aside questions, Dear Abby–style, for the quick fix that's sometimes enough to get people started paying attention to the way they deal with aggravating situations. If one acts instead of reacts when her buttons are pressed, she's able to step back, watch the play, and choose her responses—instead of shooting back a crazy, knee-jerk retaliation that will cool no one's jets.

Here's just a sampling of questions asked me so far this year. If you have such a query for the Conflict Coach, I can be reached at my Web site, www.SybilEvans.com.

Dear CC,

My boss asked me to give suggestions for revising the employee manual. I thought up some good ideas and e-mailed them to him. When the new manual came out, I saw that none of my ideas were used. He never even thanked me for my input. It gives me an empty feeling. Ignoring me is like a slap in the face and I'm seething over it. What shall I do?

Ignored and Devalued

Dear Ignored and Devalued,

You deserve to be complimented for going out of your way to make suggestions. Your boss seems an insensitive clod, but maybe he did not ignore you intentionally. Give him the benefit of the doubt and speak up, because here's the issue: A manager who asks for employee input and then discards it is a workplace demoralizer. Sadly, it happens a lot.

You need to speak up for your interests; you need to be a self-advocate.

What are your goals here? You need feedback on your work. You need not to be ignored and devalued ever again.

First, give him some of your positive reactions to the new manual. "The manual looks great—it's reader-friendly." Then remind him in a gentle way that you sent the requested recommendations for the manual and refresh his memory on your best recommendations.

You might ask, "Were *any* of the ideas that I gave you useful?" If he says yes, try to get him to give you specific feedback as to what was useful—and then why they were ignored. If he says none was useful, find out what he disliked about them. Always ask for feedback on your performance, negative or positive, and get examples so that you know how you can improve.

Whatever his response, you'll feel better that you spoke up. If it does nothing else, it will put your boss on notice that your time is valuable and he's not to ask for input unless he's serious.

Dear CC,

I asked my boss if I could leave work an hour earlier to take my son to a school concert rehearsal—no one else was available to take him. He replied, "I don't run a nursery school—we're in a crunch right now. If you have so many obligations, why don't you stay home all the time?"

I was so flabbergasted at his comment that I wanted to knee him. Please tell me what to do.

Ready to Kill

Dear Ready,

You've drawn a boss who's quick on the trigger and deals with his frustration by sharp jabs at the jugular. Do not knee him, but also do not respond by retreating, apologizing, or going on the defensive because that weakens your position.

Your error in this situation was not giving an alternative plan right away to immediately demonstrate that you're thinking responsibly.

Your objective? To defuse his anger and get your way. Do that by recognizing his concerns and allaying his fears. Reframe what he's said in a neutral way. "We're all concerned with the deadline, and I'm committed to working with you to get the job done. I have a plan that might work. I'd like to come in two hours earlier tomorrow and stay as long as it takes to complete everything."

You don't have to address every insult: Even though his "nursery school" statement was hurtful, blow it off. Don't dignify it. By bringing the conversation to a more productive business level, your commitment may not be challenged in the future.

Dear CC,

I'm a sales rep and one of the other reps is constantly making jokes about gay people and gay marriages. No one else in the unit seems to care—in fact, they mostly chuckle. I am really very hurt and don't know what to do. My brother is gay, and I feel that this is an attack on my whole family and me. I'm walking around ready to lash out at everyone—instead of only that guy.

Hurt and Angry

Dear Hurt and Angry,

You have the right to be very concerned, because today's workplace should never accept racist, sexist, or homophobic comments. Many times someone says unkind things because he feels he has a receptive audience; the more receptive it is, the more it gives him permission to be relentlessly unkind.

Don't be that receptive audience—even if you're alone in your stance. In the absence of an organizational policy that prohibits making jokes about groups, you have two choices. You can go to the Human Resources Department and discuss the problem and see what they have to say. I'd suggest first confronting the person yourself, telling him how you feel and how it can affect others. Find a private moment and say: "I'm upset when you make fun of gay people. You may not be aware of it, but some of us may have close gay friends or relatives. My brother is gay. I love him, and when you talk negatively, it really hurts me and it sends a bad message to other people who are reluctant to speak up. Please don't make those comments again."

Dear CC,

I'm a food services worker, and my male co-worker told me not to apply for an overtime job at the company because

I had a husband to support me and my co-worker needed the overtime more. I am absolutely furious. What a nerve! I've got to answer this guy. What should I say?

Need the Work

Dear Need the Work,

Your co-worker is living in the Neanderthal Age and you've got to wise him up. Guys like this are still around. But pay attention to what's *not* being said. He may indeed have some dire financial problems, and you need to use the perspective-taking tool to understand and mute the anger on both sides if you're to work together productively in the future.

Try saying something like: "Sounds like you can use the extra cash. Is there something particularly tough going on in your life now?"

He might say his son was turned down for scholarship aid or his sister desperately needed a loan. Whatever he says, show him that you understand and empathize. But then give your side of it: "We working people always want to make our lives better for our families. Whatever emergencies occur in either of our families, we BOTH deserve an opportunity to work overtime because we both do the same job for the same pay and are entitled to the same benefits."

Now, you might offer a constructive plan: "Let's both go to the boss to find out what kind of opportunities would be available for *both* of us."

When we assert ourselves in a firm and friendly way, we make ourselves strong.

Dear CC,

The other day, a teammate jokingly said to me, "Hey, old girl, you're making mistakes—you're not as sharp as you used to be." Other people giggled. These kids who think that anyone over forty is close to the grave aggravate me. I can't stand teasing like that. What shall I do?

Furious

Dear Furious,

Get un-furious. Be amused at how stupid the remark really is. And treat it that way. You can respond with humor by saying: "Sure I feel decrepit—just like Cher and Susan Sarandon feel decrepit."

However, I can understand how repeated comments like this have an abrasive effect. If the joker persists, take him aside (always allow for face-saving—if you confront him in front of others, the bully will need to retaliate and show you haven't scared him). Tell him that you really don't want to go to your employee relations representative (he'll get the implicit message). Then ask how he suggests you can both create a less hostile work atmosphere. Make it clear that you're not a sitting duck for stupid remarks. He'll be more mindful next time.

Dear CC,

I'm a film editor's secretary and lately my boss seems so irritable. Worse, he gives me confusing directions. Last week he gave me a job to do, and when I finished, he told me that the work had already been done beautifully by Nancy. Imagine—I spent 4 hours on this damn thing when he'd given it to someone else to do! This week, I was deep into a new project when he told me to drop it and start another one. He's driving me up the wall—and I'm making mistakes.

The worst thing happened an hour ago. He said, "I don't know what's wrong with you. You keep forgetting what I tell you to do, and it's because you never listen to what I say." I nearly started to cry. I ran to the ladies' room to gain composure.

Receiver of Mixed Messages

Dear Receiver of Mixed Messages,

Remember that Mae West movie, *He Done Me Wrong*? It applies to you. He done you wrong. You did the right thing by taking a timeout to regain your composure.

This is a ubiquitous issue in the workplace—the pressure that managers feel getting passed down to their subordinates. I call it the "Drop This–Do That Syndrome." Poor managers often give inconsistent messages and don't make their expectations clear. This has to affect your performance—not to mention your morale. Who likes being the target of unfair accusations?

GET OFF AUTOMATIC PILOT. Don't feed into your frustration by knee-jerk responses. Instead of crumbling and feeling weak the next time your boss sends you mixed messages, take a deep breath and tell yourself to feel strong and centered. Take your negative thoughts and dump them. Install a new tape of confident forcefulness. Then, to turn off your boss's buttons as well as your own, find a way to GET ON COMMON GROUND. You need to put your manager on notice that his style is not effective in getting out your best performance, and the way to do it is to show how you both have the same objectives.

Say: "You and I have the same aims. You want my best performance—I want to give it to you. But Bob, in order to achieve this aim, I have to get more consistent directions from you. I can tell you must be under a great deal of pressure lately, because there have been several instances when you've given me directions and then later gave me others that contradicted the first. When that happens, it's crazy—

and I make mistakes. I am sorry for the mistakes, but what can we do together to work this out so both our jobs get done quickly and efficiently?"

Conflicts get out of hand when they're not acknowledged. By stating the problem, you've taken the initiative and framed the problem as the responsibility of both.

Dear CC,

I really screwed up—I did something very wrong. I want to apologize, but I don't want to eat dirt or seem to be weak. What do you suggest?

Embarrassed

Dear Embarrassed,

Good for you—your instincts are absolutely correct. When you're wrong, apologize before you're caught and before anyone asks for your apology. It's not only the right thing to do, it's the best strategy to prevent ill feelings from sticking to you like oatmeal. People will respect you for it and emulate your decency.

There are several ways you can take responsibility for your actions without losing face. And remember—an apology doesn't even HAVE to contain the words "I'm sorry" if they're just too tough for you to get out.

First of all, always end an apology with a promise of a positive future action. Then try something like the following:

- I'm so sorry I forgot to tell you about the meeting. I realize it put you in a bad situation with our manager. What would it take for you to let go of the anger you must feel? Next time, I'll write things down.

- You're right. The cost estimates were accurate, just as you said. I miscalculated. I'll be more careful next time.
- I should have consulted with you before I approved the memo to the boss. It won't happen again.
- What I said was dead wrong and I see how troubled you are. I hope this doesn't hurt our relationship. Will you let me know if I ever again say something that bothers you? Because it's important to me that we communicate better.

HOT-BUTTON HINT

How do you solve conflict? By controlling outcomes and moving fast to solutions.

Is that your final answer?
IT'S WRONG!

The best approach: Step back, analyze the problem, look for what went wrong, empathize with the other guy to get his point of view, assert yourself in a sincere way, and stress common interests.

10

The Magic of Your Mind

> **HOT-BUTTON HINT**
>
> *There is no sport in hate when all the rage is on one side.*
>
> —Percy Bysshe Shelley

When people don't return your phone calls or e-mail, when they constantly interrupt you, take the last cup of coffee without making a new pot, or insist loudly that your political hero is a crook without letting you speak, there comes a point when something just snaps.

Here are some wonderful disciplines you can pull out of the magic of your mind at a moment's notice. Try one, try several, until you find something that calms your anger, unclenches your fists, and turns off your hot buttons. If you check the resource section in the back of this book, you'll find books that tell you more about each. You can use most of these techniques on the subway when the jostler has jostled you, in your car when the woman in the next car has just cursed you because you didn't move fast enough to suit her, when you're trapped in an airline seat and the guy in front of you has abruptly lowered his seat into your lap—or when you're in your bath. Your choice. It's all about choice and your own mind.

And this is the wonder: All you need is your mind. You can choose to be furious—or choose to be calm. I've tried both; calm is better.

Mindfulness

Thich Nhat Hanh is a Vietnamese Buddhist monk who teaches people to weave mindful meditation into their daily lives. He tells us to use everything that happens, even the daily irritations of traffic jams or critical bosses, as helpful signals calling you back to your true, mindful self. If you stay in the moment and pay attention to right now and even the most mundane daily acts, like waiting for a traffic light or watching the way the bubbles disperse as you wash dishes, says the monk, you can turn these acts into an experience of wonder and calm. The energy of mindfulness can transform that woman in the next car from a virago into a songbird—in your mind. Paying attention to the way the cool stream from the water fountain feels in your mouth or the way the steam from your coffee rises can turn off your hot buttons.

Transcendental Meditation

TM is a classic Vedic meditation technique introduced to the West by a Hindu monk named Maharishi Mahesh Yogi. It is said to induce a state of "restful alertness," and you can do it anywhere—walking to work, in your cubicle, in the airport lounge. A TM teacher gives you a personal mantra, usually a word or sound, and the technique includes repeating the mantra mentally only fifteen or twenty minutes twice a day. Like mindfulness, it energizes as it calms.

Thought-Switching

You can actually transform your thoughts from a negative and self-destructive mode to a positive and life-enhancing mode.

First, put on the emergency brake. When someone gets you so mad you could scream, resist the urge to fight fire with fire. Brake. If you can't actually leave the situation, withdraw figuratively for a timeout. Turn your thoughts elsewhere for at least ten seconds. Now conjure up an image of the most terrific place or peaceful person you know: A Cayman Island beach? Venice at dusk? The face of your lover? Concentrate on that image for a moment or so. Feel more balanced? Good.

Now, switch your thoughts.

Instead of Thinking . . .	Switch to . . .
They treat me like dirt.	I'm going to tell the boss how I felt when they did that—and then I'm going to quietly request better treatment. I can do that.
They're so damn rude—imagine shaking sand right in my face—I'm going to kick sand on their blanket when I go get ice cream.	I bet I can control this situation so it works out for me.
Push in front of me? I'll show you pushing!	Go push your way, little sad woman who probably has no friends and maybe even a terrible disease brought on by all that hostility. I'll bask in my blessings.

I said I wanted my meat well done. Why doesn't anyone listen? It's just too embarrassing to make a fuss.	I don't have to make a fuss—I'll do it quietly but firmly. I have every right to send this meat back. It'll make me stronger and happier to stand up for myself, and they'll respect me more.

Don't expect perfection. Do expect relief from fury. A totally perfect thought-switch you will never achieve—it can't happen. And you do have to practice this technique. When you get it down, you'll feel wonderfully better. The magic of your mind can release you from thoughts of retribution and lead you into a life where you'll feel swell about yourself and your power.

Breathe

The easiest anger release is deep, slow, rhythmic breathing, according to Miriam M. Gottleib, Ph.D., author of *The Angry Self.* Inhale through your nose slowly until you feel your lungs fill with air. Then exhale very slowly through your nose or mouth. Develop a steady rhythm, and don't breathe so rapidly that you hyperventilate or so slowly that you get out of breath. Try it before your button is pushed. Visualize yourself in a stressful situation (the insane motorist giving you the finger?). Let your anger build high—and then start rhythmic breathing.

Do Something Physical

Sometimes the magic of your body works as well as the magic of your mind. A client of mine tells me that when she's furious, she tears things. She methodically and deliberately shreds an old towel until it lies at a heap at her feet, and by that time she's feeling better. Some paint a room; others weed a garden; others do ten laps around the park, or a hundred sit-ups, or punch pillows. Physical activity siphons off rage.

Don't Waste Your Anger on the Person You Hate

Here's a thought: When you're in a situation that produces real fury, don't waste it on the guy who gave you the finger or the woman hogging the great Starbucks chair. Anger gives you energy and makes you feel most fully alive, actively engaged. So channel anger's energy, all that extra adrenaline, all that sudden lack of self-consciousness into some action that's rewarding for you, not for your nemesis.

- Practice the musical instrument of your choice: You'll play with much more passion.
- Write an angry letter or a love letter—both will be spontaneous and powerful.
- Sing out loud, especially if you're in the car. You'll never sound so good again.

Change Your Life: A Hot-Button Journal

Everything you read or see that's meaningful should change your life in some way, small or large. From what you've read in these pages, what can you take home? What exactly will you do to change the way you deal with conflict?

Here's one simple but useful way to change your life: Keep a hot-button journal. Fill it in whenever you feel devitalizing anger or when you've pressed someone else's buttons—and wish you hadn't. Use these five headings to track your progress:

What pushed my button today?

What I said or did in response.

How did I push someone else's button?

What happened?

Maybe I'll try—next time (or did I handle it just right this time?).

Here's what will happen: You'll gradually get into the habit of dealing with conflict in much more satisfying ways because you'll start to see patterns in the way you express your frustration. For example, when you feel fury, do you see yourself always lashing back at others, or holding the anger in? Do you often get headaches for which your doctor can find no cause? Do you sense that an awful lot of people are getting furious with you? Is it possible that the way you've been handling conflict is making you sick or making you sad?

When you isolate the patterns in your journal and recognize what usually gets you maddest, you're ahead of the game. Then you can almost anticipate what will push your buttons—or how you will push someone else's hot button.

Being aware of all this, you can choose to defuse the anger—by reconstituting the way you handle the irritating people and situations in your life. We can't rewrite the past or change a single thing that's already happened. But if you've ever been so enraged that you slammed the door in a loved one's face, or hung up the telephone on someone when her words just stabbed you, you can alter the course of such conflicts in the future. When you make the choice to resolve conflict rather than steam with anger, you'll feel so powerful. You'll feel so good.

I promise.

LAST HOT-BUTTON HINT

The harder the conflict, the more glorious the triumph.

—Thomas Paine

Now that you have the tools to handle the conflict, go for the glorious triumph!

Resources

Books

Adams, Lisa K. *Dealing With Arguments.* New York: Rosen, 1997.

Anderson, Kare. *Getting What You Want.* New York: Penguin/Plume, 1994.

Borisoff, Deborah, and David A. Victor. *Conflict Management: A Communications Skills Approach.* Englewood Cliffs, NJ: Prentice-Hall, 1989.

Brawner, Jim, and Suzette Brawner. *Taming the Family Zoo.* Colorado Springs: Navpress, 1998.

Cloke, Kenneth, and Joan Goldsmith. *Resolving Conflicts at Work.* San Francisco: Josey-Bass, 2000.

Cohen, Sherry Suib. *Secrets of a Very Good Marriage.* New York: Penguin, 1993.

Cornelius, Helen, and Shoshana Faire. *Everyone Can Win.* Australia: Simon & Schuster, 1989.

Covey, Stephen. *The 7 Habits of Highly Effective People.* London: Simon & Schuster, 1999.

Crum, Thomas F. *The Magic of Conflict.* UK: Pocket Books, 1999.

Denenberg, Richard V., and Mark Braverman. *The Violence Prone Workplace.* Ithaca, NY: Cornell University Press, 1998.

Elgin, Suzette Haden. *How to Disagree Without Being Disagreeable.* New York: John Wiley & Sons, 1997.

Ellis, Albert. *How to Control Your Anger.* London: Robert Hale, 1999.

Evans, Sybil. *Resolving Conflict in a Diverse Work Place.* Amherst, MA: Amherst Educational Publishing, 1997.

Fisher, Roger, and Scott Brown. *Getting Together: Building Relationships As We Negotiate.* New York: Penguin, 1989.

Fisher, Roger, and William Ury. *Getting to Yes.* London: Arrow, 1997.

Gottlieb, Miriam. *The Angry Self.* Phoenix: Zeig, Tucker & Co., 1999.

Gottman, John. *Why Marriages Succeed or Fail.* London: Bloomsbury, 1998.

Gray, John. *Men Are from Mars, Women Are from Venus.* London: Thorsons, 1993.

Hanh, Thich Nhat. *The Miracle of Mindfulness.* London: Rider, 1991.

Hendrix, Harville. *Getting the Love You Want.* New York: Henry Holt, 1998.

Horn, Sam. *Tongue Fu!* New York: St. Martin's Press, 1996.

Hudson Institute. *Workplace 2020.* Indianapolis: Hudson Institute, 1997.

Jacobs, Bruce A. *Race Manners: Navigating the Minefield Between Black and White Americans.* New York: Arcade Publishing, 1999.

Johnston, Marianne. *Dealing with Fighting, Dealing with Anger.* New York: Rosen, 1996 (children's book).

Kabat-Zinn, Jon. *Mindfulness Meditation.* London: Piatkus, 1994.

Kottler, Jeffrey A. *Beyond Blame.* London: Routledge, 1993.

Mahesh Yogi. *Science of Being and Art of Living: Transcendental Meditation.* New York: Penguin, 1994.